S0-BHU-584

Guy Debord

Guy Debord

Translated by Donald Nicholson-Smith,
with a Foreword by T. J. Clark
and a New Afterword by the Author

Anselm Jappe

University of California Press
Berkeley   Los Angeles   London

University of California Press
Berkeley and Los Angeles, California

University of California Press, Ltd.
London, England

© 1993, 1995, 1999 by Anselm Jappe

English translation copyright © 1999 by the
Regents of the University of California

Foreword copyright © 1999 by T. J. Clark

Original Italian edition published in 1993 by
Edizioni Tracce, Pescara, Italy. Revised edition,
in French, published in 1995 by Via Valeriano,
Marseilles.

Library of Congress Cataloging-in-Publication Data

Jappe, Anselm, 1962–
      [Guy Debord. English]
      Guy Debord / Anselm Jappe; translated from
   the French by Donald Nicholson-Smith; with a
   foreword by T. J. Clark.
         p.   cm.
   Includes bibliographical references and index.
   ISBN 0-520-21204-5 (alk. paper).
   —ISBN 0-520-21205-3 (pbk. : alk paper)
      1. Debord, Guy, 1931-   2. Radicals—
   France—Biography.   I. Title.
   HN440.R3 D43613   1999
   303.48′4—dc21
      [b]   98-37465
                                                CIP

Manufactured in the United States of America
10   09   08   07   06   05   04   03   02
12   11   10   9   8   7   6   5   4   3   2
The paper used in this publication meets the minimum requirements of ANSI/NISO Z39.48-1992
(R 1997) (Permanence of Paper). ∞

Contents

Foreword

A book about Guy Debord—and Anselm Jappe's is far and away the best we have so far, I think—ultimately stands or falls by what it has to say about two interlinked puzzles that stand at the heart of Debord's life and work. Such a book need not spell out these puzzles exactly as I do (you will see that Jappe's terms are different), but I believe it ought to be driven and haunted (as Jappe's undoubtedly is) by a similar sense that broad questions about the nature of Debord's achievement constantly come up and get harder to answer the more unavoidable they seem. The questions are these. First, how are we to understand the obvious (but scandalous) fact that in Debord's case politics was largely *writing*—that it turned on the building of an inimitable polemical and expository style, assembled over decades, born from a series of engagements with, on, and against the French language? Second, what does it mean that this, the *only* political writing of our time—the only such writing to have a chance of surviving its circumstances, I believe, the writing that will be seen by future ages to have kept the possibility of politics alive—issued from a situation so thoroughly at odds with the century, or with most of the terms in which the century chose to present itself? Why was distance and embattlement, of which Debord was the ultimate exponent, so often the source of insight and sanity in his case, not "paradise for a sect"? What does it tell us about the *age* that its true voice—its adequate description—came so exultantly from the margins?

Because Jappe succeeds in posing these two questions concurrently, and knows full well that answering one of them involves answering both, he manages to talk about Debord's achievement as one of voice, or language, without falling in with those in France who have been trying since Debord's death, and even before it, to turn him into "a master of French prose." At all events, the maneuver is futile. For a start, part of the work on the language Debord was involved in turns on an agonized, and deeply funny, running battle with the notions of mastery and Frenchness lurking in the phrase above—"mastery" *equaling* "Frenchness," which in turn equals clarity, authority, classical balance, skeptical levity, etc. A great deal of the agony/comedy in Debord's prose is provided by the business of its continually swallowing, and half-regurgitating, monstrous Hegelian, un-French, unclear turns of phrase and thought—so that the reader is typically plunged, in a sentence or two, from icy Retz or La Rochefoucauld aphorisms, shining with hate-filled economy, on to smothering, fuzzy (inspiring) rigmarole, full of unrepentant dialectical tricks, like the best bits of Feuerbach or the young Marx. (And there is no "like" about it a lot of the time: the quotations and paraphrases are verbatim. Jappe tracks many of these down.) This is "writing," sure enough. I'd be inclined to say great writing. But it was not done by someone who was only or essentially a writer (or a master of French prose), any more than he was an "artist," "filmmaker," "politician," or even "revolutionary." All of these identities, Debord never tired of telling us, are what now stand in the way of the activities they once pointed to.

Political writing of the highest order is rare. Moments at which a particular language is opened to a further range of possibilities—a new tone, a new conception of human purposes, a sharper or wilder rhetorical ascent—in any case happen infrequently. And moments at which this opening depends on the creation of a specifically political voice, rather than an ethical, lyric, or epic one, are truly few and far between. The Rousseau of the *Discourses* would be one, Burke in the *Reflections* another. (The Debord–Rousseau comparison is inescapable, I think, even down to the confidence with which right-thinking commentators go on trying to reduce the politics of both to personal deficiency, thinking that doing so will lay the politics finally to rest. That never quite seems to happen.) But the fact that both my points of comparison come from the late eighteenth century only puts the Debord puzzle in sharper relief. For Burke and Rousseau were working with a political imagery and argumentation already formed and enriched by many others, in a previous half-century's conversation. They had seen the imagery and argumentation taken up in actual political practice, by despots and revolutionaries, and put to the test of reality. The terms of the conversation had changed constantly as a result. In a word, they were the least isolated of men. They did not need to *invent* a political language—still less to wrest the possibility of one from a surrounding farrago of lies and soundbites. They did not live in the midst of a terrible, interminable contest over how best to debauch and eviscerate the last memory—the last trace—of political aspiration. Those who complain of Debord's paranoia should look again at what he was trying to do, and why he might have thought, in the 1970s and 1980s, that almost everything and everybody stood in his way.

One main merit of Jappe's book is that it manages to see and speak to Debord's embattledness and isolation, and also to his being a social animal. For no one was better, over whole stretches of his life, at making himself enough of a community for the purposes of the moment; and if that community had nothing to do with the official "political" culture of Sartre, Garaudy, and de Gaulle, then so much the better. Writing was one social activity among others. The room on the rue Saint-Jacques where *The Society of the Spectacle* got written was at once an austere cell—with nothing on the shelves, I remember, but a few crucial texts (Hegel, Pascal, Marx, Lukács, Lautréamont's *Poésies*) laid open at the relevant page—and the entryway to Debord's minuscule apartment, through which friends and comrades continually passed. The process was meant to be seen, and interrupted. One moment the deep, ventriloqual dialogue with *History and Class Consciousness*; the next the latest bubble for a *comics détourné*, or the best insult yet to Althusser and Godard.

Those names lead me finally to Debord's hostility to the very idea of "representation," which everyone these days (except Jappe) is supposed to think the weirdest and most naïve part of his worldview. For what else can there be (says everyone) *besides* representation? What could Debord possibly have meant by the notions brought on in his writing to represent representation's opposite—"lived experience," for instance, or "imagination," or, worse still, "poetry"? Do they not lead us inevitably back to a Rousseau-and-Lukács realm of transparency and face-to-faceness and therefore usher in a politics of purity and purging to match? Not necessarily, is Jappe's answer. In the end, in our present age of "information," it may even be this side of Debord's politics—for the moment the most despised, the most outdated—that will prove the kernel of future action. For supposing we take Debord's writing as directed not to anathematizing representation in general (as everyone has it) but to proposing certain tests for truth and falsity in representation and, above all, for truth and falsity in representational *regimes*. Why should there not be an alternative to our current "totalitarian dictatorship of the fragment"? Why is it so difficult to think (and demand and construct) "representation" as plural rather than as singular and centralized: representations as so many fields or terrains of activity, subject to leakage and interference between modes and technologies, and constantly crossed and dispersed by other kinds of activity altogether: subject, as a result, to retrieval and cancellation—to continual reversals of direction between object and image, and image and receiver? Why should a regime of representation not be built on the principle that images are, or ought to be, transformable (as opposed to exchangeable)—meaning disposable through and through, and yet utterly material and contingent; shareable, imaginable, coming up constantly in their negativity, their non-identity, and for that reason promoted and dismantled at will? "History," to take up one of Debord's favorite quotations from Lukács, "is the history of the unceasing overthrow of the objective forms that shape the life of man."

I know that in the age of symbol management it is sometimes hard to tell Debord's utopia apart from the one on offer from Microsoft. But they are different, in every respect; the one is a nerveless parody of the other; and the fact that Debord's imagining of other worlds shares so much with that of his opponents is potentially his imagining's strong point. It is what lets *The Society of the Spectacle* go on haunting the non-world of cyberspace—until the moment, which is surely not far off, when the bourgeoisie begins to fall out of love with the speed-up of the last two decades, and no longer gets higher and higher on the details (the gadgetry) of its own proletarianization. Political writing is always instrumental as well as utopian. Debord's is no exception. Only sometimes writing has to reconcile itself to the idea that its time of instrumentality—its time as a weapon—lies a little in the future. Jappe's book is true to its subject, above all, because it reads Debord, and helps us read him, with that future in mind.

T. J. Clark
May 1998

Translator's Acknowledgments

I wish to thank Bruce Elwell and John Simmons for reading the translation manuscript and offering help on many points. Thomas Y. Levin graciously supplied me with some hard-to-find documents. To Mia Rublowska I am indebted for all kinds of aid, tangible and intangible. Above all I must express my gratitude to Anselm Jappe, who reviewed the text with me word by word and displayed seemingly inexhaustible patience in dealing with my queries. This English-language edition embodies the author's latest revisions. Needless to say, however, all shortcomings of translation should be laid at my door.

D. N.-S.

Abbreviations

The following abbreviations are used throughout this book for frequently cited works; the particular editions used are indicated. For Debord's works, citations are generally to a current French edition and to an English translation where one exists. Full publication histories for Debord will be found in Bibliography 1. Citations to Marx and Engels refer wherever possible to the eight-volume selection published by Penguin Books, in association with *New Left Review*, beginning in the nineteen-seventies; these volumes are still in print (1998), with pagination unchanged, as Penguin Classics.

Bandini	Mirella Bandini, *L'Estetico, il politico: Da Cobra all'Internazionale Situazionista 1948–1957* (Rome: Officina Edizioni, 1977).
Berréby	Gérard Berréby, ed., *Documents relatifs à la fondation de l'Internationale Situationniste* (Paris: Allia, 1985).
Capital I/III	Karl Marx, *Capital*, vol. 1, trans. Ben Fowkes (Harmondsworth, England: Penguin/New Left Review, 1976); vol. 3, trans. David Fernbach (Penguin/New Left Review, 1981).
Comm.	Debord, *Commentaires sur la société du spectacle, suivi de Préface à la quatrième édition italienne de "La Société du Spectacle"* (Paris: Gallimard, 1992); Eng.: *Comments on the Society of the Spectacle*, trans. Malcolm Imrie (London: Verso, 1990).
CEL I	Henri Lefebvre, *Critique de la vie quotidienne I: Introduction*, second edition (Paris: L'Arche, 1958); Eng.: *Critique of Everyday Life I: Introduction*, trans. John Moore (London: Verso, 1991).
CEL II	Henri Lefebvre, *Critique de la vie quotidienne II: Fondements d'une sociologie de la quotidienneté* (Paris: L'Arche, 1961).

Dérive	Libero Andreotti and Xavier Costa, eds., *Theory of the Dérive and Other Situationist Writings on the City*, trans. Paul Hammond, Gerardo Denís, and others (Barcelona: Museu d'Art Contemporani/ACTAR, 1996).
EW	Karl Marx, *Early Writings*, ed. Quintin Hoare, trans. Rodney Livingstone and Gregor Benton (Harmondsworth, England: Penguin/New Left Review, 1974).
Films	Debord, *Society of the Spectacle and Other Films*, trans. Richard Parry and others (London: Rebel Press, 1992).
Grundrisse	Karl Marx, *Grundrisse: Foundations of the Critique of Political Economy (Rough Draft)*, trans. Martin Nicolaus (Harmondsworth, England: Penguin/New Left Review, 1973).
HCC	Georg Lukács, *History and Class Consciousness*, trans. Rodney Livingstone (London: Merlin Press/Cambridge, Mass.: MIT Press, 1968).
In Girum	Debord, *In Girum Imus Nocte et Consumimur Igni*, trans. Lucy Forsyth (London: Pelagian Press, 1991).
IS	*Internationale Situationniste* (1958–69). Citations supply the issue number followed by the page number and thus apply to all reprint editions of the Situationist journal. Much material from *IS* exists in English translation in *SIA, Oct., Dérive,* and *Passage*, which are cited accordingly, with references to the latter sources generally given only when the text is not to be found in *SIA*.
OCC	Debord, *Oeuvres cinématographiques complètes* (Paris: Gallimard, 1994).
Oct.	"Situationist Texts on Visual Culture and Urbanism: A Selection," trans. John Shepley, *October* 79 (Winter 1997).
Pan.	Debord, *Panégyrique*, vol. 1 (Paris: Gallimard, 1993); Eng.: *Panegyric*, vol. 1, trans. James Brook (London: Verso, 1991).
Passage	Elizabeth Sussman, ed., *On the Passage of a Few People through a Rather Brief Moment in Time: The Situationist International 1957–1972* (Cambridge, Mass.:

MIT Press/Boston: Institute of Contemporary Art, 1989).

Pot. *Guy Debord présente Potlatch (1954–1957)* (Paris: Gallimard, Collection Folio, 1996). Some material from *Potlatch* exists in English translation in *SIA*, *Oct.*, and *Dérive*, which are cited accordingly.

Pref. Debord, "Préface à la quatrième édition italienne de 'La Société du spectacle,'" in *Comm.*, pp. 91–112; Eng.: *Preface to the Fourth Italian Edition of "The Society of the Spectacle,"* second edition, trans. Michel Prigent and Lucy Forsyth (London: Chronos, 1983).

Prelims. Debord and P. Canjuers, *Préliminaires pour une définition de l'unité du programme révolutionnaire* (1960), in Bandini, pp. 342–47; Eng.: "Preliminaries toward Defining a Unitary Revolutionary Program," in *SIA*, pp. 305–10.

PW I/II/III Karl Marx, *Political Writings*, ed. David Fernbach, 3 vols. (Harmondsworth, England: Penguin/New Left Review, 1973–74). Vol. 1, *The Revolutions of 1848;* vol. 2, *Surveys from Exile;* vol. 3, *The First International and After.*

Rapp. Debord, *Rapport sur la construction des situations et sur les conditions de l'organisation et de l'action de la tendance situationniste internationale*, in *Internationale Situationniste 1958–69* (Paris: Arthème Fayard, 1997); Eng.: partial translation in *SIA*.

SIA Ken Knabb, ed. and trans., *Situationist International Anthology* (Berkeley: Bureau of Public Secrets, 1981).

SS Debord, *La Société du spectacle* (Paris: Gallimard, 1992); Eng.: *The Society of the Spectacle*, trans. Donald Nicholson-Smith (New York: Zone, 1994). Citations are to sections (§§), not page numbers, and thus apply to all editions.

VS Debord and Gianfranco Sanguinetti, *La Véritable Scission dans l'Internationale* (Paris: Arthème Fayard, 1998); Eng.: *The Veritable Split in the International*, third edition revised, trans. Lucy Forsyth and others (London: Chronos, 1990).

A Note on Quotation from English Translations

Existing English translations have generally been followed in quoted matter, and citations to them are given in all cases. Sometimes, however, I have modified them according to my own lights.   —*Translator*

Part 1 | The Concept of the Spectacle

Must We Burn Debord?

Some historical periods display a strong belief in the power of critical thought. Cases in point are the reign of Ch'in Shih Huang Ti, the Chinese emperor who organized the first book-burnings in history, or the age that condemned Anaxagoras and Socrates, or the one that burned Bruno and Vanini at the stake. As recently as twenty years ago, in the Iran of the Shah, a schoolteacher was sent to prison for life because she owned a copy of Hegel's *Science of Logic*.

Our own era, however—meaning the last few decades in the West—has (not unreasonably) treated its thinkers as completely harmless individuals. Many a self-proclaimed sworn enemy of the world as it is has fallen rapturously into the welcoming arms of academia or of television. Guy Debord, though, must surely be numbered among the very few people deemed quite beyond the pale. For a long time, in fact, the police showed far more interest in him than did the agencies normally responsible for the diffusion of ideas. A time came, however, when this attitude could no longer prevent the theories developed by Debord and his Situationist friends from leaving their mark, despite all obstacles, on the spirit of the times. Since then another way of obscuring Debord's thinking has come into play, namely trivialization: there must be very few present-day authors whose ideas have been so widely applied in a distorted form, and generally without attribution.

That we live in a "society of the spectacle" is acknowledged by almost everyone—by television producers, by President Jacques Chirac, by the lowliest of mere spectators. The phrase seems practically de rigueur in every discussion of the invasion of life by the mass media, every denunciation of the effects on children of being stuck from babyhood on in front of the television screen; likewise the "spectacularization" of information is universally deplored apropos of the reporting of tragic events such as wars and catastrophes. Occasionally a slightly better informed commentator will mention that these terms are derived from the title of a book by a certain Debord, who is thus by implication depicted as a kind of less well-known Marshall McLuhan. Further details are rarely supplied.

Whether such "disinformation" is to be regretted is an open question. As an Austrian socialist of the first half of this century said, "When I began reading Marx, I was surprised never to have heard his name mentioned at school. When I began to understand Marx, I was no longer surprised in the least."

When Marx's theories are reduced to a simple economic doctrine concerning the supposedly inevitable pauperization of the proletariat, it is easy enough to trumpet the error of his thought. Here is a Marx eminently suitable for classroom discussion. A similar intent informs the presentation of Debord's ideas as nothing more than a theory of the mass media; a few specific points are then summarily conceded and the remainder of what he says passed over in silence. Nor is such a juxtaposition of Debord and Marx particularly arbitrary: a period that seeks to use the collapse of Soviet bureaucratic despotism and the seeming triumph of the Western model of social organization as weapons with which to deliver the coup de grace to everything remotely related to Marxist thought could hardly fail to be irked by one of the few theories of Marxist inspiration that has been confirmed repeatedly by the developments of the last thirty years.

There is another reason, too, why an analogy between Debord and Marx is not an arbitrary one: Debord's theories cannot be properly grasped unless they are first properly located within Marxist thought in general. Some people will doubtless find this surprising and question the idea that Debord might be of interest on account of his interpretation of Marx. Was not Debord first and foremost the representative of an artistic avant-garde that sought to transcend art by means of "*détournements*," "*dérives*," play, and "unitary urbanism"? Surely the fulcrum of Situationist agitation was the "revolution of everyday life"? These things certainly played an important part, yet placing all the emphasis on them means playing down Debord's theoretico-practical activity, burying him in effect in the great cemetery of past avant-gardes, and ultimately according him no significance for the present time save that of some "father of the video neo-avant-garde" or "precursor of punk" (and these labels are not made up). This kind of incomprehension is likewise betrayed by the ever more prevalent use of the word "Situationism"— a term the Situationists themselves firmly rejected from the outset on the grounds that it perversely froze their ideas into a dogma (*IS* 1/13; *SIA*, 45).

The chief concern of this study is the *relevance to the present time* of the notion of the "spectacle," as developed by Debord, and its utility in the construction of a critical theory of contemporary society. The intention is to show that the spectacle is the most highly developed form of a society based on commodity production and its corollary, the "fetishism of commodities." It is hoped that the real significance of this last concept will be clarified by showing the extent to which it constitutes a key to the understanding of the world of today, where the results of human activity are so antagonistic to humanity itself that they now threaten it with extinction through ecological catastrophe or war. We shall be touching on the pertinence for the present day of a central portion of Marx's thought, the critique of the fetishism of commodities, and in this context considering Debord's relationship to those minority strands in Marxism which have defined themselves in terms of that pivotal topic.

The main aim is to advance understanding of the theoretical issues while shedding light on the relationship between Debord and his contemporaries. Certain issues, among them the question of revolutionary organization, will be given short shrift here, because, whatever importance they once had, discussion of them now tends to resemble the byzantine debate on the human versus the divine nature of Christ. Nor shall we devote much space to anecdotal and biographical details, which have been fairly well documented elsewhere.[1] We will, however, be considering Debord's practical activity, his life, and what might be called his "myth," for they partake of an overarching desire for a rich life full of passion, not of passive contemplation, and embody a will to destroy whatever at present makes such a life impossible.

Aside from a growing disgust for those who used Marx to justify their gulags and their *nomenklatura*, it seemed in the nineteen-sixties that a good many Marxist or supposedly Marxist theories were outdated. These were years when capitalism showed no signs of any inability to increase its productive forces; it even seemed quite capable of ensuring a somewhat more equitable distribution than formerly of what it produced. This gave the lie to the belief that a revolution would be made by workers suffering ever greater poverty. Critical social thought proceeded to

1. See Bibliography 2.

ask the most general, most simple, yet least frequently raised question: what use was being made of the immense accumulation of means now at society's disposal? Had life, as actually experienced by ordinary individuals, become richer? The answer, clearly, was negative. Whereas the power of society overall appeared to be limitless, the individual was deprived of any control over his own world.

Unlike many others, Debord did not interpret this state of affairs as an inevitable reversal of progress, or as the fate of modern man, to which there was no alternative but an improbable return to the past. Rather, he attributed the situation to the fact that *the economy had brought human life under the sway of its own laws.* Consequently, no change emanating from *within* the economic sphere would be sufficient so long as the economy itself was not subordinated to the conscious control of individuals. In what follows, an attempt will be made to explain, on the basis of Debord's own statements, how this claim differs from similar-sounding formulations that even the Pope might utter. The modern economy and its existence as a detached sphere will be analyzed here as the consequences of the *commodity,* of *exchange-value,* of *abstract labor,* and of the *form of value.* These are the topics that need addressing.

This has in fact been the concern, since the time of the First World War, of a minority tendency within Marxism that assigns central importance to the problem of *alienation,* considered not as epiphenomenal but as crucial to capitalist development. It is true that this still implies a very philosophical approach; the essential point, however, is the stress laid on the fact that the economy, once it has achieved autonomy, and no matter what form its development takes, can only be antagonistic to human life. The leading figure in this strain of Marxism is the Georg Lukács of *History and Class Consciousness* (1923), who took up and further elaborated the Marxian critique of the "fetishism of commodities" in view of the transformations that had occurred in social reality since Marx's time. Later still, armed with the arguments of both Marx and Lukács, Debord would attempt to construct a theory of a particular variant of commodity fetishism that had arisen in the interim and that he called "the spectacle."

It is thus essential, if one is effectively to grasp the ideas set forth by Debord in *The Society of the Spectacle* (1967), to attend closely to his sources, to which he owes more than might at first be supposed. This is in no sense to diminish the originality of Debord's work, one of whose chief merits is that it adapts the earlier theories to a very different period. As he himself remarks in his autobiographical *Panegyric* (1989), "Men more knowledgeable than I have explained very well the origin of what has come to pass" (*Pan.*, 83; Eng., 77)—following which observation he quotes his own earlier paraphrase of the Marxian theory of exchange-value (*SS* §46). *The Society of the Spectacle* does not contain many quotations as such;[2] when they do occur, their purpose is to buttress Debord's assertions rather than to acknowledge his sources. A careful reading of the book reveals, however, that Debord hews narrowly to the Lukácsian tradition in Marxism, refining certain aspects of it and sharing certain of its problems. To trace the development of the critique of alienation in Marx, Lukács, and Debord is not, however, to endorse Debord's claim, apropos of *The Society of the Spectacle*, that "there have doubtless not been three books of social criticism of such importance in the last hundred years" (*OCC*, 183–84; *Films*, 133).[3]

Debord's writings are not easily susceptible of paraphrase: for one thing their stylistic elegance militates against it, and for another there is a danger of "overinterpretation." Inevitably, therefore, it will be necessary to quote a good deal. As Debord himself emphasized, he wrote little (*Pan.*, 42; Eng., 34), and only when it seemed to him necessary. No text of his was ever written to order, at the request of an editor or under the pressure of a contractual deadline. Any attempt at exegesis must confront the problem that Debord's work, for all its succinctness, claims to have said everything essential,[4] explicitly refusing interpretation and demanding to be followed, so to speak, to the letter. For a very long time Debord approved of no reading of his thought that was not strictly literal, indeed tantamount to a pure reproduction of the original text.

The Spectacle—Highest Stage of Abstraction

The concept of "the society of the spectacle" is often taken to refer exclusively to the tyranny of the television and other such means of communication. For Debord, however, the "mass media" are but a "limited" aspect of the spectacle—"its most stultifying superficial manifestation"

2. Not overt quotations, that is. Very many passages of Debord's book are "*détournements*" of statements by other authors.

3. Unfortunately, we are not told what the other two books might be, or whether indeed they include *Capital*, which was published almost exactly a century before *The Society of the Spectacle* (14 September 1867–14 November 1967).

4. In this respect (and in this respect only), there is a parallel to be drawn between Debord and Wittgenstein.

(*SS* §24). Invasion by the means of mass communication is only seemingly a deployment of instruments that, even when badly used, remain essentially neutral; in reality the operation of the media perfectly expresses the entire society of which they are a part. The result is that direct experience and the determination of events by individuals themselves are replaced by a passive contemplation of images (which have, moreover, been chosen by other people).

This perception is at the heart of all Debord's thinking and action. In 1952, when he was twenty years old, he called for an art that would *create* situations rather than reproduce already existing situations. Five years later Debord's founding platform for a Situationist International (SI) contained a first definition of the spectacle: "The construction of situations begins beyond the modern collapse of the notion of spectacle. It is easy to see how closely the very principle of the spectacle, namely non-intervention, is bound to the alienation of the old world" (*Rapp.*, 699). The twelve issues of *Internationale Situationniste* (1958–69) attest to the increasing importance assumed by the notion of the spectacle in Situationist thinking. Its systematic analysis, however, awaited the appearance, in 1967, of the 221 theses that constitute Debord's *The Society of the Spectacle*.[5]

In contrast to the first stage of the historical development of alienation, which may be described as a downgrading of "being" into "having," the spectacle is characterized by a subsequent downgrading of "having" into "appearing" (*SS* §17). Debord's analysis is based on the everyday experience of the impoverishment of life, its fragmentation into more and more widely separated spheres, and the disappearance of any unitary aspect from society. The spectacle consists in the reunification of separate aspects at the level of the *image*. Everything life lacks is to be found within the spectacle, conceived of as an ensemble of independent representations. As an example here, Debord evokes celebrities, such as actors or politicians, whose function it is to represent a combination of human qualities and of *joie de vivre*—precisely what is missing from the

5. The ideas of the Situationists are not identical in every regard to the ideas of Guy Debord, as Debord himself stressed in 1957 and again in 1985. For my present purposes, apart from books, shorter works and articles signed by Debord, I have also taken into consideration, though to a lesser degree, the many unattributed articles in *Internationale Situationniste;* these expressed the collective opinions of the Situationists, and it is unlikely, in view of Debord's relationship to the organization, that ideas not espoused by him would have been presented in this way as "ideas of the group." On the other hand, all citations here to writings signed by other Situationists are clearly identified as to their authors.

actual lives of all other individuals, trapped as they are in vapid roles
(*SS* §60–61). "Separation is the alpha and omega of the spectacle" (*SS*
§25), and individuals, separated from one another, can rediscover unity
only within the spectacle, where "images detached from every aspect of
life merge into a common stream" (*SS* §2). Individuals are reunited
solely "in [their] separateness" (*SS* §29), for the spectacle monopolizes
all communication to its own advantage and makes it one way only.
The spectacle speaks, "social atoms" listen. And the message is One: an
incessant justification of the existing society, which is to say the spectacle itself, or the mode of production that has given rise to it. For this
purpose the spectacle has no need of sophisticated arguments; all it needs
is to be the only voice, and sure of no response whatsoever. Its first prerequisite, therefore, and at the same time its chief product, is the passivity of a contemplative attitude. Only an individual "isolated" amidst
"atomized masses" (*SS* §221) could feel any need for the spectacle, and
consequently the spectacle must bend every effort to reinforce the individual's isolation.

The spectacle has two main foundations: "incessant technological
renewal" and the "integration of State and economy." And in its most
recent phase it has three main consequences: "generalized secrecy; un-
answerable lies; an eternal present" (*Comm.*, 22; Eng., 11–12).

The spectacle is thus not a pure and simple adjunct to the world,
as propaganda broadcast via the communications media might be said
to be. Rather, it is the entirety of social activity that is appropriated by
the spectacle for its own ends. From city planning to political parties of
every tendency, from art to science, from everyday life to human passions and desires, everywhere we find reality replaced by images. In the
process, images end up by becoming real, and reality ends up transformed
into images.

Such images, furthermore, are necessarily distorted. For if on the one
hand the spectacle is society in its entirety, at the same time it is also a
part of society, as well as the instrument by means of which this part
comes to dominate the whole. The spectacle does not reflect society
overall; it organizes images in the interest of one portion of society only,
and this cannot fail to affect the real social activity of those who merely
contemplate these images.

By subordinating everything to its own requirements, the spectacle is
obliged to falsify reality to the point where, as Debord puts it, reversing
Hegel's well-known proposition, "in a world that *really* has been turned
on its head, truth is a moment of falsehood" (*SS* §9). Every power needs

lies in order to govern, and the spectacle, as the most highly developed power that has ever existed, is correspondingly the most mendacious. All the more so, too, because it is the most superfluous and hence the least justifiable.

The problem lies not, however, in the "image" or "representation" as such, as so many twentieth-century philosophies argue, but rather in the society that needs such images. It is true that the spectacle makes particular use of sight, "the most abstract of the senses, and the most easily deceived" (*SS* §18), but the problem resides in the *independence* achieved by representations that, having escaped from the control of human beings, proceed to address them in a monologue that eliminates all possible dialogue from human life. Such representations, though born of social practice, behave as independent beings.

It will be evident by this time that the spectacle is the heir of religion, and it is significant that the first chapter of *The Society of the Spectacle* has a quotation from Feuerbach's *Essence of Christianity* as its epigraph. The old religion projected man's own power into the heavens, where it took on the appearance of a god opposed to man, a foreign entity. The spectacle performs the same operation on earth. The greater the power that man attributed to gods of his own creation, the more powerless he himself felt; humanity behaves similarly with respect to powers that it has created and allowed to escape and that now "reveal themselves to us in their full force" (*SS* §31). The *contemplation* of these powers is in inverse proportion to the individual's experience of real life, to the point where his most ordinary gestures are lived by someone else instead of by the subject himself. In this world, "the spectator feels at home nowhere" (*SS* §30). In the spectacle, as in religion, every moment of life, every idea, and every gesture achieves meaning only from without (*Prelims.*, 343–44; *SIA*, 307).

All of which implies neither a fatality nor the inevitable result of technological development. The split that has come about between real social activity and its representation is the consequence of splits within society itself. It is the most ancient of all separations, that of power, which has given rise to all the others. Beginning with the dissolution of primitive communities, every society has experienced the establishment within itself of an institutional power, a separate authority, and all such power has a "spectacular" dimension to it. Only with the advent of the modern era, however, has power been able to accumulate the adequate means, not only to extend its domination to every aspect of life, but also actively to mold society in accordance with its own requirements. It has achieved this thanks chiefly to a material production tending continually to re-create everything needed to promote isolation and separation, from automobiles to television.

This "spectacular" trend in capitalist development has imposed itself gradually, beginning in the 1920s and gaining enormously in strength after the Second World War. And it has continued to accelerate. In 1967, Debord described the spectacle as "the self-portrait of power in the age of power's totalitarian rule over the conditions of existence" (*SS* §24) and seemed to feel that an almost unsurpassable situation had been reached. In 1988, however, he acknowledged that the spectacle's grip over society in 1967, as seen with the benefit of twenty years' hindsight, had clearly not yet been perfected (*Comm.*, 18; Eng., 7).

The foregoing remarks do not apply solely to Western capitalist societies, for all modern sociopolitical systems pay tribute to the regime of the commodity and the spectacle. Just as the spectacle is a totality within a society, so too it is a totality on a worldwide scale. A real antagonism, that between a proletariat demanding life and a system "where the commodity contemplates itself in a world of its own making" (*SS* §53), is concealed by *spectacular* antagonisms between political systems that are in actuality mutually supportive. Such antagonisms, however, are not mere phantoms, for they reflect the uneven development of capitalism in different parts of the world.

Thus, alongside countries where the commodity has been able to develop freely, we have their pseudo-negation in the form of societies dominated by a state bureaucracy, such as the Soviet Union, China, or numerous third-world nations. In 1967, Debord classified such regimes, together with the fascist governments that arose in Western countries in periods of crisis, as instances of "concentrated spectacular power." The relatively feeble economic development of these countries, as compared with that of societies ruled by "diffuse spectacular power," is compensated for by *ideology*, which is the ultimate commodity; and the acme of ideology is the requirement that everyone identify with a leader—with a Stalin, a Mao, or a Sukarno. The spectacle in this concentrated form lacks flexibility, and its rule depends in the end on a police force. Its negative image nevertheless has a part to play in the "worldwide division of spectacular tasks" (*SS* §57), for the Soviet bureaucracy and its extensions in Western countries (i.e., the traditional Communist parties) stand in an illusory manner for resistance to diffuse spectacular power. Inasmuch as no alternative to one or other of these forms appears to exist, real opponents within either spectacular system may often take the opposing system as their model—something that often happens, for example, in third-world revolutionary movements.

It was already clear to Debord when he wrote *The Society of the Spectacle* that whichever version of the spectacle could offer the wider choice of commodities must eventually prevail (*SS* §110). Each individual commodity promises access to an "already questionable satisfaction allegedly derived from the *consumption of the whole*" (*SS* §65), and as soon as the inevitable moment of disillusion occurs another commodity appears that makes the same promise. In the struggle waged among various objects, a struggle in respect of which man is a mere spectator, any given commodity is liable to wear itself out, yet the spectacle as a whole merely gets stronger. As Debord writes in one of the finest formulations in his book, "the spectacle is the epic poem of this strife—a strife that no fall of Ilium can bring to an end. Of arms and the man the spectacle does not sing, but rather of passions and the commodity" (*SS* §66). Exchange-value has come to dominate use-value (*SS* §46), and the detachment of the commodity from any genuine human need has succeeded, with the advent of patently useless objects, in attaining a quasi-religious level: Debord evokes the collecting of promotional key chains, which he characterizes as "indulgences" of the commodity (*SS* §67). What such an instance demonstrates is that the commodity no longer contains so much as an "atom" of use-value but that it is henceforward consumable *qua commodity*.[6]

The spectacle is thus not bound to a particular economic system. Rather, it betokens the victory of the *category* of the economy as such within society. The class responsible for the establishment of the spectacle—the bourgeoisie—owes its position of dominance to this triumph of the economy and its laws over all other aspects of life. The spectacle is "both the outcome and the goal of the dominant mode of production," "the omnipresent celebration of a choice *already made* in the sphere of production, and the consummate result of that choice" (*SS* §6). Not just work, but likewise other sorts of human activity—what is known as "free time"—are organized in such a way as to justify and perpetuate the reigning mode of production. Economic production has been transformed from a means into an end, and the spectacle is its form of expression: with its "essentially tautological" character (*SS* §13), the

6. As early as the nineteen-thirties, Theodor W. Adorno asserted that henceforward exchange-value could be consumed and use-value exchanged, and that "all enjoyment that achieves emancipation from exchange-value thereby acquires subversive characteristics" (*Dissonanzen*, in *Gesammelte Werke*, vol. 14 [Frankfurt: Suhrkamp, 1977], 24–25).

spectacle's aim is simply the reproduction of the conditions of its own existence. Instead of serving human desires, the economy in its spectacular stage continually creates and manipulates needs that are all reducible to the single "pseudo-need for the reign of an autonomous economy to continue" (SS §51).

"The economy" should therefore be understood here as one portion of global human activity that holds sway over all the rest. The spectacle is nothing more than this autocratic reign of the commodity economy (see, for instance, Comm., 14; Eng., 2). An economy become autonomous is in itself a form of alienation; economic production is founded on alienation; alienation has indeed become its chief product; and the economy's domination of the whole of society entails that maximum diffusion of alienation which is precisely what constitutes the spectacle. "The economy transforms the world, but it transforms it into a world of the economy" (SS §40).

Clearly the term "economy" is not being used here to mean simply material production—without which, of course, no society could exist. The economy in question is *an economy that has become independent* and in so doing subjugated human life. This is a consequence of the triumph of the *commodity* within the prevailing mode of production.

In the second chapter of *The Society of the Spectacle*, Debord examines the steps whereby "the entire economy then became what the commodity, throughout this campaign of conquest, had shown itself to be—namely, a process of quantitative development" (SS §40). Debord's account of the predominance of exchange-value over use-value does not depart significantly from Marx's, though his phraseology can be colorful: "Starting out as the condottiere of use-value, exchange-value ended up waging a war that was entirely its own" (SS §46).[7] And whereas Marx evokes the law of the falling rate of profit, Debord speaks of a "falling rate of use-value, which is a constant of the capitalist economy" (SS §47): an increasing subordination of all use, even the most banal, to the requirements of the growth of the economy—to a sheerly quantitative criterion. For even though the progress of the economy may have solved the immediate problem of survival in part of the world, the question of survival in the larger sense continues to rear its head, because an abundance of commodities is nothing more than a shortage for which material provision has been made.

---

7. Debord was indeed so much taken with this formulation that he quoted himself twenty years later (Pan., 83–84; Eng., 77).

In conceiving of alienation, of the spectacle, as a process of abstraction, and accounting for it in terms of the commodity and the *structure* of the commodity, Debord is elaborating upon some fundamental ideas of Marx's that, not surprisingly, have met with little success in the history of "Marxism." For Hegel, alienation is constituted by the objective and sensible world inasmuch as the subject fails to recognize this world as his own creation. The "young Hegelians"—Feuerbach, Moses Hess, or the early Marx—likewise see alienation as an inversion of subject and attribute, of concrete and abstract, but their conception is the exact opposite of Hegel's in that the true subject for them is man in his sensual and material existence. Man is alienated when he becomes the attribute of an abstraction that he has himself posited but that he no longer recognizes as such and that thus appears to him to be a subject in its own right. Man therefore comes to be determined by a now autonomous creation of his own. Feuerbach discerns alienation in the projection of human powers into the heaven of religion, leaving earthbound man powerless; but he also recognizes it in the abstractions of idealist philosophy, for which man in his material existence is merely a phenomenal form of the universal Spirit. Hess and the young Marx identify the state and money as two other fundamental alienations, as two abstractions in which man alienates himself in his capacities as a member of a collectivity and as a worker. This means by extension that the phenomenon of alienation does not affect all "humanity" to the same degree but that a specific alienation weighs down on one part of it, namely that part which is obliged to work without possessing the means of production. The worker's product does not belong to him and thus appears to him as an alien and hostile force. In all forms of alienation, the concrete individual has value only inasmuch as he partakes of the abstract, inasmuch as he possesses wealth, is a citizen of a state, a man before God, or a "self" in the philosophical sense. In this context, human action has no end of its own and serves the sole purpose of permitting man to attain what he has already himself created, which, though conceived exclusively as a means, has been transformed into an end. Money is the most obvious example here.

The spectacle is in effect the most highly developed form of this tendency toward abstraction, as witness Debord's observation that its "very manner of being concrete is, precisely, abstraction" (*SS* §29). The devaluing of life to the benefit of hypostasized abstractions now affects all aspects of existence; and these abstractions, which have now assumed the role of subject, no longer appear as things but, even more abstractly, as *images*. The spectacle may be said to incorporate all older forms of alienation: Debord describes it variously as "the material reconstruction of the religious illusion" (*SS* §20), as "money *for contemplation only*" (*SS* §49), as "inseparable from the modern State" (*SS* §24), and as "ideology in material form" (the title of the last chapter of *The Society of the Spectacle*).[8]

The notion of alienation as the inversion of subject and attribute, and as the subordination of the "essence of man" to what that essence produced, was superseded in Marx's thinking after a few years on the grounds that it was still too philosophical in character. In the *Communist Manifesto* (1848), Marx and Engels poked fun at the "German *literati*" because, "beneath the French criticism of the economic functions of money, they wrote 'alienation of the essence of man'" (*PW I*, 91). But the concept of alienation, in the sense of abstraction, comes back into play in Marx's later work on the critique of political economy, which in addition reveals the *historical origins* of the process of abstraction. In the first chapter of Volume I of *Capital*, Marx analyses the *form of the commodity* as the core of all capitalist production and shows that the process of abstraction is at the heart of the modern economy, not simply an unpleasant side effect of it. It should be borne in mind that Marx is not yet speaking here of surplus-value, or of the selling of labor-power, or of capital. He thus sees all the most highly developed forms of the capitalist economy as deriving from this primal structure of the commodity, which he compares to the "cell-form" of the body,[9] and from the antagonisms between concrete and abstract, between quantity and quality, between production and consumption, and between the social relationship and what that relationship produces.[10]

Marx stresses the *dual character* of the commodity: aside from its utility (its use-value), it also possesses a value that determines the relationship whereby it is exchanged for other commodities (its exchange-value). The material qualities of each commodity are necessarily distinct

---

8. It is worth noting once again that the spectacle implies a continual reversing of thing and image: things that were merely "ideal," such as religion and philosophy, take on material form, while things that had a certain material reality, such as money and the state, are reduced to mere images.

9. Marx, "Preface to the First Edition," *Capital I*, 90.

10. Consequently, nothing could be further from the truth than the claim of some commentators that Marx's reasons for starting out with the analysis of value were purely methodological ones and that this analysis is meaningful only when viewed through the lens of the later analysis of surplus-value. Thus Louis Althusser counsels those reading Volume I of *Capital* for the first time to skip Part One, and he makes no bones about his conviction that the pages on the fetishistic character of the commodity are a harmful residue of Hegelianism that has had an extremely pernicious effect on the development of what he considers to be Marxism (see "Preface to *Capital* Volume One" [1969], in Althusser, *Lenin and Philosophy and Other Essays*, trans. Ben Brewster [New York: Monthly Review Press, 1971], 81 and 95).

from those of all others, so that in this sense commodities have no common measure. But at the same time all commodities have a common substance which makes them exchangeable in that each possesses a different quantity thereof. This "substance of value" is identified by Marx as the *quantity of abstract labor-time* needed to produce a particular commodity. Qua exchange-value, commodities have no specific qualities, and diverse commodities may be distinguished from one another only in a quantitative way. The value of a product is thus constituted not by the specific concrete labor that has created it but rather by *abstract labor:* "With the disappearance of the useful character of the products of labour, the useful character of the kinds of labour embodied in them also disappears; this in turn entails the disappearance of the different concrete forms of labour. They can no longer be distinguished, but are all together reduced to the same kind of labour, human labour in the abstract."[11] Thus the qualitative character of the different forms of labor that produce different products is lost. The value of a commodity is nothing more than a "crystal" of a "substance"—of "homogeneous human labour," which is merely "an expenditure of human brains, muscles, nerves, hands, etc.," and the only measure of which is the *time* it takes to perform.[12] The time in question is always that which is needed *on average* to manufacture a particular product in a given society under given working conditions; more complicated jobs have a value that is simply a multiple of that of simpler ones (i.e., of a greater quantity of simpler labor). In the seemingly trite formula "10 lb. of tea = 20 yards of linen," Marx recognized the most general formula for all capitalist production: two concrete things take the form of something else that connects them, namely abstract labor, whose ultimate form is money.

A commodity must nevertheless always have a use-value, and answer a need, whether real or artificial. A commodity's value always appears as a use-value, which, in the exchange process, is simply the "bearer" of exchange-value. To be realized, use-value must "become the form of appearance of its opposite, value."[13] The process whereby the concrete becomes abstract is here understood by Marx not in an anthropological sense but as the consequence of a determinate *historical* phenomenon. The spread of the commodity is indeed a phenomenon of the modern period. The subordination of quality to quantity and of concrete to ab-

---

11. *Capital I,* 128.
12. Ibid., 128, 134.
13. Ibid., 148.

stract is implicit in the structure of the commodity, but not all human activity is founded on exchange and hence on the commodity.

So long as different human communities, villages for instance, continue to produce what they need for themselves, restricting exchange to the role of an occasional way for dealing with surpluses, use-value will determine production. Each particular job is part of a division of tasks within the community with which it is directly associated, and it thus retains its qualitative character. This is why Marx says that the social relation here is produced *along with* material production. Relations between men may be brutal in such circumstances, but they continue to be clearly recognizable for what they are, as for instance when serfs of the glebe or slaves realize that they are relieved of part of what they produce by their masters. Only when a certain threshold is passed in the development and volume of exchange does production itself come to be defined essentially in terms of the creation of exchange-value. The use-value of each product will thenceforward reside in its exchange-value, and other use-values will be reachable only through exchange-value serving as intermediary. Labor itself becomes labor-power to be sold for the purpose of performing abstract labor. Access to use-value, which is to say access to the concrete, is possible only via the mediation of exchange-value, or, more specifically, of money.

In modern society, individuals are isolated within a production system where everyone produces according to their self-interest. The social links between such individuals are established only a posteriori, thanks to the exchange of commodities. Their concrete being or subjectivity is perforce alienated in the mediation of abstract labor, which erases all differences. The capitalist mode of production entails the extension of the characteristics of the commodity to the entirety of material production and to the entirety of social relations. Men merely exchange units of abstract labor, objectified as exchange-value, which can then be reconverted into use-value.

The value of products is created by men, but unbeknownst to them. The fact that value always appears in the shape of a use-value, of a concrete object, gives rise to the illusion that a product's concrete characteristics are what determine its fate.[14] Herein lies the famous "fetishism of the commodity and its secret" in discussing which Marx makes an

---

14. If "one ton of iron and two ounces of gold" have the same market value, common sense suggests that a natural relationship exists here; in reality the relationship concerned is between the quantities of labor that have produced the one and the other (ibid., 167).

explicit comparison to the religious illusion, where the products of human fancy appear to take on a life of their own.[15] In a society where individuals encounter one another solely through exchange, the transformation of the products of human labor and of the relations that preside over it into something apparently "natural" further implies that the whole of social life seems to be independent of human volition and that it manifests itself as a seemingly autonomous and "given" entity that is subject to no rules but its own. Indeed, in Marx's view, such social relations do not merely *appear* but actually *are* "material [*sachlich*] relations between persons and social relations between things."[16]

On those rare occasions when the Marxist tradition has addressed the issue of "commodity fetishism," it has almost always treated it as a phenomenon strictly confined to the sphere of consciousness, that is to say, as a false idea of the "real" economic situation. But this is but one aspect of the matter. As Marx himself cautions, "the belated scientific discovery that the products of labour, in so far as they are values, are merely the material expressions of the human labour expended to produce them, marks an epoch in the history of mankind's development, but by no means banishes the semblance of objectivity possessed by the social characteristics of labour."[17] In point of fact, the concept of "fetishism" implies that the whole of human life is subordinated to the laws dictated by the nature of value and in the first place to the necessity for value to increase continually. The abstract labor embodied in commodities is utterly indifferent to whatever effects it may have on the plane of use. Its aim is purely and simply to have produced a greater quantity of value, in the form of money, by the end of its cycle than it had at the beginning.[18] This means that in the dual character of the commodity it is already possible to discern capitalism's most fundamental trait, namely, the necessity for the system to be in a permanent state of crisis. Far from being a "neutral" factor (as the Marxists of the workers' movement tended to believe), which only becomes problematic in the context of the extraction of "surplus-value" (i.e., exploitation), value leads on the contrary to an ineluctable clash between "economic" rationality on the one

15. Ibid., 163, 165.
16. Ibid., 166.
17. Ibid., 167.
18. With interest-bearing capital, that is to say, with "money that produces more money," the tautologous character of the production of value achieves its clearest expression: "M [money]—M' [more money]. Here we have the original starting-point of capital, money in the formula M—C [commodity]—M', reduced to the two extremes M—M', where M' = M + ΔM, money that creates more money. This is the original and general formula for capital reduced to an absurd abbreviation" (*Capital III*, 514).

hand, entailing the creation of more and more value irrespective of concrete content, and real human needs on the other. From the point of view
of value, the trafficking of plutonium or contaminated blood is worth
more than French agriculture. There is nothing aberrant about this: it is
simply the working of the logic of value.[19] Clearly value is in no sense
an "economic" category; rather, it is a complete social form that itself
causes the splitting of society into different sectors. Nor, therefore, is the
"economy" an imperialist sector that has subjugated the other areas of
society to its will, as Debord's phrasing might at times lead one to think,
for the economy is itself constituted by value.

There are in fact two competing views to be found in Marx, the one
envisaging liberation *from* the economy, the other liberation *by means
of* the economy; nor may the two be simply assigned to different phases
of his thought, as some would like to do. In his critique of value, Marx
thoroughly exposed the "pure form" of the society of the commodity.
At the time, this critique constituted a bold piece of anticipation; only
today is it able truly to apprehend the essence of social reality. Marx himself was not aware, and his Marxist successors even less aware, of the
gap that existed between his critique of value and the content of the
greater part of his work, in which he scrutinized the empirical forms of
the capitalist society of his era. He could not have perceived how laden
that era still was with precapitalist features, and consequently many of
the characteristics he described were still very different from, even sometimes opposed to, what was to emerge later from the gradual victory of
the commodity-form over all the relics of precapitalist times. Marx thus
treated as essential traits of capitalism features that were in reality expressions of a still unfinished form of the system. Among such features,
for example, was the creation of a class that had of necessity to be excluded from bourgeois society and its "benefits." The Marxism of the
workers' movement, from social democracy to Stalinism, and including
all the more or less highly elaborated variants produced by the intellectuals, retained only this side of Marx's thought. And even if the movement

19. In the German journal *Krisis*, no. 13 (1993), one of the few publications to have
elaborated upon these arguments in recent years, Ernst Lohoff writes as follows: "The
contemplative and affirmative tone with which Hegel has reality evolve from the starting-
point of the concept of 'Being' is utterly foreign to the Marxian account [of value]. For
Marx 'value' cannot embody reality, but it subordinates reality to its own form, which
form it then destroys, and in so doing destroys itself. The Marxian critique of value does
not accept value as a positive basic principle, nor does it argue in its name. It interprets its
self-sufficient existence in terms of appearance. And indeed the large-scale construction of
the mediation known as the commodity absolutely does not lead to any definitive triumph
of that form, but coincides instead with its crisis" (p. 126).

often distorted it still more, it nevertheless had good reason to refer to this view of things, which was valid as applied to capitalism's ascendant phase, when the issue was still the imposition of capitalist forms upon pre-bourgeois ones.[20] The high point of this phase was the period epitomized by the names of Ford and Keynes—a time when the Marxism of the workers' movement enjoyed its greatest triumphs. The crisis that erupted in the nineteen-sixties, by contrast, arose not as before from shortcomings of the commodity system but instead from that system's total victory. And it was now that its most fundamental contradiction came to the fore, a contradiction grounded in the structure of the commodity itself. As we shall see, the relevance of Debord's thought lies in his having been among the first to interpret the present situation in the light of the Marxian theory of value, whereas his shakier contentions are made at points where his thinking is still under the influence of the Marxism of the workers' movement. One of the last voices of an old kind of social criticism, Debord was at the same time one of the first voices of a new stage.

There are two implications of the critique of commodity fetishism that Debord had the great foresight to grasp. The first is that economic exploitation is not the sole evil of capitalism, for capitalism necessarily entails the rejection of life itself in *all* its concrete manifestations. Second, none of the many variant arrangements *within* the commodity economy can ever bring about decisive change. It is therefore quite fruitless to expect any good outcome to flow from the development of the economy and an adequate distribution of its benefits. Alienation and dispossession are the very essence of the commodity economy, nor could that economy ever function on any other basis, so that whenever the economy progresses alienation and dispossession must needs likewise progress. Debord made a genuine rediscovery here, for it must be remembered that "Marxism" was no more inclined than bourgeois science to practice the "*critique* of political economy"; instead it practiced political economy *tout court,* considering the abstract and quantitative sides of labor while ignoring the contradiction with its *concrete* side.[21] This brand of Marxism failed to see that the subordination of the whole of life to economic requirements was one of the most contemptible results of capitalist de-

20. The Situationists, who detested dogmatism, and "isms" in general, maintained that they were Marxists "just as much as Marx was when he said 'I am not a Marxist'" (*IS* 9/26; *SIA,* 141).

21. Marx identifies the "purely economic" view with "the bourgeois standpoint" (*Capital III,* 368); this passage is also cited by Lukács (*HCC,* 243).

velopment; it treated this result instead as an ontological fact and judged that bringing it to the fore was in itself a revolutionary act.

Debord's use of the terms "image" and "spectacle" should be understood as an extension of Marx's idea of the commodity-form. All these concepts reduce the multiplicity of the real to a unique, abstract, and equal form. And indeed the image and the spectacle occupy the same position in Debord's thought as the commodity and its derivatives do in Marx's. The first sentence of *The Society of the Spectacle* is a *détournement* of the first sentence of *Capital*: "The whole life of those societies in which modern conditions of production prevail presents itself as an immense accumulation of *spectacles.*" Likewise, Debord substitutes the word "spectacle" for the word "capital" in another sentence borrowed from Marx: "The spectacle is not a collection of images; rather, it is a social relationship between people that is mediated by images" (*SS* §4).[22] According to Marx, money accumulated beyond a certain threshold is transformed into capital; according to Debord, capital accumulated beyond a certain threshold is transformed into images (*SS* §34). The spectacle is the equivalent not merely of goods, as is money, but also of all possible forms of activity, the reason being, precisely, that "whatever society as a whole can be and do" has been commodified (*SS* §49). The "essentially tautological" character of the spectacle (*SS* §13) perfectly echoes the tautological and self-referential character of abstract labor, of which the only goal is to increase the mass of objectified dead labor and which in effect treats the production of use-values merely as a means of reaching that goal.[23] The spectacle is conceived of by Debord as a visualization of the abstract link that exchange establishes between individuals, just as, for Marx, money was the materialization of that link. And images in their turn assume material form and exert a real influence on society: this is why Debord insists that "ideological entities have never been mere fictions" (*SS* §212).

Debord and Lukács

Marxian thought is thus at once a *record* and a *critique* of the reduction of all human life to value, that is to say, to the economy and it laws.

22. Cf. *Capital I*, 932: "capital is not a thing, but a social relation between persons which is mediated through things."
23. Whereas labor under its concrete aspect invariably produces a qualitative transformation, as for instance when cloth is transformed into a coat, no such transformation occurs under its abstract aspect, merely an *increase in value* (money, objectified dead labor). This is the origin of labor's tautological character.

Nevertheless, generations of Marx's adversaries and followers have interpreted his testimony as an *apology* for this reduction. It must seem surprising, from their point of view, that Debord should invoke Marx and at the same time deem the economic sphere antagonistic to the totality of life. Debord, however, can legitimately lay claim to illustrious predecessors in his interpretation of Marx. One of these is Georg Lukács, who writes: "It is not the primacy of economic motives in historical explanation that constitutes the decisive difference between Marxism and bourgeois thought, but the point of view of totality" (*HCC*, 27). This "point of view" is for Lukács closely bound up with the rediscovery of the "fetishism of the commodity." The return of this concept, at least as a modish term, began in the nineteen-fifties, but this should not be allowed to obscure the poor treatment it has received in general from "Marxists." From Marx's death until the nineteen-twenties, it fell into almost total oblivion: Engels in his last period paid it no attention, nor did Luxemburg, Lenin, or Kautsky; all founded their condemnation of capitalism on growing pauperization, on difficulties of accumulation, or on the falling rate of profit. The first to revive the "fetishism" concept in any serious way was Lukács, in his *History and Class Consciousness* (1923),[24] and only after the Second World War did the notion begin to find a slightly larger following in the Marxist camp.

On its first publication, Lukács's book created an uproar in which praise and condemnation were intermingled. In 1924, it was damned by the Third International, and a parallel anathema was issued by German social democracy. A few years later Lukács too distanced himself from his own book, which quickly became at once legendary and impossible to come by, so that few people were able to be influenced by it. But the official demise of Stalinism stimulated the search for a different kind of Marxism, and eventually, in 1957 and 1958, a few chapters of this *livre maudit* were published in the French journal *Arguments;* in 1960 a French translation of the entire work appeared over the author's own objections. Lukács, since he manifestly could not prevent the rediscovery of his book, proceeded to authorize a new German edition (1967), adding a preface that incorporated very significant self-criticism.

History and Class Consciousness attained an almost cultlike status in the nineteen-sixties, and it exerted a profound influence on Debord;

24. Another attempt to explore these themes should also be mentioned: Isaac I. Rubin's *Essays on Marx's Theory of Value* (Detroit: Black and Red, 1972; Montreal: Black Rose, 1973); this work was first published in Moscow in 1924 and barely noticed at that time.

clearly it supplied the initial orientation for his development of Marxian themes. Debord himself does not refer overmuch to this connection,
however: his direct quotation of Lukács is confined to two sentences serving as epigraph for the second chapter of *The Society of the Spectacle;*
elsewhere he quotes a few lines from the young Hegel's "The Difference
between the Philosophical Systems of Fichte and Schelling" that would
seem to have been taken from Lukács's book (*HCC*, 139). As for Lukács's theories, Debord explicitly evokes only his conception of the party
as that "mediation between theory and practice" whereby proletarians
cease to be "mere 'spectators'"; and he adds that what Lukács is really
describing here is "everything that the [Bolshevik] Party *was not*" (*SS*
§112).[25]

The entire run of the journal *Internationale Situationniste* contains
just one reference to Lukács, but the choice of matter quoted is characteristic: "The primacy of the category of totality is the bearer of the
principle of revolution in science" (*IS* 4/31; *HCC*, 27). That category is
indeed as central for Lukács—whose reiteration of this is one of the very
few points where he continues, in his 1967 preface, to see validity in his
book (*HCC*, xx–xxi)—as it is for Debord.

We have seen that in Debord's view the spectacle is at once economic
and ideological in nature, at once a mode of production and a type of
everyday life, and so on. The Situationists deemed it necessary to pass
a *global* judgment here, one that could not be dazzled by the variety of
choices seemingly on offer within the spectacle; they consequently rejected all change of a partial kind. According to *The Society of the Spectacle*, the degree of alienation now imposed on them puts workers "in
the position of having either to reject [their impoverishment] in its totality or do nothing at all" (*SS* §122). At least in its "diffuse" variant,
the spectacle always appears in a variety of guises: different political tendencies, contrasting life styles, antagonistic artistic attitudes. The spectator is urged to express an opinion, or to choose one such false alternative or another, so that he never questions the whole. The Situationists
stressed the necessity of rejecting existing conditions *en bloc*, in fact they
made this attitude into an epistemological principle: "The only possible
basis for understanding this world is to oppose it; and such opposition

25. The Situationists nonetheless approved in theory of this conception of organization and strove to apply it to themselves. See their pamphlet *De la Misère en milieu étudiant* (Strasbourg: Union Nationale des Étudiants de France/Association Fédérale Générale des Étudiants de Strasbourg, 1966), 25; English trans: "On the Poverty of Student
Life," in *SIA*, 334. (This pamphlet is discussed in Part 2, pp. 82–83.)

will be neither genuine nor realistic unless it contests the totality" (*IS* 7/9–10; *SIA*, 81).

Lukács[26] for his part explained that the more bourgeois thought succeeded in understanding particular "facts" about social life, the less it was able to apprehend it in its totality. This incapacity corresponded perfectly to the actual fragmentation of social activity and in particular to the growing compartmentalization of work. Bourgeois science, along with the kind of "vulgar" Marxism it influenced, so typical of the Second International, allowed itself to be misled by such alleged contradictions as that between the economic and the political spheres. Only authentic Marxism—and Lukács states explicitly that the method of authentic Marxism was derived from Hegel—was able to identify isolated facts as mere *moments* of an overarching *process*.

Bourgeois science takes the apparent independence of "things" and "facts" for the truth and strives to discover the "laws" that govern them. It looks upon economic crises or wars not as the more or less distorted outcome of human actions but rather as events obeying their own laws. This science remains prisoner to the commodity fetishism which it is the task of a genuine critique to dispel. This is why, according to Lukács, it may legitimately be said that "the chapter [of *Capital*] dealing with the fetish character of the commodity contains within itself the whole of historical materialism" (*HCC*, 170)—a truly unheard-of assertion in 1923. Lukács uses the term "reification" to refer to the operation whereby fetishism transforms processes into things.

Apropos of the commodity, Lukács maintains that "at this stage in the history of mankind there is no problem that does not ultimately lead back to that question and there is no solution that could not be found in the solution to the riddle of commodity-*structure*" (*HCC*, 83). "Our intention here," he announces, "is to *base* ourselves on Marx's economic analyses" (*HCC*, 84), and he sees his personal contribution as an analysis of the commodity as the "universal category" of total social being (*HCC*, 86). The transition from a society in which the commodity appears only in occasional acts of exchange to one in which commodities are produced systematically was not a purely quantitative change, as bourgeois economists like to believe. It was also a qualitative transition whereby the commodity was transformed from a simple mediation between productive processes into a central factor in a mode of production whose very character it came to determine (*HCC*, 83ff.).

26. In the context of the present discussion, "Lukács" refers exclusively to the Lukács of *History and Class Consciousness*.

Lukács lays far more emphasis than Marx on the "contemplative" aspect of capitalism. In his view, each individual is capable of recognizing no more than the tiniest portion of the world as of his own making, while the vast remainder lies beyond the range of conscious activity and may only be contemplated from afar. This is not to say that "activity" of a sort—even frenzied and harrowing activity—is impossible; the decisive fact, however, is that the worker's function in the productive process is reduced to a passive role circumscribed by a preestablished plan that unfolds as automatically as a conveyor belt.

In contrast to other times, there is but a difference of degree in the reification undergone by the various classes of society. Whoever works must sell his labor-power as a *thing;* and in the case of the bureaucrat this sale includes brain-power. But the entrepreneur contemplating the progress of the economy or the advance of technology is likewise reified, as is the technician "faced with the state of science and the profitability of its application to technology" (*HCC*, 98). Under capitalism every individual is restricted to wresting whatever advantage he can from a system "the 'laws' of which he finds 'ready-made'" (*HCC*, 98). Taking issue directly with Engels, Lukács asserts that industry and scientific experimentation are based on a contemplative attitude toward "facts" whose actual motion appears as coagulated (*HCC*, 132).[27] More and more, man becomes a mere passive observer or spectator (*HCC*, 90, 100, 166) of the independent movement of commodities, which to him seems like a kind of "second nature" (*HCC*, 128)—a phrase also used by Debord in *The Society of the Spectacle* (§24). Likewise enveloped in this false consciousness is the "economistic" version of Marxism, which sees all social change as governed by economic laws.

Contemplation is obviously related to *separation*, since the subject can contemplate only that which is opposed to him inasmuch as it is separate from him. Lukács, far more than Marx, associates reification with the division of labor, a phenomenon that had made great "progress" in the half-century that had intervened between Marx's day and the Lukács of 1923. Whereas for the medieval artisan the productive process constituted an "organic, irrational [. . .] unity" (*HCC*, 88), modern productive activities are part of an extended *calculation* in accordance with

---

27. In his 1967 preface, Lukács vigorously reversed this judgment, asserting that it is in fact activity, not passivity, that is characteristic of the bourgeoisie. But one may perfectly well become active, even frantically so, on the basis of a "fact" or a "law" whose validity one accepts in a passive way, which suggests that *History and Class Consciousness* was nearer the mark than its author was later prepared to admit.

which individual tasks that are in themselves meaningless are reassembled by "specialists." Such fragmented labor is less capable than ever of producing a social bond whereby human beings can encounter one another on an individual and concrete basis.

What Debord and Lukács have in common in a specific sense is their unswerving rejection of every form of contemplation, which they see as an alienation of the subject. They both identify subject and activity, and for Debord contemplation, or "non-intervention," is the diametrical opposite of life. "There can be no freedom apart from activity, and within the spectacle all activity is banned" (SS §27).

Lukács broadens the critique of the contemplative nature of capitalist society with a stiff harangue against "the contemplative duality of subject and object" (HCC, 148). Pre-Hegelian philosophy looked upon the object—whether conceived in idealist fashion as a 'thing-in-itself' or in the manner of eighteenth-century materialism—as an entity separate from and independent of the activity of the subject. It took the Hegelian dialectic to discover that the duality is resolved in the *process*, and Marx then proceeded to identify this process with the concrete historical process that "truly eliminates the—actual—autonomy of the objects and the concepts of things with their resulting rigidity" (HCC, 144). Indeed "the nature of history is precisely that every definition degenerates into an illusion: *history is the history of the unceasing overthrow of the objective forms that shape the life of man*" (HCC, 186). Whereas science can only search for "those 'laws' which function in—objective— reality *without the intervention of the subject*" (HCC, 128), thus perpetuating the split between subject and object, theory and praxis, the class struggle, by reconstituting the unity of subject and object, will thereby reconstruct the *total man*.

In the spectacle, a fragmented society is *illusorily restored to wholeness;* and Debord's analysis of this process is the point at which he goes beyond *History and Class Consciousness*. It is instructive in this regard to compare statements by the two authors. Thus Lukács writes that "mechanization makes of them [the workers] isolated abstract atoms whose work no longer brings them together directly and organically; it becomes mediated to an increasing extent exclusively by the abstract laws of the mechanism which imprisons them" (HCC, 90). And here is Debord: "The generalized separation of worker and product has spelled the end of any comprehensive view of the job done, as well as the end of direct personal communication between producers. . . . Consistency and communication become the exclusive assets of the system's managers" (SS §26). Clearly for Debord "abstract laws" are no longer a pure mediation and have been reorganized into a coherent system. In 1923, Lukács recorded the passing of all totality and implicitly adopted Max Weber's notion of the "disenchantment of the world"; Debord similarly evokes continued global domination by "a *banalizing* trend" (SS §59), but he sees this as arising from a spurious reconstruction of the totality, from a *totalitarian* dictatorship of the fragmentary.

This development is particularly striking when Debord extends reification to realms beyond that of work. The young Marx found fault with political economy because it saw, not the man, but merely the worker, leaving all other aspects to be seen only by "the eyes of doctors, judges, grave-diggers, beadles, etc."[28] In contrast, the spectacle "attends to" the whole man and appears to lavish on him, in the spheres of consumption and free time, all the attention that in reality is refused him both in the sphere of work and everywhere else (SS §43). Even dissatisfaction and rebellion are liable to become cogs in the machinery of the spectacle (SS §59).

No genuine mending of splits can occur solely at the level of thought: only activity can transcend contemplation, and mankind truly knows only what it has *done*. For Lukács, proletarian theory thus has no value save as a "theory of praxis" in the process of self-transformation into a *"practical theory* that overturns the whole world" (HCC, 205). Debord likewise asserts that it is "within the historical struggle itself" that "the theory of praxis [must be] verified by virtue of its transformation into theory-in-practice" (SS §90); with Marx, says Debord, the negation of the existing order passed from the theoretical plane to that of "revolutionary practice—the only true agent of [that] negation" (SS §84). And when Debord warns that "no *idea* could transcend the spectacle that exists—it could only transcend ideas that exist about the spectacle" (SS §203), he is merely summing up one of the favorite themes of *Internationale Situationniste*, which was continually rebuking all proprietors of more or less exact truths for failing to test them practically.

The real philosophical pivot of *History and Class Consciousness* is the demand that the subject countenance no independent object apart from itself; in other words, Lukács's work theorizes an identity of subject and object. This is also one of the main reasons why the later Lukács

28. Karl Marx, *Economic and Philosophical Manuscripts*, trans. Gregor Benton, in *EW*, 335.

rejected his own work. In his preface of 1967, he denounced the notion of an identical subject-object as hopelessly idealist in character, since it sought to abolish all objectivity along with alienation. The conception of alienation proposed in *History and Class Consciousness* unknowingly implied an acceptance of the Hegelian identification of subject and object and failed to take into account the Marxian definition of objectification: "a natural means by which man masters the world and as such it can be either a positive or a negative fact. By contrast, alienation is a special variant of that activity which becomes operative in definite social conditions" (*HCC*, xxxvi). All work involves objectification, and so too does language; alienation, on the other hand, occurs only when "the essence of man [comes] into conflict with his existence" (*HCC*, xxiv). By identifying the two notions, *History and Class Consciousness* unintentionally defined alienation as "an eternal '*condition humaine*'"—a "fundamental and crude error," according to the later Lukács, which "certainly contributed greatly" to the book's success (ibid.), as likewise to the rise of German and French existentialism.

In point of fact, the critique of capitalist alienation and that of simple objectivity coexist in *History and Class Consciousness*, and it is very difficult to disentangle them. It is reasonable to enquire, therefore, to what extent a similar unintended confusion is to be found in Debord's work. The need to draw a distinction between alienation and objectification was of course clearly felt well before 1967; suffice it to recall the publication in 1932 of the *Economic and Philosophical Manuscripts*, where Marx argues that for Hegel alienation was identical to the objectification of the Spirit, and hence as necessary as it was transient.

Debord was in fact at pains to avoid Lukács's "fundamental and crude error," and he reminds us that Marx emancipated himself from "the unfolding of the Hegelian Spirit on its way to its rendezvous with itself in time, its objectification being indistinguishable from its alienation" (*SS* §80). Debord certainly does not define objectification as something necessarily bad; so far from rejecting the loss of the subject in the shifting objectifications which time brings, and from which that subject is liable to emerge enriched, Debord hails this as a genuinely human phenomenon—the complete opposite of the alienation that confronts the subject with hypostasized abstractions that are absolutely *other*. "As Hegel showed, time is a *necessary* alienation, the medium in which the subject realizes itself while losing itself. . . . The opposite obtains in the case of the alienation that now holds sway. . . . This is a *spatial alienation*, whereby a society which radically severs the subject from the activity that it steals from it separates it in the first place from its own time. Social alienation, though in principle surmountable, is nevertheless the alienation that has forbidden and petrified the possibilities and risks of a *living* alienation within time" (*SS* §161). For Debord, as for Lukács before him, one of the fundamental modes of reification is the *spatialization of time*.[29] Using Hegelian terms, as he acknowledges, Debord contrasts "restless becoming in the progression of time" (i.e., "*necessary* alienation") with a space characterized by the absence of movement (*SS* §170). On several occasions, Debord observed that the Situationist attitude consisted in identifying oneself with the passage of time.

Like the Lukács of *History and Class Consciousness*, Debord was led to assume that reification clashes with a subject that is in its essence immune to it. Such a subject, even one existing here and now, must be at least in part the bearer of demands and desires different from those created by reification. What seems to be entirely absent from either *History and Class Consciousness* or *The Society of the Spectacle* is any hint that the subject might be under attack, within itself, from forces of alienation capable of conditioning its unconscious in such a way as to cause it to identify actively with the system in which it finds itself. According to the Situationists (no doubt Debord was the least naïve in this regard), it would suffice for empirical subjects to reach understanding amongst themselves without intermediaries in order for them to arrive at revolutionary positions. Debord seems to conceive of the spectacle as a force exerted *from without* upon "life." Indeed he asserts that the spectacle is the society itself and at the same time just a part of that society (*SS* §3). Although the spectacle tends to invade "lived reality" (*SS* §8), the latter remains distinct from it, even the opposite of it. There must after all be such a thing as a substantially "healthy" subject, otherwise it would make no sense to speak of the "falsification" of a subject's activity. Inasmuch as Debord describes the subject's world as a distorted reflection of the subject (*SS* §16), then it is not the subject that is alienated but that world. Yet the objective world would have no independent existence if it were

29. Some observations on this subject will be found in Martin Jay, *Downcast Eyes: The Denigration of Vision in Twentieth-Century French Thought* (Berkeley: University of California Press, 1993), chapter 7 of which is entitled "From the Empire of the Gaze to the Society of the Spectacle: Foucault and Debord" (see especially pp. 416ff.). A somewhat less superficial account might have been expected from Jay, a historian of philosophy well known for his work on the Frankfurt School. It is certainly worth noting, however, how quickly Debord seems to be losing his "marginality" in the eyes of the academic world.

merely a "faithful reflection" of its producer. We seem to be back in the presence of Lukács's "identical subject-object."

Debord identifies the reification-resisting subject with the *proletariat*,[30] just as Lukács did in *History and Class Consciousness*. Both authors locate the essence of the proletariat not in economic conditions but in its opposition to reification. For Lukács, class consciousness is not an empirical datum that may be found immediately in the class as a whole or even in each proletarian; instead it is a datum *in itself* that is assigned de jure to the proletarian class. Although reification affects all classes, the bourgeoisie is not uncomfortable with this situation for the simple reason that the rule of the commodity is also *its* rule. The only class with an interest in the transcendence of reification is the proletariat, because the worker always finds himself, no matter what, to be the *object* of events: inasmuch as he is obliged to sell his labor-power as a commodity, he himself is inevitably capitalism's main commodity. At the same time, inasmuch as he is aware of being reduced to a mere object of the labor process, he may eventually realize that he is in reality the author, or subject, of that process; hence "his consciousness is the *self-consciousness of the commodity*" (*HCC*, 168). Thus reification is destined to be transcended precisely when it reaches its highest level: once every human element has been taken away from the life of the proletariat, that class will by the same token be able to see clearly that every "objectification" embodies a relationship between men that is mediated by things (*HCC*, 176). Starting from the most obvious form of reification, the relationship between wage-labor and capital, the proletariat will eventually discover all its other forms. And it will find itself unable to abandon this path until it has reconstituted the totality—that "total process . . . uncontaminated by any trace of reification . . . which allows the process-like essence to prevail *in all its purity* [and which represents] the authentic, higher reality" (*HCC*, 184).

Almost alone among observers in the nineteen-sixties, Debord insists that the proletariat continues to exist, and he describes it as "the vast mass of workers who have lost all power over the use of their own lives" (*SS* §114). Proletarians are "people who have no possibility of altering the social space-time that society allots for their consumption" (*IS* 8/13; *SIA*, 108). Both Lukács and Debord emphasize that in modern society the *condition* of the proletarian, so long as this is not defined solely in

---

30. Debord wavers even more than the Lukács of *History and Class Consciousness* between stressing the alienation of "man," of "the individual," and stressing the alienation of "the worker."

terms of wages, is in the process of becoming the condition of the entire
society. The subordination of all aspects of life to the exigencies of the
commodity, to the laws of calculation and quantification, means that
"the fate of the worker"—that is to say reification—"becomes the fate
of society as a whole" (*HCC,* 91). Debord for his part writes that "the
triumph of an economic system founded on separation leads to the *proletarianization of the world*" (*SS* §26); thus a good portion of the work
of the middle classes is now carried out under proletarian conditions
(*SS* §114), and the proletariat is de facto larger than ever.[31] Even as-
suming that purely economic demands could be met, the spectacle can
never offer a qualitatively rich life, for its very foundation is quantity
and banality. The proletariat is deprived not only of material wealth but
also of all the possibilities of human enrichment that it likewise creates.
The spectacle excludes it by definition from access to the entire range of
humanity's products, thus prohibiting it from putting into *free play* what
the economy of the spectacle uses to foster the unrelenting growth of its
alienated and alienating production system. This is why the proletariat
turns out to be the enemy of what exists, and the "negative at work,"
regardless of any quantitative increase that might be made in the doling
out of survival. In face of the totality of the spectacle, the project of the
proletariat cannot but be total itself, nor can it be confined to some "re-
distribution of wealth" or some "democratization" of society.

   The real social contradiction is therefore that between those who
want, or rather those who are obliged to maintain alienation, and those
who would abolish it; between those who cannot, either in thought or
in action, transcend the subject-object split, and those whose thought and
action tend on the contrary toward such a transcendence. The great importance assigned by the Situationists to "subjective" factors led them
to place significantly more stress on the manifestations of false consciousness—on the bureaucratic character of workers' parties, for instance. It
also allowed them to play down the significance of facts that seemed to
contradict their theory. It made it easy, notably, to assume that the proletariat is revolutionary in its essence, or *in itself:* if it does not demonstrate its revolutionary character in any flagrant way, even if almost all

---

31. Twenty years later, in *Comments on the Society of the Spectacle,* Debord reversed the terms of this proposition: he now saw the middle classes, of whom he had originally said that they would be absorbed into the proletariat, as occupying the whole of social space, the rule of the spectacle being their expression. Although the conditions of their
lives had been proletarianized in that they had no power over those lives, they lacked the
class consciousness of the proletariat. From this point of view, therefore, even Debord
eventually admitted that the proletarian class had been absorbed by the middle class.

of its concrete actions have to be viewed as "reformist," the reason can be said to be that the class has simply not yet attained its *being-for-itself*, not yet arrived at a consciousness of its true being, on account of its illusions and through the fault of those with an interest in manipulating those illusions. The question is not to determine what the workers *are* at present but rather what they *can become*—for only thus is it possible to grasp what in truth they *already are* (*VS*, 122; Eng., 111). Such an account is clearly very general, and a far cry from Marx's, according to which the proletariat is the revolutionary class not just because it has the most serious reasons for dissatisfaction but also because its place in the production process, its cohesion, and its massive concentration in particular areas together give it the means to overthrow the existing order.

For Debord, the concrete form assumed by the proletariat qua identical subject-object is that of *workers' councils*, thanks to which proletarians can first conduct the struggle and later organize a future free society. Around 1920, Lukács too sympathized with the idea of workers' councils, having participated in the Hungarian Council Republic (or Commune) of 1919. In workers' councils, activity in the first person is supposed to replace mere contemplation of the actions of a party or leader: "in the power of workers' councils . . . the proletarian movement becomes its own product; this product is the producer himself" (*SS* §117). Here all separation and all specialization are abolished, for revolutionary workers' councils vest "all decision-making and executive powers in themselves" (*SS* §116). The power of such councils will "transform the totality of existing conditions," for it aspires to "recognize itself in a world of its own design" (*SS* §179).

In the historical process, according to *The Society of the Spectacle*, subject and object are already identical *in themselves;* historical struggle is the struggle to make them coincide *for themselves*. Modern history "has no goal aside from what effects it works upon itself. . . . As for the *subject* of history, it can only be the self-production of the living: the living becoming master and possessor of its world—that is, of history" (*SS* §74). This "becoming master" must emphatically not be taken as implying that the development of the forces of production brings first the bourgeoisie and then the proletariat to power. The most serious reproach directed at Marx in *The Society of the Spectacle* is that he capitulated, "as early as the *Manifesto*," to a linear view of history that "identifies the proletariat with the bourgeoisie with respect to the revolutionary seizure of power." The fact is that "the bourgeoisie is the only revolutionary class ever to have been victorious" and that its victory in the political sphere was a consequence of its prior victory in the sphere of material production (SS §86–87). Given that its economy and its state are nothing but alienations, and the negation of all conscious life, the task of the proletariat can in no sense be to seize hold of those same instruments, the result of which could only be a new enslavement like that already established in Russia and other countries. Debord joins Lukács in opposition to a purely *scientific* explanation of history: the motor of history for both authors is the class struggle, but this struggle is not a pure reflection of economic processes. Debord expresses his approval of Marx's assertion that "it is the *struggle*—and by no means the *law*—that must be understood" (a formulation that would be equally at home in *History and Class Consciousness*); and in the same context he immediately quotes Marx and Engels's well-known statement in *The German Ideology*: "We know only a single science, the science of history" (SS §81).[32] In Debord's view, the Marxian attempt to draw lessons with a scientific value from failed revolutions of the past merely opened the door to the later degeneration represented by working-class bureaucracies. Instead of placing itself under the leadership of one chief or another, or trusting to the unfolding of what appears to be a natural process, what is really required is the organization of the "practical conditions of consciousness" of proletarian action (SS §90).

History and Community as the Essence of Man

We have already noted that the existence of a subject whose activity can be reified obviously implies the existence of a "human essence" that can serve as a yardstick by which to determine what is "healthy" and what is "alienated." When, in 1967, Lukács criticizes his own failure to distinguish in *History and Class Consciousness* between alienation and reification, he states that in reality alienation exists only when "the essence of man [comes] into conflict with his existence" (HCC, xxiv), and from this he deduces the need for a "Marxist ontology."

Debord nowhere considers constructing an "ontology," but this does

---

32. Lukács says of the Hegelian analysis of bourgeois society that "it is only the *manner* of this deduction, namely the dialectical method, that points beyond bourgeois society" (HCC, 148), while Debord notes that although Hegel's *conclusions* are negated by the existence of the proletariat, "the validity of [his] *method* is confirmed" thereby (SS §77).

not necessarily rule out his having any conception of a "human essence." Marx, in his *Economic and Philosophical Manuscripts* of 1844, conceives of such an essence in terms of man's belonging to his natural species, his *Gattungswesen*. He sees human history as part of natural history, and the natural history of man is, precisely, the production of human nature, which has occurred within history: "The eye has become a *human* eye, just as its *object* has become a social, *human* object," for "the *cultivation* of the five senses is the work of all previous history" (*EW*, 355, 352, 353). This humanization of nature, whereby man produces himself and becomes human himself, is understood by Marx as an organic exchange with nature and as a development of productive capabilities in the broadest sense.

In Debord, likewise, we find the conception of a human essence that is not fixed, not given, but rather identical with the historical process, understood as man's self-creation in time: "Man . . . is one with time" (*SS* §125). To appropriate one's own nature means first and foremost to appropriate the fact of being a historical being. In the fifth and sixth chapters of *The Society of the Spectacle*, which are the least often read, Debord offers a brief interpretation of history. He considers this historical life of man and the consciousness that he has of it to be the chief results of man's increasing domination of nature.

So long as agricultural production predominated, life remained tied to natural cycles and took on the aspect of an eternal return; historical events, such as invasions by enemies, seemed like problems of completely external origin. Time had a purely natural and "given" quality. It began to acquire a social dimension only with the accession of the first ruling classes to power. Not only did these classes appropriate whatever material surplus their society contrived to produce but, inasmuch as they were not obliged to spend all their time working, they were also able to give themselves over to adventures and wars (*SS* §128). Historical time came into existence at the pinnacle of society even as, at the bottom, things remained unchanging from generation to generation (*SS* §132). Historical time meant a time that was irreversible, a time in which events were unique and never repeated themselves. Out of this time came a wish to remember such events and to transmit that memory; this was the earliest form of historical consciousness. For a small number of people, history was already taking on a direction, a sense, a meaning. The first attempts to understand it emerged from the "democracy of society's masters" characteristic of the Greek *polis* (*SS* §134). Within that community of free citizens, at least, the problems of society could be debated openly, and in this context the conclusion was reached that the resolution of such problems depended on the power of the community, not on that of some divinity, destiny, or holy king. The material basis of society remained nonetheless bound to cyclical time. This contradiction gave rise, over another long period, to the compromise of semihistorical religions, in other words to the monotheistic religions, for which irreversible time, in the shape of a time of waiting for final redemption, is combined with a devaluation of concrete history, deemed a mere preparation for that final event (SS §136).

The democratization of historical time was unable to progress until the moment when the bourgeois class, with the coming of the Renaissance, began to transform work itself (SS §140). In contradistinction to earlier modes of production, capitalism *accumulates*, and never returns to the same point; it is continually transforming the processes of production and above all the most fundamental of those processes, namely labor itself. Thus for the first time in history the very foundations of society were set in motion and could therefore be expected to accede to linear and historical time. At precisely the same moment, however, society as a whole lost its historicity (if by historicity we mean a sequence of qualitative events), for the new irreversible time was that of "the mass production of objects," and hence the *"time of things"* (SS §142). The leveling out of all quality by the commodity system was also manifested in the end of all traditional freedoms and privileges, as too in the complete loss of autonomy of different places.

In cyclical societies, dependence on the blind forces of nature obliged submission to the decisions of those in power, whether these were based on real considerations, such as irrigation in the ancient Orient, or on imaginary ones, as with the the seasonal rites of priest-kings (SS §132). The commodity economy presented itself as the heir of nature, and the bourgeoisie presented itself as that economy's manager. The fact that the true basis of history was the economy, that is, a product of man, was meant to remain in the unconscious; the very possibility of a history that was conscious and lived by all had to be confined to the shadows. It is in this sense that Debord interprets Marx's famous remark in *The Poverty of Philosophy* according to which the bourgeoisie, having taken power, felt that there once was history but "there is no longer any history" (SS §143).

Time under the rule of the commodity differs radically from time in earlier periods. It is a time all of whose moments are abstractly equivalent, varying only in a quantitative sense: such moments function, in fact, exactly like exchange-value. The importance for modern production of "exactly measurable," spatialized time was analyzed as early as *History and Class Consciousness* (*HCC*, 90). Debord notes that the cyclical aspect has been reinstated in daily experience, in the temporality of consumption: "Day and night, weekly work and weekly rest, the cycle of vacations" (*SS* §150). In the capitalist economy, time has become a commodity that, just like all the others, has lost its use-value in favor of exchange-value. The organization of pseudo-events and the creation of seemingly interesting "units of time" have become one of society's chief industries, as witness the marketing of vacations.[33] By contrast, irreversible and historical time can only be *contemplated* in the actions of others—never experienced directly in one's own life. "The pseudo-events that vie for attention in the spectacle's dramatizations have not been lived by those who are thus informed about them" (*SS* §157). Furthermore, whatever real experience the individual manages to achieve in his daily life is alien to official time and remains unintelligible to him, for he lacks the tools to relate his own lived experience to the lived experience of society at large and thus invest it with greater meaning.

It is interesting to observe how Debord applies Marxian economic categories to historical time considered as the main product of society. Thus in primitive societies power extracts "temporal surplus value" (*SS* §128); masters enjoy "the private ownership of history" (*SS* §132); "the main product that economic development transformed from a luxurious rarity to a commonly consumed item was thus history itself"—albeit only the history of *things* (*SS* §142); and time is "raw material for the production of a diversity of new products" (*SS* §151). According to Marx, the violent expropriation of the means of production of small independent producers, as well as those of peasants and craftsmen, was a prerequisite for the establishment of capitalism. Debord adds that the necessary precondition of the subjugation of workers to "time-as-commodity" is "the violent expropriation of their time" (*SS* §159).

The spectacle must deny history, because history proves that laws are nothing, whereas process and struggle are all. The spectacle is the reign of an eternal present that claims to be history's last word. Under Stalinism, it took the form of a systematic manipulation and rewriting of the past. In countries where the diffuse spectacular system holds sway, by contrast, the mechanism is subtler. To begin with, it eliminates all opportunities for people to share experiences or projects without interme-

---

33. The Club Méditerranée, as one of the earliest and most advanced examples of the alienation of everyday life, was a frequent polemical target of the Situationists.

diaries or to recognize themselves in their own actions and in the effects of those actions. The complete disappearance of historical intelligence creates socially atomized individuals with no choice but to contemplate the seemingly unalterable progression of blind forces. All those faculties that might allow such individuals to perceive the contrast between the falsification wrought by the spectacle and earlier forms are likewise eradicated.

The antagonism between human life and the economy is emphasized even more strongly by Debord than by Marx and Lukács. Lukács underlines the fact that even in earlier societies divided into estates the economy was already the basis of all social relations, although that economy had not "objectively reached the stage of being-for-itself" (HCC, 57). In the modern period, by contrast, "economic factors are not concealed 'behind' consciousness but are present in consciousness itself (albeit unconscious or repressed)" (HCC, 59). In another passage, Lukács evokes "the first time [that] mankind consciously takes its history into its own hands—thanks to the class consciousness of a proletariat summoned to power" (HCC, 250), thus bringing to an end the necessity merely to interpret and follow along behind the objective course of the economic process.[34] This is the point where the proletariat's conscious will makes its entrance, a will that Lukács calls "violence," in the sense that it means a rupture with the self-regulation of the system. From the moment when the real possibility of the "realm of freedom" arises, "the blind forces really will hurtle blindly towards the abyss, with ever-increasing and apparently irresistible violence, and only the conscious will of the proletariat will be able to save mankind from the impending catastrophe" (HCC, 70). Material production in the society of the future will be "the servant of a consciously directed society; it [will] lose its self-contained autonomy (which was what made it an economy, properly speaking); as an economy it [will] be annulled" (HCC, 261).

For Debord, the development of economic forces was necessary, for it was only thus that the economy could eventually cease being the *unconscious basis* of society. As the economy's sway is extended to the whole of life, it is simultaneously revealed to be a creation of mankind, and mankind becomes conscious of this. The autonomous economy "breaks

34. The text quoted here is "The Changing Function of Historical Materialism," originally a speech given in 1919 during the Hungarian Council Republic; according to Lukács's preface (1923) to *History and Class Consciousness,* this essay still contains "the echoes of those exaggeratedly sanguine hopes that many of us cherished [at that time] concerning the duration and tempo of the revolution" (HCC, xli).

all ties with authentic needs to the precise degree that it emerges from a *social unconscious* that was dependent on it without knowing it. . . . By the time society discovers that it is contingent on the economy, the economy has in point of fact become contingent on society. . . . Where economic id was, there ego shall be" (*SS* §§51–52). The task of the proletariat is to become "the class of consciousness" (*SS* §88), consciousness meaning "direct possession by the workers of every moment of their activity" (*SS* §53) instead of subordination to what they have created in an unconscious manner.

History and Class Consciousness reminded all Marxists who had forgotten it that crises are not solely attributable to quantitative causes, to relationships based on the relative importance of economic factors, but also to a kind of revolt of use-value (*HCC*, 106–7). Debord likewise emphasizes the qualitative rather than quantitative nature of economic crises. He thus saw the recession of the seventies, when it arrived, as merely an exacerbation of the general crisis of the spectacular system, asserting that even the economic aspect was due to a sharpening of the class struggle in which wage demands were coupled with a rejection by the working class of such junk consumer goods as modern housing (*VS*, 28; Eng., 24–25).

Debord's search for a subject or principle necessarily antagonistic to the spectacle led him to an explicit invocation of the proletariat, but also to a number of somewhat vague concepts, among them the Feuerbachian *Gattungswesen*, or "species-being," mentioned above, which was also taken up by Lukács in his last period. The fact is that we are getting close here to one of the limits of Debord's theory.

The logic of the value-form requires that in a society based on commodity production—defined by Marx as "a social formation in which the process of production has mastery over man, instead of the opposite" (*Capital I*, 175)—social processes assume the character of blind forces. This is not a pure illusion, as is thought by those who look "behind" the "laws of the market" or "technical imperatives" for an acting subject. True, for individuals under capitalism "their own movement within society has for them the form of a movement made by things, and these things, far from being under their control, in fact control them."[35] This means that in capitalism—as in earlier types of society, characterized by other forms of fetishism, including fetishism in the strict sense—no sub-

35. Ibid., 167–68.

jects, whether individual or collective, are ever real actors in history; the blind process of value has created them, and they must follow its laws or be ruined. What is not implied here is that history is itself a process without a subject, as claimed by structuralism and systems theory: the absence of a subject, which is only too real in present society, does not constitute an ontological and immutable fact; rather, it represents capitalism's chief defect. Debord clearly points up, if succinctly, the *unconscious* nature of a society ruled by value. At the same time, however, he bases himself on the aspect of Marx's thought that assigns a central role to the concepts of "classes" and "class struggles"—concepts that were also primary for the workers' movement. Overemphasis on the "class struggle," however, can lead to a misapprehension of the nature of the classes that have been created by the development of value and that have no meaning outside this development. The proletariat and the bourgeoisie cannot be anything but the living instruments of variable capital and fixed capital: they have their roles to play, but they are in no sense the directors of economic and social life. Their conflicts, which is to say class struggles, pass of necessity via the mediation of an abstract *form* that is equal for all: money, commodity, state. Thenceforward such struggles are merely struggles over distribution within a system that nobody now seriously challenges. The logic of the commodity-form always decreed that social classes must become one category among others and that all categories must eventually be detached from their empirical bearers. This outcome is manifest today: the modern individual is truly a "man without qualities," able to assume a multitude of interchangeable roles, all of which are in reality alien to him. One may be at one and the same time a worker and a co-owner of a firm; likewise one may be simultaneously pro-ecology qua resident and anti-ecology qua worried wage-worker with a job at risk. Even the ruling classes have lost all mastery, and now the only thing at stake in economic competition is a more comfortable place within the general alienation. In the last reckoning, the development of society, which appears even to the most powerful as an inevitability to which they must adapt if they are to preserve their short-term interests, is a threat to all classes.

The existence of a powerful proletariat, united not only by working conditions but also by an entire culture and style of life, and more or less excluded from bourgeois society, was in reality nothing but a precapitalist relic, an "estate" in the feudal sense, and not a direct result of capitalist development at all. It was precisely class struggles that helped capitalism realize itself by allowing the laboring masses to be transformed into abstract and equal "monads" participating fully in the money system and in the state. The secret historic mission of the proletarian movement was to destroy remnants of precapitalism, to generalize abstract forms such as those of the law, money, value, and commodities, and thus to impose the pure logic of capital. These tasks often had to be carried out despite the resistance of the bourgeoisie itself, which was still determined to defend such actually pre-bourgeois forms as low wages and the barring of workers from the exercise of political rights—things the workers' movement too identified incorrectly with the essential nature of capitalism. The Marxism of this movement was perforce a "sociologizing" one to the extent that it reduced the advances of capitalist society to the conscious activity of social groups treated as a *preexisting factor*. The workers' movement therefore partook in a sense of the typical illusion of the bourgeois subject, which believes that it is making decisions when in reality the fetishistic system is the agent.

This is not to say that these results of capitalist development in any way mitigate the system's contradictory character. They merely eliminate the illusion that the antagonistic portion of the system is one of the poles constituted by the logic of capitalism itself. Quite rightly, Debord had no truck with the propaganda put about in the fifties and sixties, at the height of the Fordist era, to the effect that harmony had now replaced social conflict and that the disappearance of the working class in the traditional sense was the proof of it. On the other hand, when Debord deems it possible, under present-day conditions, for a subject to exist that is by definition "outside" the spectacle, he seems to be forgetting what he had himself said regarding the unconscious character of the commodity economy; and he seems to forget it a second time when he identifies this subject with the proletariat. No doubt an attachment to such concepts appeared to him to betoken a salutary radicalism, but in actuality it was a conflation of capitalism and its earlier and unfinished forms. In consequence, Debord is noticeably prone to vacillation when it comes to defining the proletariat, which he sometimes equates in sociological fashion with the workers and sometimes depicts as the mass of people who are deprived of everything (SS §114).[36] He had set out in search of possible real occupiers of a place already assigned within a tele-

---

36. We should not be surprised, in this context, to see Gianni Vattimo, Turin prophet of what he himself calls "weak thinking," proclaiming that "a large majority of us are proletarians. . . . Proletarians not in terms of property but in terms of the quality of life" (*La Stampa*, 11 October 1990, cited in *Il Manifesto*, 12 October 1990).

ological vision of history, the place of the adversaries of the spectacle. The Situationists called in the proletariat when an agent was required to "realize art" (*IS* 1/8), much as Engels had once called it in as the heir of classical German philosophy. On several occasions, this problem was implicitly confronted: "for the first time, theory as the understanding of human practice [must] be recognized and directly lived by the masses [and] workers [must] become dialecticians" (*SS* §123). Elsewhere Debord was to say that "it is not so much a matter of the Situationists being Councilist as it is of the Councils needing to become Situationist";[37] and the SI conceived its role vis-à-vis the workers as one of waiting to be approached by them (*IS* 11/64).

The critique of the economy as a now autonomous agency, and of separations in general, reposes inevitably on the concept of *totality*. For Debord, the concept seems to refer to *human community* in the sense of "a harmonious society" that is able to "manage its power" (*OCC*, 246–47; *In girum*, 47). Its opposite is "the totalitarian dictatorship of the fragment" (*IS* 8/33)—"one of those fragments of social power which claim to represent a coherent totality, and tend to impose themselves as a total explanation and organization (*IS* 6/6; *Dérive*, 109). When, with the advent of the spectacle, ideology reaches its apogee, this "is no longer the voluntaristic struggle of the fragmentary, but rather its triumph" (*SS* §213).

If the nature of man lies in his historicity, this historicity implies that community is an authentic human need. Debord says that "community . . . is the *true social nature* of man, human nature" (*IS* 10/11; *SIA*, 160). But community is corroded by exchange: the spectacle means "the dissolution of all common and communicable values, a dissolution produced by the annihilating victory of exchange-value over use-value on the battlefield of the economy" (*IS* 10/59).

Genuine community and genuine dialogue can exist only when each person has access to a direct experience of reality, when everyone has at their disposal the practical and intellectual means needed to solve problems. In the past, these preconditions have sometimes been partially met: the ancient Greek *polis* and the Italian republics of the Middle

---

37. In an internal SI document (1970), reprinted in *Débat d'orientation de l'ex-Internationale Situationniste* (Paris: Centre de Recherche sur la Question Sociale, 1974), 7, cited by Pascal Dumontier, *Les Situationnistes et mai 1968: Théorie et pratique de la révolution (1966–1972)* (Paris: Gérard Lebovici, 1990), 187.

Ages constitute the most highly developed examples, although only certain portions of the population were affected. But villages, neighborhoods, guilds—even local taverns—can also nourish forms of direct communication whereby each individual retains control over at least part of his own activity. Where the spectacle holds sway, by contrast, a *fragment* of the social totality, having detached itself from collective discussion and collective decision making, issues orders via *unilateral communication*. This occurs wherever subjects no longer gain access to the world through personal experience but instead by means of images, which are infinitely more manipulable and which in themselves imply passive consent. The Situationists were convinced that direct communication between subjects was sufficient in itself to banish social hierarchies and autonomous representations: "Wherever there is communication, there is no State" (*IS 8/30; SIA*, 115).

In earlier times, activities of an economic kind were liable to have non-economic determinants. In medieval society, for example, productive power could be subordinated to considerations of tradition, as when guilds limited production in order to maintain a particular standard of quality; or a nobleman might dissipate his fortune for the sake of prestige alone. It is worth recalling that almost all societies prior to the society of the commodity economy devoted their surpluses to feast and luxury rather than reinvesting them in a new spiral of production. The communitarian social forms of old, whose dissolution was an absolute precondition, according to *History and Class Consciousness*, of society's contriving "to satisfy all its needs in terms of commodity exchange" (*HCC*, 91), were thus social forms incompletely subordinated to economic yardsticks. Indeed, in his early works Lukács looked back with nostalgia to former times, such as the medieval period, which had been "filled with meaning"; and something of this attitude survives in *History and Class Consciousness*, where he contrasts a former "organic unity" to the present-day rule of "calculation" (*HCC*, 88, 103). Lukács's reference to Ferdinand Tönnies (*HCC*, 131) is instructive in this regard. Tönnies introduced the distinction between *society* and *community*, viewing society as a purely external bond mediated by exchange among people in a state of permanent competition with one another, and community as an ensemble of concrete personal associations together constituting an organic unity which is the source of individual actions. Similarly, Debord condemns the society of the spectacle as a society without community (*SS* §154). In essence, Lukács and Debord both agree with Marx, for whom the unraveling of the old social bonds deprived men of the security and plenitude that membership in an estate had hitherto vouchsafed them; only in this way, however, could the free individual, no longer determined by such affiliations, have emerged.[38] In his *Critique of Hegel's Doctrine of the State*, the young Marx applauds Hegel for defining "the separation of the state from civil society as a *contradiction*."[39] In modern society, man is divided: in the political realm he is a *citizen*, member of an abstract community; in social and economic life he is a *bourgeois*. The contradiction inheres in the fact that something that was originally one is now split into two antagonistic parts; the old estates were communities that, in a rough and ready way, "sustained" the individual in his integrity, assigning him a status at once legal, moral, social, and economic. In contradistinction to the relationship between the person who is a "free" seller of his own labor-power and the person who buys that labor-power, the relationship between a feudal lord and his serf was not a purely economic one but extended to all aspects of existence. The classes of the present day are based exclusively on *social* differences.[40] The isolation, abstraction, and separations attendant upon modern society are thus an inevitable stage along the way to the reconstitution of a free community.

A comparable teleology of Hegelian inspiration is to be found in *The Society of the Spectacle*: "In the course of this development [of the commodity economy] all community and critical awareness have ceased to be; nor have those forces, which were able—by separating—to grow enormously in strength, yet found a way to *reunite*" (*SS* §25). Here Debord clearly expresses the idea not just that the various splits within the overall unity are destined to be mended but also that these separations were in fact a necessary precondition of growth and reunification at a higher level. The same sort of determinism seems to inform the thesis according to which "unitary societies" or "myth-based societies" are *obliged* to break down into independent elements, after which a totalizing and reconstitutive tendency inevitably comes into play, which is at first expressed in art and then in its negation; this is the connection in which

38. Cf. for example the first chapter of Marx and Engels, *The German Ideology* (Moscow: Progress Publishers, 1968), especially the discussion of "Natural and Civilized Instruments of Production and Forms of Property," pp. 81–86; or the section on "forms which precede capitalist production," in *Grundrisse*, 471–79.

39. Karl Marx, *Critique of Hegel's Doctrine of the State* (§§ 261–313), trans. Rodney Livingstone, in *EW*, 141.

40. Cf. ibid., 146–47. As a matter of fact, "Marxism" could perfectly well have deduced from this account of Marx's that in the last analysis social classes have a *quantitative* character and that consequently they are not a determining but merely a derivative factor in the functioning of a commodity-based society.

Debord quotes the lines mentioned above, from Hegel's "The Difference between the Philosophical Systems of Fichte and Schelling," which he had found in *History and Class Consciousness* (*SS* §180; *HCC,* 139). The reunification of the forces that have been separated cannot come about until the development of the commodity economy has revealed the domination of the economy over society and completed the mastery of nature.

At bottom, Debord is in agreement with the Lukács who, in the preface of 1967 to *History and Class Consciousness,* quotes Marx in support of his—Lukács's—self-critical observation that he had earlier failed to understand that the development of the productive forces by the bourgeoisie had an objectively revolutionary function. That development, though occurring at the expense of so many human beings, was the necessary precondition of a finally liberated society (*HCC,* xvii–xviii). Implicit for both Lukács and Debord, it would seem, is the theory that the proletariat must inherit the world created by the bourgeoisie, a world that will thus merely change managers. This view is nevertheless clearly at odds with the proposition that the bourgeois mode of production is alienating by virtue of its very structure and that consequently the proletariat must not simply succeed the bourgeoisie as master of this system. One might reasonably question, too, the underlying assumption that all the sufferings of the past are acceptable in that they were necessary to arrive at the present state of the forces of production, which is confidently expected, by a more tortuous path, to precipitate the revolution—just as all the "economistic" theories say it will.

This "determinist" dimension of Debord's thinking may likewise be discerned in the claim that another factor has played a vital role in history, namely the consciousness of *the gap between what exists and what is possible.* Whereas the category of the *sacred* formerly expressed "what society *could not deliver,*" the spectacle, "by contrast, depicts what society *can deliver,* but in this depiction what is permitted is rigidly distinguished from what is possible" (*SS* §25). The domination of nature should lead society immediately to ask the question "What for?" and then to use its mastery to transcend labor and replace it with free activity. But nature's transformation, the great achievement of the bourgeoisie, is used instead by that class to buttress existing hierarchies (*IS* 8/4–5; *SIA,* 103) and to keep the true nature of the functioning of society from becoming conscious. The fact that the forces of production must eventually subvert the relations of production remains true for the Situationists in a sense broader than the traditional one: not as "an au-

tomatic short-term judgment passed on the capitalist production system" but rather as a "judgment . . . passed on the development, at once
niggardly and reckless, which this self-regulating system arranges for itself, as compared with the *grandiose development that is possible*" (*IS*
8/7; *SIA*, 104).

This kind of finalism is reminiscent of *The Phenomenology of Mind*.
The Situationists, however, were in many respects immune to the excessive optimism to which such a position often gives rise. Debord cautioned that critical theory "expects no miracles from the working class.
It views the reformulation and satisfaction of proletarian demands as
a long-term undertaking" (*SS* §203). He further noted that "a critique
capable of surpassing the spectacle must *know how to bide its time*"
(SS §220). Even during the most intense moments of May 1968, the SI
warned against triumphalism.

All the same, in a more general way the Situationists persisted in thinking that postwar European society represented the last stage of a class society now several centuries old, which could be followed only by a general upheaval. As early as 1957, Debord was writing over-optimistically
that the culture epitomized by a Françoise Sagan "signals a probably unsurpassable stage in bourgeois decadence" (*Rapp.*, 694). In 1965 he announced "the decline and fall of the spectacular commodity economy" (*IS*
10/3–11; *SIA*, 153–60). After 1968, the Situationists, like Hegel contemplating Napoleon or, later, the Prussian state, and like Marx during the
1848 revolution, thought that an "upside-down world was about to be
set back on its feet" and that history was on the point of being realized.
In 1969, reproducing an extreme example (extreme, at any rate, for its
time—October 1967) of the replacement of real experience by images,
the Situationists' journal commented: "having carried its invasion of social life thus far, the spectacle was soon to experience the beginning of
a *reversal* in the relationship of forces. In the following months [i.e., in
1968], history and real life resumed their assault upon the heaven of the
spectacle" (*IS* 12/50).

In Part 2 we shall see how this came about.

Part 2 | The Practice of Theory

The Letterist International

"We did not seek the formula for changing the world in books, but by wandering" (*OCC*, 251; *In girum*, 50–51). Debord's reformulation of the theories of Marx, as described in Part 1, was not the product of academic research and even less of militant political action in either the small or large left-wing parties. The working out and dissemination of Debord's theory was more of a passionate adventure than a lecture series on Marxology.

It was in the Latin Quarter of Paris, in cafés avoided by respectable students, but just a stone's throw from the prestigious École Normale Supérieure, where the future élite were preparing their careers, that the young Guy Debord set out on a journey thanks to which he too would leave a certain mark on the world. Looking back later, he expressed the certitude that the disorder that overtook the world in 1968, and that would never be completely eradicated, had its source at a few café tables where, in late 1952, a handful of somewhat strayed young people calling themselves the "Letterist International" (LI) used to drink too much and plan systematic rambles that they referred to as *dérives*. "It is wonderful to see," observed Debord apropos of this period in his film *In girum imus nocte et consumimur igni*, "that disturbances with the tiniest and most ephemeral of origins have eventually shaken the order of the world" (*OCC*, 246; *In girum*, 46–47). From that time forward, Debord and his friends were "in possession of a very strange power of seduction: for no one has approached us since then without wishing to follow us" (*OCC*, 252; *In girum*, 51). The Debordian adventure proceeded logically from this starting-point: it had become necessary "to discover how to live the days that came after in a manner worthy of such a fine beginning. You want to prolong that first experience of illegality for ever after" (*OCC*, 246; *In girum*, 46).

For a clearer understanding of Debord's ideas, then, we need to pay attention to his deeds. Referring to himself, Debord quotes Chateaubriand: "Of the modern French authors of my time, I am therefore the only one whose life is true to his works" (*Pan.*, 53; Eng., 46); the great rarity of such consistency explains "why those who expound various thoughts about revolutions to us ordinarily abstain from letting us know how they have lived their lives" (*OCC*, 220; *In girum*, 26)—something Debord does not fail to do.

Debord's singularity is further underscored by the fact that he could write: "We did not go on television to say what it was that we had understood. We did not hanker after grants from the scientific research bodies, nor for praise from newspaper intellectuals. We brought fuel to the flames" (*OCC*, 252–53; *In girum*, 52). The significance of Debord's early activities, which at the time passed virtually unnoticed, is pointed up by his conviction that the animosity that was always directed at him went back to those days: "Some think that it is because of the grave responsibility that has often been attributed to me for the origins, or even for the command, of the May 1968 revolt. I think rather that what has displeased people so persistently about me is what I did in 1952" (*Pan.*, 35; Eng., 25). But what *did* Debord do in 1952, aside from making a curious film (so to speak) and helping found the Letterist International? According to him, it was in 1952 that, with "four or five scarcely recommendable people from Paris," he set out in search of, and indeed glimpsed, "the 'North-West Passage' of the geography of real life" (*Pref.*, 100; Eng., 10). This quest eventually developed into a social war in which theories were units of varying strength "which must be engaged at the right moment in the combat" (*OCC*, 219; *In girum*, 25). That he, Debord, should have been "a sort of theoretician of revolutions" was thus "the falsest of legends" (*OCC*, 218; *In girum*, 24), for the development of a theory was but *one* element, albeit an important one, in a complex set of interactions.[1]

The point of departure was "the supersession of art," which was to be achieved by starting out from a "modern poetry" in the throes of "self-destruction" (*Pref.*, 100; Eng., 10). "After all, it was modern poetry, for the last hundred years, that had led us there. We were a handful who thought that it was necessary to carry out its programme in reality" (*Pan.*,

---

1. Some years later, however, Debord would write that, of all the epithets applied to him by the French press, "theoretician" was the only one (except for *enragé*) to which he had no objection: the attribution went "without saying, although I have not been just a theoretician, nor have I been a specialist in that capacity; still, I have indeed been a theoretician also, and one of the best" (*Considérations sur l'assassinat de Gérard Lebovici* [Paris: Gallimard, 1993], 88).

35; Eng., 24). There is no doubt that Debord always remained faithful to this vow.

The "supersession of art" first presented itself to Debord in the garb of Letterism. Born in Paris on 28 December 1931, Debord had aspired since his adolescence to a life full of adventures. His models being Lautréamont, whom the Surrealists had deemed the supreme exemplar of the individual utterly at war with all bourgeois values, and the pre-Dadaist adventurer Arthur Cravan, Debord was hardly tempted to pursue either an artistic or a university career (*Pan.*, 20; Eng., 23). In 1951, at the Cannes film festival, he ran across a group showing a film called *Traité de bave et d'éternité* [Treatise on Slobber and Eternity] to a chorus of boos and hisses. The film had no images, and onomatopoeic poetry and multifarious monologues were all it had for a sound track. This group was Isidore Isou's Letterists.

Isou, a Rumanian born in 1924, had begun as early as 1946 to urge the Parisian cultural establishment to undertake a renewal not just of the arts but of the entirety of civilization.[2] Reembracing the iconoclastic goals of the Dadaists and early Surrealists, Isou meant to complete the self-destruction of artistic forms initiated by Baudelaire; for him the leap needed to achieve this end was the reduction of poetry to its smallest component, namely the *letter*. The letter was at once a graphical element, suitable for use in collage, and a sound element, suitable for use in onomatopoeic declamation, and hence a link between poetry, painting, and music. With a small number of followers, Isou extended this procedure and others to every artistic and social realm, including cinema and architecture. From the point of view of art history, it should certainly be acknowledged that the Letterists owed a great deal to Dada (one has merely to think of Kurt Schwitters's *Ursonate*), but it is also true that they originated not a few of the ideas with which the "avant-garde" artists of the nineteen-sixties bedazzled the public.

Isou's Letterism already embodied in large measure the spirit that would later animate Debord and the Situationists, as much in their fidelity to Letterism as in their transcendence of it. The chief thing the two movements have in common is the conviction that the whole world must be torn down then rebuilt not under the sign of the economy but instead under that of a generalized *creativity*. The entirety of traditional

2. A standard account of Letterism is Jean-Paul Curtay, *La Poésie Lettriste* (Paris: Seghers, 1974).

art was certified dead by both groups, while the alternative to it was another invention of Isou's, namely *détournement*, a collage-like technique whereby preexisting elements were reassembled into new creations. According to Isou, art always goes initially through "amplic phases," during which a rich panoply of expressive means is developed, then through "chiseling phases," which first strive to perfect the work then gradually strip away all the resulting refinements.[3]

Other themes that would later assume prime importance for Debord were the desire to transcend the division between artist and spectator and the incorporation of action and emotion, or in other words life style, into the arts. The Letterist promotion of youth as a sociological category and at the same time a potentially revolutionary force was another genuine anticipation of the sixties—one that Debord would never completely embrace but that left a significant mark on him nevertheless. The same may be said of Isou's propensity for inventing new forms of expression, rather than executing works of art, and then claiming paternity for anything resembling his techniques. Last but not least, the Letterists already manifested an inclination to believe that their little group had been chosen to preside over the palingenesis of the world, a conviction attended by an agreeable megalomania but also, inevitably, by sectarianism and chronic squabbling.

The Isou group was also much given to organizing small scandals, which was still fairly easy at that time. They disrupted theatrical performances, gallery openings, and film festivals. All this, combined with their nonconforming life style, made the Letterists attractive even to some young people whose interests were not strictly of an artistic kind. A particularly tumultuous scandal was provoked at Easter 1950, when a young man dressed as a Dominican appeared in the pulpit of Notre Dame Cathedral and informed the congregation that "God is dead." This action ended with an attempted lynching, the impostor's arrest, and headlines in all the papers.

Debord writes that no sooner was he fully independent than he found himself feeling "quite at home in the most ill-famed of company" (*OCC*, 222; *In girum*, 27). His own contribution was not long in coming: on 30 June 1952, he showed his first film, *Hurlements en faveur de Sade* (*Howlings in Favor of Sade* [*OCC*, 9–18; *Films*, 9–22]), an early (and never used) scenario for which had previously appeared in the sole num-

3. According to Isou, Baudelaire destroyed the anecdote, Verlaine the poem, Rimbaud the verse, and Tzara the word, which he replaced by the nothing; only Isou had the courage to reduce everything to letters, thus giving form to the nothing.

ber of the Letterist journal *Ion* (April 1952).[4] The outrage caused by this film was not of the kind that its audience probably expected from the title: the screen is sometimes dark, sometimes white, but always blank, while the soundtrack consists of quotations from the widest variety of sources, observations on the life of the Letterists, and a few theoretical propositions, all frequently interrupted by long stretches of silence. The work ends with twenty-four minutes of complete silence and complete darkness. Though first shown by a film club self-described as "avant-garde," the film was cut short after a mere twenty minutes by an utterly indignant audience.[5] In the first moments of the film the following words are heard: "Cinema is dead. Films are no longer possible. If you want, let's have a discussion" (*OCC*, 11; *Films*, 12). The intent of the provocation was to transcend the passivity of the spectator: Debord was no longer concerned, as the two or three earlier Letterist films had been, with the search for a new *aesthetic;* on the contrary, he wanted to draw a line under even the most recent art. In consequence, he and his friends were very soon at loggerheads with Isou and his faithful followers, whose cult of "creativity" constituted in their eyes a dangerous form of idealism. Debord and those in his camp wanted their action to be informed by a social critique of Marxist inspiration, though still in a somewhat vague way, and they rebuked the so-called "old Letterists" or "right-wing Letterists" for being too positive, for being "artists." In November 1952, at a meeting in Aubervilliers, four people founded the Letterist International.[6] One may be sure that at the time hardly anyone took note of this announcement by a few young "marginals" in a dive in the Paris *banlieue*, especially considering that such declarations must have been

4. This first script is reproduced in Berréby, 109–23. For an account of the genesis and exhibition of *Howlings in Favor of Sade*, see Thomas Y. Levin, "Dismantling the Spectacle: The Cinema of Guy Debord," in *Passage*, 81–85.

5. A screening in London in 1957 drew a large crowd, doubtless attracted by the title (*IS* 12/105). In 1991, when a German version (obviously not difficult to produce!) was shown in Berlin, the notoriety of Debord's first film, now so utterly out of circulation, again lured a good number of enthusiasts. The occasion proved that in forty years the film had lost none of its power to scandalize: furious spectators interrupted the performance and stole all the copies on hand of a book on the SI whose appearance the showing was intended to publicize. Just such a rude challenge to passivity had of course always been Debord's purpose.

6. For his part, Isou has proceeded tirelessly, until the time of this writing, with his multifarious work, waiting imperturbably for the day when the whole world recognizes him as one of humanity's great geniuses. Irked, however, by the realization that his sometime follower's reputation surpasses his own, Isou has for more than thirty years been waging a grotesque hate campaign against Debord; the title of one of his lampoons gives the measure here: *Contre le cinéma situationniste, néo-nazi* (1979). Interestingly, after the ritual attacks associated with the break itself, Debord paid no further attention to Isou; and when, in 1979, Isou proposed to Debord's publisher and friend Gérard Lebovici that

two a penny in certain circles at the time. Nevertheless, forty years later, the sheet of paper on which the four set forth their principles in twenty lines would be treated as a historic document and reproduced in a large illustrated volume.[7] This surprising fact must undoubtedly be attributed to the intervening "career" of Guy Debord.

Before tracing the itinerary of this extraordinary organization, let us pause for a moment to examine the historical context in which it came into being.

The nineteen-twenties in France, especially the first half of the decade, were highly effervescent, and to some degree this effervescence persisted into the thirties. In contrast, the political and cultural climate after the Liberation, apart from a brief moment of euphoria, was distinctly gray, and certainly at a very far remove from any kind of revolutionary break-through. Surrealism had no doubt lost much of its original innovative-ness as early as 1930; after the Second World War, however, the move-ment's decadence was brutally patent: for one thing, Surrealism was now welcome in the temples of bourgeois art, just as it was in the world of advertising; and meanwhile many of its adepts had taken a distinctly mystical turn. Only outside France could Surrealism still exert an influ-ence, at least indirectly, as it did on the CoBrA movement in Denmark, Belgium, and Holland, or via Marcel Mariën's Belgian group. In France, on the other hand, what emerged was a new, slightly "avant-gardist" academicism in painting—the so-called Paris School. On the literary front, the well-worn values, the Mauriacs and Gides, remained firmly in place, while any real innovative tendencies were apparently exhausted.

Things were even more clear-cut in the political sphere. The only seem-ing opposition to the bourgeois forces was the French Communist Party, evicted from the government in 1947 but commanding a quarter of the popular vote and immense respect, even from the other parties, on ac-count of its role in the Resistance and its "national" policies. Completely in thrall to the USSR of Stalin, the party displayed a delusional dogma-tism that led it, for example, at the beginning of the nineteen-fifties to denounce an "absolute pauperization of the proletariat" or to rave about a "proletarian logic." In France more than in any other Western coun-

---

he publish some of his—Isou's—writings, in which he compared Debord to Göring, Lebo-vici's response, certainly inspired by Debord, was curiously mild (see Champ Libre, *Cor-respondance*, vol. 2 [Paris: Champ Libre, 1981], 49–51). Is a kind of respect for Debord's first "master" to be discerned here?

7. See Robert Ohrt, *Phantom Avantgarde* (Hamburg: Nautilus, 1990), 64.

try, the Communist Party conducted a veritable reign of terror over the intellectuals, successfully silencing any thinking on the Left that did not correspond to its manuals. It is hard to identify a single intellectual of that period (except of course for bourgeois intellectuals) who did not at least for a time fall into line, and this goes too for all those who just a few years later would constitute swarms of professional anti-Stalinists. After 1945, the journal Les Temps Modernes sought to develop a critique of Stalinism, but significantly three of its four founders—Maurice Merleau-Ponty, Raymond Aron, and Albert Camus—soon joined the liberal camp, while the fourth, Sartre, even more significantly, engaged in obscene mental contortions in defense of the "socialist character" of the Soviet Union and (as he was able to write as late as February 1956) the "extraordinary objective intelligence" of the French Communist Party.

Small groups of Trotskyists, anarchists, or followers of Bordiga also emerged, but in addition to their inability to make their voices heard they were hindered by their authoritarian structures and their theoretical sterility. The Trotskyists could not even decide whether the Soviet Union was a class society. It was against the background of disagreements of this kind that "Socialisme ou Barbarie" was formed in 1949; this group and its journal of the same name (see below, pp. 90–93) soon became the only passable theoretical voice of independent Marxism in France. To begin with, however, this position did not differ significantly from that of the "left communists" of the nineteen-twenties, and certainly no attempt was made to connect Marxist revolutionary theory with the avant-garde injunction to "change life." It is thus not absurd to claim that the Letterism of Isidore Isou, for all its limitations, represented the only truly ground-breaking movement in France's postwar period.[8]

Just as the activity of the Situationists in the sixties was an attempt to respond to the new social conjuncture created by a modernizing capitalism, so the early stages of that activity in the years of the Letterist International cannot be detached from the rapid and radical change that France underwent in the fifties. At the beginning of that decade, France's economy was rather backward in comparison with the economies of the country's northern neighbors; for instance, the percentage of the population employed in agriculture was 27 percent, as against 13 percent for

8. A view shared by Richard Gombin, a sociologist much more interested by Marxist groups than by artistic tendencies; see his Les Origines du gauchisme (Paris: Le Seuil, 1971), 79; Eng. trans. by Michael K. Perl: The Origins of Modern Leftism (Harmondsworth, Middlesex: Penguin Books, 1975), 60.

the Netherlands. Within a very few years, however, France caught up with the most highly developed countries. Productivity was soon increasing at a faster rate in France than anywhere else in the world, and between 1953 and 1957 French industrial output rose by 57 percent even though the average increase for all European countries was only 33 percent.[9] Nor was economic growth the only factor here; rather, a qualitative transition occurred that profoundly affected daily life and introduced the "style" so succinctly described by the French as *métro-boulot-dodo*. The high point of the activity of the young members of the Letterist International corresponds exactly to the brief period between 1954 and 1956, which some sociologists now think witnessed the culmination of "a second, silent French revolution" that wrested the country violently from "its still traditional framework" and ushered in the "alienation" of our time.[10] France's first television program was broadcast in 1953. In 1955 washing machines appeared on the market for the first time, and the same year the first *grands ensembles*, or high-rise "moderate-income housing," went up in Sarcelles—a kind of development that would soon ravage the outskirts of all French cities. Between 1954 and 1956 French consumer spending on household appliances doubled. In 1957 there were six times as many college students in France as there had been twenty years earlier. This particularly sudden eruption of modernity, which in many other countries had begun arriving much earlier, meant that capitalist modernization was easier to *see coming* in France than it was elsewhere;[11] and the young generation was especially sensitive to the change. The significance of the LI and the SI lies in the fact that they were among the first people to see these new developments as the bases of a new class struggle. The question so often repeated in their publications—"Will these modern means help realize human desires?"—takes on its full resonance only if it is placed in the context of the most thoroughgoing restructuring of daily life that France had ever known.

The activity of the Letterists (as the dissidents of the LI called themselves simply, not wishing to concede this title to those still loyal to Isou) cannot be separated from a Paris that was still for a time the cultural capital of the world, a place where the various factions of the intelli-

9. These figures are from Cornelius Castoriadis, "Perspectives de la crise française" (1958), in *La Société française* (Paris: Union Générale d'Éditions, Collection 10/18, 1979), 108 and 139.

10. "Matériaux pour servir à l'histoire intellectuelle de la France, 1953–1987," *Le Débat* 50 (May–August 1988): 174.

11. As pointed out in "Discours préliminaire," *Encyclopédie des Nuisances* 1 (November 1984): 13.

gentsia could assume that their quarrels were of world-historical significance simply by virtue of where they were conducted. Later, Debord
would evoke the beauty of the Paris of his youth, "when for the last
time, it shone with so intense a fire" (OCC, 227; *In girum*, 31). In those
days, young people from every corner of the globe continued to come
to Paris, and sleep under the bridges if need be, just so as to be there.
The center of the city was still inhabited by a *people* in the old meaning
of the word, descended from the same populace that had so often in the
past risen to throw off the yoke of its masters. A few years later all of
this came to an end, as the Situationists were the first to record.[12] May
1968 was itself an attempt by the young to take back a city that had
long represented a space of freedom for them but that by the 1960s had
changed completely.[13]

The new "International" was comprised of a dozen or so young people, some of them North Africans or foreigners living in Paris (this was
the extent of the group's internationalism). The Letterists despised existentialism, even though in a sense they were themselves objectively a
sort of extremist wing of it, for they too incarnated a tragic antagonism
between subjectivity and the outside world.[14] Even if everything did not
always go swimmingly in the three or four bars where they juggled their
slim resources and avoided the attentions of the police, they had a very
high opinion of themselves, disdaining the world around them along with
all those who, unlike them, were not determined to break with the bourgeois life style.[15] They looked upon themselves (at any rate after certain
purely nihilistic elements had been expelled) as an avant-garde that had
moved beyond art itself, and they expressed the firm conviction that their
"works—though practically inexistent—would leave their mark on history" (*Pot.*, 180). Rejecting the dismal life offered by the whole society
in which they lived, the Letterists wanted their epic to be based on the
quest for passion and adventure. This was not the sixties, when the "Underground" was fashionable and widely accepted, but a time when a

12. See "La Chute de Paris" [The Fall of Paris], *IS* 4/7–9.
13. See Louis Chevalier, *L'Assassinat de Paris* (Paris: Calmann-Levy, 1977), for example p. 19; this is a book that was much appreciated by Debord.
14. Debord, however, in his film *On the Passage of a Few Persons through a Rather
Brief Period of Time*, which celebrated the Letterist milieu in Saint Germain des Prés, had
this to say: "These people also scorned 'subjective profundity.' They were interested in
nothing but an adequate, concrete expression of themselves" (OCC, 21; *Films*, 25).
15. Many documents and iconographic items relating to the life of the young Letterists will be found in Greil Marcus, *Lipstick Traces* (Cambridge, Mass.: Harvard University Press, 1989), and in Ohrt, *Phantom Avantgarde*. Both Marcus and Ohrt draw too on
interviews given them by various sometime Letterists.

group of this kind inevitably remained isolated and surrounded by enemies. All of this conferred an extraordinary intensity upon encounters
and events; looking back later, Debord would often sing the praises of
this heroic period, though he always noted that for many of the participants the adventure did not have a happy ending.

In 1953, after a number of expulsions, the LI crystallized around a
solid core of members, notable among them, aside from Debord, being
Debord's wife Michèle Bernstein, Mohamed Dahou, Jacques Fillon, and
Gil J. Wolman, who had made a Letterist film in 1952. Apart from the
sporadic distribution of *cartes de visite* bearing such messages as "If you
think you have genius, or if you think you have only a brilliant intelligence, write the Letterist Internationale," or "Create a little situation
for yourself with no prospects,"[16] the Letterists addressed the public by
means of small mimeographed bulletins. Thus between 1952 and 1954
four numbers of *Internationale Lettriste* appeared and between 1954 and
1957 twenty-nine issues of *Potlatch*. In all likelihood, nobody would now
remember the LI had not Debord made his start there, but as a matter
of fact the Letterists' pronouncements are certainly memorable on their
own account. For instance: "The most dazzling displays of intelligence
mean nothing to us. Political economy, love, and urban planning are
means we must master in order to solve a problem that is first and foremost of an ethical kind. Nothing can release life from its obligation to
be absolutely passionate. We know how to proceed. The world's hostility and trickery notwithstanding, the participants in an adventure that
is altogether daunting are gathering, and making no concessions. We consider generally that there is no honorable way of living apart from this
participation." Below this text appear seven signatures, in the best Surrealist tradition (*Pot.*, 17–18). "Even though almost everything that happens in this world provokes our anger and disgust," asserted the Letterists, "we are nevertheless more and more able to find it amusing" (*Pot.*,
156; *Dérive*, 53); and they rejected the common idea that life is sad
(*Pot.*, 39; *Dérive*, 45). In their refusal of work and vague aspirations to
"revolution," in their promotion of subjective experience, and in their
after all very real degree of cultivation, the Letterists closely resembled
the early Surrealists; the difference was that the young Letterists were
more uncouth, more negative—but also more sincere.

They were, indeed, very young. In the summer of 1953 their average
age was about twenty-one. Or, more precisely, according to calculations

16. Reproduced in Berréby, 265–67.

made some years later, the LI's average age was twenty-three at the time of its foundation and dropped to 20.8 years a few months later as a consequence of internal purges (see *IS* 3/17). Some measure of the absolute seriousness with which the young Letterists took their activities is given by this propensity to statistical exactitude, as too by the characterization of purges within the group as "lively factional struggles and the expulsion of superannuated group leaders" (*Pot.*, 43); by the fact that their paper could report a Letterist meeting held to decide on the exact texts of short inscriptions to be written in chalk at certain places in the city; or by their long discussion, at another meeting, of whether all churches should be demolished or merely converted to other uses. Their pursuit of adventure, passion, and play was supposed to be conducted with a rigor reminiscent of a revolutionary organization on the Leninist model. Under pain of expulsion, every gesture, every word of a member had to correspond to the spirit of the group, and all contact with excludees, even on a private basis, was strictly taboo. These were times of extreme eclecticism in every sphere, yet the Letterist International demanded of its members that they break utterly with all aspects of the world outside, as much on the plane of thought as on that of lived experience. The value of an individual was measurable by reference to what that individual was satisfied with—a yardstick to which Debord remained firmly loyal ever afterwards. This total refusal to compromise with the outside ("We have no truck with those who do not think as we do" [*Pot.*, 166]), or even with each other ("Sooner change one's friends than change one's ideas" [*Pot.*, 185]), was possibly more typical of the Letterists and Situationists than any other single trait, and it would earn them countless rebukes and accusations of "Stalinism." And indeed the overwhelming majority of the members of these organizations ended up being expelled on the basis of motions brought by Debord. It is no coincidence that a *détournement* of a remark by Saint-Just may be found twice in the very few pages, dating from the earliest days, of *Internationale Lettriste:* "Human relations must be founded on passion, or else on terror."[17]

Still, Letterist discipline differs from the Leninist variety in that Leninist rigor is invariably bound up with tactical considerations and the desire to recruit as many adherents as possible, each of whom is expected merely to express formal agreement with the party's principles, whereas the LI or SI sought to retain a minimum of members only but required that the participation of each be flawless. The justification for

17. Ibid., 154 and 157.

this attitude was the need for self-defense of a group operating under difficult conditions and convinced that the degeneration of other groups was
caused by an excess of internal tolerance. It is worth pointing out, however, that this characteristic combination of a quest for disorder with a call
for rigor is yet another feature linking the young Letterists to Surrealism, which had been responsible for introducing expulsions, splits, and or-
thodoxies into the world of art. The relationship between the Debord
tendency and the original Surrealists is an ambiguous one, but the young
Letterists' view of the version of Surrealism contemporary with them
could not have been clearer: they called it "a festering, theosophical
agony" (Pot., 176).[18] Breton in particular was the butt of a near-Oedipal
hatred. In 1953 a twenty-line "manifesto" announced that "present-day
society is divided solely into Letterists on the one hand and snitches on
the other, and among the latter André Breton is the most notorious."[19] In
Potlatch, the Letterists evoked "bourgeois inquisitors like André Breton
or Joseph McCarthy" (Pot., 80) and voiced sentiments such as the following: "From Gaxotte [an ultrareactionary historian] to Breton, those people whom we find ridiculous all think it sufficient to denounce us solely
on account of our non-adherence to their own views of the world—views
which turn out to be all much of a muchness" (Pot., 107). For Breton's
sixtieth birthday, some Belgian allies of the Letterists sent out fake invi-
tations to several hundred people asking them to an alleged talk by Breton at the Hotel Lutétia on "the eternal youth of Surrealism." The moral
of this hoax, according to Potlatch, was that "no claim, no matter how
idiotic, will now occasion surprise so long as it has been approved by
[Surrealist] doctrine" (Pot., 240).

At the same time, the Letterists maintained that "the set of demands
once laid down by Surrealism" was a "minimum" (Pot., 44). They certainly acknowledged the positive role played by early Surrealism, though
less by virtue of its works than by virtue of its attempts to "change

18. The sole direct contact between the LI and the French Surrealists was destined to
end badly. In the fall of 1954, the two groups agreed to mount a protest together against
the official festivities marking the Rimbaud centenary. The Surrealists backed out, however, deeming a joint text written for the occasion, "Ça commence bien!" [A Good Start!],
to be too "Marxist." In a leaflet they accused the Letterists of being Stalinists, falsifiers,
and publicity hounds (Pot., 87–90), and the Letterists responded with a flyer of their own,
"Et Ça finit mal!" [And a Bad End!] (for this whole exchange, see Berréby, 274–78). Surrealism's most ferocious epigones never forgave the Letterists for this episode, and almost
thirty years afterwards they were still accusing them of having laid a "trap" for the Surrealists and of being dogmatists bent on subordinating artistic freedom to politics (see the
comments on this exchange in José Pierre, Tracts surréalistes et déclarations collectives II:
1940–1969 [Paris: Le Terrain Vague, 1982], 359–63).

19. Berréby, 154.

life" and go beyond art. Surrealism had been a still artistic destruction of art, however, and now a much more important task had to be tackled, neither expressive nor aesthetic in character, namely "the conscious construction of new affective states" (*Pot.*, 106).

The "construction of situations" was indeed the key concept of the young Letterists; this was something that could not be arrived at merely by asserting some dogma but called for research and experiment.[20] Debord evoked the construction of situations in his earliest writings—specifically in the already cited single issue of *Ion* (1952)—and the notion was still in evidence fifteen years later in the context of a discussion by him of the way in which the spectacle prevents people from determining their own destinies. The program envisaged did not change, but in the first decade it was essentially conflated with the *supersession of art*.

In the nineteen-fifties it was easy enough to show that cultural innovation was nonexistent, and the Letterists ridiculed everything that was touted as "new"—and most especially Alain Robbe-Grillet—as the palest of imitations of historic avant-garde achievements, imitations that no one would have dreamt of taking seriously just a few years earlier. For the Letterists, however, it was not a matter of waiting for some genuinely new artistic tendency to come along: "All abstract painting since Malevich has amounted to breaking down open doors," they wrote (*Pot.*, 215); as for the cinema, its "entire field of possible discoveries" had been exploited to the limit (*Pot.*, 139); while "onomatopoeic poetry and neoclassical poetry have simultaneously demonstrated the utter depreciation of this product" (*Pot.*, 209). The Letterists, even Isou's old guard, had always felt that the successful realization of any newly conceived artistic technique condemned all future exponents of that technique to the status of boring imitators.

Potlatch offered an original explanation for this stagnation of art: here too "the relations of production [had] entered into contradiction with the necessary development of the forces of production" (*Pot.*, 274; *Oct.*, 88). Just as the strengthening of man's domination of nature had superseded the idea of God, so likewise new technological advances would make the supersession of aesthetics possible and necessary. The church was "a sort of monument to everything not yet dominated in the world" (*Pot.*, 205). Art was the heir to religion,[21] for it expressed the fact that man was not capable of using the new means now available to make

20. The word "Situationist" appeared for the first time in 1956 (*Pot.*, 227).
21. An announcement circulated in 1956 by the Movement for an Imaginist Bauhaus proclaimed that "Art Is the Opium of the People" (see Bandini, 275).

a different everyday life for himself (*Pot.*, 170; *Dérive*, 56); it was precisely because a new order of things had emerged as a possibility that the
mere *voicing* of disagreement was now useless. This is the sense of Debord and Wolman's assertion that Letterism was not a "literary school"
but rather an experimental search for a new "way of living" (*Pot.*, 186).
Potlatch called for the unity of art and life, not to lower art to the level
of life as it was presently lived, but instead to raise life to the level
promised by art. The richness of life that art promised, just like the techniques for intensifying sensation that were characteristic of artistic practice, ought to be attainable within the realm of everyday experience. In
this way the Letterists hoped to go beyond the Surrealists. Breton had
spoken of "beauty, which has quite obviously never been envisaged here
with anything but passionate aims in mind"; yet the Surrealists had been
content merely to write books in which they loudly proclaimed the necessity of *living* the new values instead of just *describing* them.[22] In 1925
they had declared: "(1) We have nothing to do with literature. But we are
quite capable, if need be, of making use of it like everyone else. (2) Surrealism is not a new means of expression, nor a simpler one. . . . (3) We
are determined to create a Revolution."[23] Things did not work out quite
according to plan, however.

If poetry in books was dead, it was "now to be found in the form
of cities," and it could be "read on people's faces." But merely seeking
poetry out wherever it might be was not enough, for the beauty of cities, or of faces, had to be *constructed*: "the new beauty will be SITUA-
TIONAL" (*Pot.*, 41). Unlike the Surrealists, the Letterists expected to
find little in the nooks and crannies of reality, in dreams, or in the unconscious; reality itself had instead to be remade. "The adventurer is one
who makes adventures happen rather than one to whom adventures happen" (*Pot.*, 51)—an admirable motto that would be a good epigraph for
Debord's whole journey. The function of the arts henceforward would
be to combine into a new style of life, and in the early days the Letterists spoke in this connection of an "integral art." The situations that the
future Situationists were forever pursuing always had a material aspect,
and the complete and authentic construction of situations meant a new

22. André Breton, *Nadja* (1928; Paris: Gallimard, Collection Folio, 1988), 188–89;
Eng. trans. by Richard Howard (New York: Grove Press, 1960), 159.

23. *Déclaration du 27 janvier 1925*, in José Pierre, ed., *Tracts surréalistes et déclarations collectives I: 1922–1939* (Paris, Le Terrain Vague, 1980), 34; Eng. trans. by Richard
Howard, in Maurice Nadeau, *The History of Surrealism* (New York: Collier, 1967),
103.

urbanism in which all the arts would be mobilized in the creation of a passion-filled atmosphere.

The Letterists' interest in urbanism arose from their notion of "psychogeography," by which they meant the systematic observation of the effects produced by different urban ambiances upon the emotions. In this vein they published several descriptions of the zones into which the city could be subdivided from the psychogeographical point of view, as well as accounts of specific places considered in this light.[24] Such findings were the product of what the Letterists called *dérives*—rambles based on "a technique for passing hastily through varied ambiances."[25] A *dérive* would take the best part of a day, during which the explorers would allow themselves to be guided "by the solicitations of the terrain and of chance encounters." The role of chance would be reduced as familiarity with the territory grew, and it would thus become possible to *choose* which solicitations to respond to. But only a "unitary urbanism" represented a complete solution: the creation of ambiances that did not merely allow feelings to find expression but actually provoked new feelings. Interest in an antifunctionalist architecture of this kind grew during the period of Letterist agitation, becoming one of the earliest points of convergence with the other European artistic groups that subsequently joined with the Letterists to found the Situationist International.

Rather than create entirely new forms, the Letterists wanted to take already existing elements and rearrange them. To this appropriative technique, derived in part from Dadaist collage, in part from a kind of distorted quotation favored by both Marx and Lautréamont, they gave the name of *détournement*. *Détournement* involves a quotation, or more generally a re-use, that "adapts" the original element to a new context. It is also a way of transcending the bourgeois cult of originality and the private ownership of thought. In some cases the products of bourgeois civilization, even the most insignificant ones, such as advertisements, may be reemployed in such as way as to modify their meaning; in other cases, the effect may be to reinforce the real meaning of an original element—a sentence of Marx's, say—by changing its form. Dadaist collage restricted itself to the devaluing pole of the "devaluing/revaluing" dialectic that is the basis of all *détournement* (*IS* 10/59; *SIA*, 176). In the first

---

24. See for example *Potlatch*, 109–10, and Berréby, 300 and 324–26.
25. See Guy Debord, "Théorie de la dérive," *Les Lèvres Nues* 9 (1956); reprinted in Berréby, 312–19, and in part in *IS* 2/19. Also Debord's "Introduction à une critique de la géographie urbaine," *Les Lèvres Nues* 6 (1955); reprinted in Berréby, 288–92.

instance, this technique is indeed "the negation of the value of the previous organization of expression" (*IS* 3/10; *SIA*, 55), but the elements reused acquire a new meaning, and from the outset Debord sought to go beyond the pure negativity of Dada. Systematized theoretically in 1956, in an article by Debord and Wolman, *détournement* became a Letterist and Situationist trademark.[26] Instances of its application include Asger Jorn's repainted *kitsch* pictures, comic strips with rewritten bubbles, and Debord's films, almost entirely composed of preexisting cinematic elements. The supreme example must be *The Society of the Spectacle*, identifying all of whose textual *détournements* calls for considerable erudition.[27] The creations of the past were thus neither deprecated nor regarded with undue respect but rather—in terms that Debord employed as late as 1960—"used for propaganda purposes." Some borrowings were made over and over again in Debord's work, cases in point being the passage from the *Communist Manifesto* on "the heavy artillery with which [the bourgeoisie] batters down all Chinese walls";[28] a sentence from Bossuet's *Panégyrique de Bernard de Clairvaux* ("Bernard, Bernard, this green youth will not last forever");[29] and the metaphor of the search

26. Guy Debord and Gil J. Wolman, "Mode d'emploi du détournement," *Les Lèvres Nues* 8 (1956); reprinted in Berréby, 302–9.

27. Here are a few of the *détournements* of Marx and Hegel to be found in *The Society of the Spectacle*: for §4, see *Capital I*, 932; for §9, see Hegel, *The Phenomenology of Mind*, trans. J. B. Baillie, rev. 2d ed. (1949; London: Allen and Unwin/New York: Humanities Press, 1966), 99; for §35, see *Capital I*, 163, and "Speech at the Anniversary of the *People's Paper*," *PW II*, 300; the quoted material in §43 is from Marx's *Economic and Philosophical Manuscripts*; for §74, see Marx and Engels, *Manifesto of the Communist Party*, *PW I*, 70–71; for §107, see Hegel, *Phenomenology*, 505; for the last sentence of §114, see Marx, "A Contribution to the Critique of Hegel's Philosophy of Right: Introduction," *EW*, 256; for §164, see Marx to Ruge, September 1843, in "Letters from the Franco-German Yearbooks," *EW*, 209; for §188, see Hegel's *Philosophy of Right*, trans. T. M. Knox (London: Oxford University Press, 1967), 13; for §191, see Marx, "Hegel's Philosophy of Right," *EW*, 250; for §202, see Marx, "Preface to *The Critique of Political Economy*," in Marx and Engels, *Selected Works* (Moscow: Progress Publishers/New York: International Publishers, 1968), 183.

As for other authors, the latter portion of §14 appropriates a well-known sentence of Eduard Bernstein's; §21 refers to Freud's celebrated principle in the *The Interpretation of Dreams* according to which "dreams are the *guardians* of sleep" (*Standard Edition*, vol. 4, p. 233); and §207 is a *détournement* of Lautréamont's formulation promoting *détournement*.

In many ways *The Society of the Spectacle* comes very close to obeying Walter Benjamin's injunction to write a book composed entirely of quotations.

Appended to the 1998 edition of Debord and Sanguinetti's *La Véritable scission dans l'Internationale* is a list, drawn up by Debord, of some of the *détournements* to be found in that work.

28. Berréby, 305; also *IS* 3/10: *SIA*, 55; *SS* §165. (Original: Marx and Engels, *Manifesto of the Communist Party, PW I*, 71.)

29. See. *Pot.*, 114; Debord and Jorn, *Mémoires* (1959); *OCC*, 241; *In girum*, 42–43.

for the North-West Passage (*Pref.*, 19; Eng., 10), taken from Thomas De Quincey's *Confessions of an English Opium-Eater*. In the broadest sense, Debord's whole conception of society is founded on *détournement:* all the elements needed for a free life are already to hand, both culturally and technologically speaking; they have merely to be modified as to their meanings, and organized differently (see for example *IS* 7/18).

It was not very hard to set forth "utopian" programs such as that of "unitary urbanism"; Isou's old-guard Letterists had done something of the sort, as had many others. What made the LI different was its search for *practical means* with which to realize the program, and from the outset the young Letterists tended to embrace the traditions of political revolution. In 1954 Debord wrote that "at least the best reasons for civil war will not be in short supply" (*Pot.*, 28). The LI called upon "proletarian revolutionary parties to organize armed intervention in support of the new revolution" in Spain.[30] Yet the French Communist Party aroused no sympathy whatsoever among the Letterists, and one might well ask who the said revolutionary parties were. The fact is that in its first few years of existence the LI was simply a *bohème* that placed vague hopes in a somewhat mythical "revolution."

It was nevertheless during this period that the Letterists laid the groundwork for projects developed later. Despite the continuing presence of a proletariat in the classic sense, they were among the first to glimpse the unprecedented way in which the social question was beginning to reframe itself. What would happen to the increasing amount of free time available to the population in general? Would modern technology allow people to live lives governed by play and desire, or would it merely create new forms of alienation? "The real problem of revolution is the problem of leisure time. Economic constraints and their moral corollaries are in any event bound soon to be destroyed and transcended. The organization of leisure . . . is already a necessity for the capitalist State, as it is for its Marxist heirs. On all sides, however, the only response has been the inescapable stupefactions of sports stadium and television set. . . . Unless this question is not openly addressed before the collapse of the reigning system of economic exploitation, that change will be nothing but a travesty" (*Pot.*, 50–51). Uttered in 1954, these were truly prophetic words at a time when the phenomenon evoked was in its infancy, and the fact that they came neither from a sociologist nor

30. Berréby, 156.

from a professional Marxologist makes them all the more striking. In a perfectly consistent manner, the Letterists rejected trade-unionism and purely economic demands in order to pose "the problem of the survival or destruction of the system"; and they did this on the basis of a well-nigh "existentialist" principle, namely, that "life passes, and we can expect no compensations aside from those that we have to invent and build ourselves" (*Pot.*, 30–31). They took note of the total degeneration of the Left, which was incapable even of offering concrete support to the cause of a free Algeria, but their basic detachment with respect to "politics" meant that they confined themselves to very brief comments on domestic and international developments without ever attempting more detailed analysis.

The secret of the seductiveness of Situationist theories in the nineteen-sixties lay in their desire to combine the content of the new revolution, as heralded by art, with the practical means for realizing it, including those of the old workers' movement. This goal was already clearly embraced in the early days of the LI, but it was several years before the Letterists managed to give it a consistent programmatic form. First, as Debord would put it later, the LI had to get beyond its "self-satisfied nihilism," "excessive sectarianism," and "inactive purity" (*Pot.*, 263). A first step in this direction was the group's collaboration with the Belgian magazine *Les Lèvres Nues*, edited by the Surrealist Marcel Mariën, where a number of Letterist articles appeared. But the Letterists' friendship with the Danish painter Asger Jorn turned out to be an even more productive connection. Jorn, along with the Dutch painter and architect Constant (Constant Nieuwenhuys), had organized the group CoBrA between 1948 and 1951, striving to recover the revolutionary spirit of Surrealism through an art that was expressionist in character.

In 1955, in Italy, Jorn and the Piedmontese painter Pinot (Giuseppe) Gallizio founded the "Experimental Laboratory" of the International Movement for an Imaginist Bauhaus, which the LI had also recently joined. Jorn had many friends in different European countries; so did Debord; and the outcome of many contacts among all these people was a first congress, dedicated to the search for a common platform, held at Alba in the Italian Piedmont in September 1956, with participants from eight countries. In the following months quite a few of these would fall by the wayside, but in July 1957, in Cosio d'Arroscia on the Ligurian coast, eight people decided to found the Situationist International. A few months later the new organization had members in Italy, France, Great

Britain, Germany, Belgium, Holland, Algeria, and Scandinavia. Most of
them were painters, and as a practical matter their common ground did
not extend very far beyond the theme of unitary urbanism and of experimentation aimed at the creation of "new ambiances" capable of fostering new types of behavior and opening the way to a civilization founded
on play.

Debord clearly acknowledged that this alliance between Letterist radicalism and forces still developing within the framework of artistic activity might be seen as "a step backwards," but he argued that the Letterists could no longer continue to "conduct an external opposition" and
must now "seize control of modern culture and use it for our own purposes" (*Pot.*, 262). To be at once "*in* and *against*" a decaying cultural
sphere (*Pot.*, 269) obviously exposed one to the risk of regression, yet it
also opened up the prospect of a broader-based project of supersession.
This possibility was very much in phase with the apparent dissipation
of postwar apathy, and the LI evoked a "general revolutionary renewal
characteristic of the year 1956," which witnessed not only important developments in Algeria and Spain but above all large-scale revolts in Poland and Hungary (*Pot.*, 249; *SIA*, 15). The traditional Left had totally
discredited itself and culture had reached such a state of decay that no
one could be unaware of it. The moment might well therefore be aus-
picious for the emergence of a new revolutionary force, even one still
struggling to achieve its own coherence.

The Situationists and Art

The first years of Situationist agitation unfolded within the world of art,
within the world of culture and its problems. Debord nevertheless asserted at the outset that "the problems of cultural creation can now
be solved only in conjunction with a new advance in world revolution"
(*Rapp.*, 696; *SIA*, 21). This statement is from "Report on the Construction of Situations and on the Prerequisites for the Organization and Action of the International Situationist Tendency" (1957), in which Debord
set forth a provisional platform for the new Situationist International.
This text, some twenty pages in length, constitutes the first systematic
presentation of Debord's ideas and indeed the longest piece of writing
its author, who was then twenty-five, would publish until *The Society
of the Spectacle* appeared in 1967.

Couched in his characteristically efficient style, so impervious to any
kind of linguistic fashion, drawing at once from the young Marx and

from Hegel but also from seventeenth-century prose and from Saint-Just, Debord's "Report" defined culture as reflecting and prefiguring the use of the means available in a given society. Modern culture, however, had lost ground relative to the growth of the means at its disposal, and, contrary to the view of so-called orthodox Marxism, such delay in the development of the superstructure (i.e., culture) was quite capable of holding up change at the base of society. The neutralization of artistic avant-gardes had therefore become one of the chief goals of bourgeois propaganda. Debord surveyed the advances in consciousness embodied in Futurism, in Dadaism (whose "dissolution was rendered inevitable by its exclusively negative character" [*Rapp.*, 691; *SIA*, 18] but whose stamp remained on all succeeding avant-gardes), and in Surrealism. Praising the fecundity of Surrealism's original agenda, Debord located the source of the movement's degeneration in its overestimation of the unconscious. When the Surrealists' paean to the irrational was co-opted by the bourgeoisie as a way of beautifying the complete irrationality of its world, one was confronted by an especially flagrant instance of the perversion after 1945 of the purposes of the old avant-gardes. What had once been a protest against the emptiness of bourgeois society was now being fragmented and dissolved into "ordinary aesthetic commerce" (*Rapp.*, 692; *SIA*, 20) as a *positive* expression of that same emptiness. This could be done either by "dissimulating the nothingness," after the fashion of existentialism, or else by "joyously affirming an absolute mental nullity," after the fashion of Beckett or Robbe-Grillet (*Rapp.*, 693). It went without saying that for Debord the "socialist realism" of the Eastern European countries operated at an even lower level. No positive value was accorded to any tendencies save those which had now come together to form the Situationist International (CoBrA, Letterism, the Imaginist Bauhaus).

The first task of the Situationist International would consist in a vast experimentation with available cultural means in order to engage in that "battle of leisure" which was the true new theater of the class struggle (*Rapp.*, 698–99; *SIA*, 24). The development of a "science of situations" would be the proper response to the "spectacle," to non-participation. The arts would not be negated but would all contribute to the unity of material ambiance and behavior that constituted a "situation." "In a classless society, one might say, there will be no painters but at most Situationists who engage in painting among other activities" (*Rapp.*, 700).[31]

31. This is a *détournement* of Marx and Engels: "In communist societies there are no

There was no longer any place for the work of art that sought to "fix emotions" and strove to endure; all Situationist techniques, from the *dérive* to the "constructed situation," implied "a wager on the passing of time." Art should no longer express the passions of the old world but rather invent new passions: instead of merely translating life, it should extend life's boundaries. The main function of "hyper-political propaganda" was to "destroy . . . the bourgeois idea of happiness" (*Rapp.*, 701). The "theater of operations" would be everyday life: "What changes our way of seeing the streets is more important than what changes our way of seeing painting" (*Rapp.*, 700; *SIA*, 24). The Situationists thus aspired not simply to a political revolution, nor solely to a "cultural" one: they envisaged the creation of a new civilization and a genuine transformation of humanity.

For the first four years of the SI's existence, the pivot of the group was the collaboration between Debord and Asger Jorn, who complemented each other well precisely because they were so different. Until 1960 the contributions of Constant, who joined in 1958, and of Gallizio, were also important. The first expulsions occurred a few months after the SI's foundation, but replacements were not long in coming, among them a whole group of German painters known as SPUR and numerous Scandinavians. In June 1958 the first number of the journal *Internationale Situationniste* was published, with its trademark metallic cover. It would appear roughly twice a year until 1961, after which publication was much less frequent, though issues were more voluminous.

According to the Situationists, the freedom conceded in the cultural sphere served as a cover for the alienation that reigned in every other realm of activity, yet culture was nevertheless the only area where the question of the use of the means at society's disposal could be posed in its entirety (see for example *Prelims.*, 345; *SIA*, 308). In one way or another, all Situationist activity during this period was pursued under the banner of experimentation and *détournement* (see IS 3/10–11; *SIA*, 55–56). Gallizio invented "industrial painting," which he produced on a large scale on long rolls and sold by the meter. Jorn, who by this time already enjoyed a solid European reputation, bought old pictures at flea markets and painted over them. Constant, an architect by profession, worked out elaborate projects for a utopian city called "New Babylon."[32]

---

painters but at most people who engage in painting among other activities" (*The German Ideology* [Moscow: Progress Publishers, 1968], 443).

32. These projects, developed continuously over more than a decade, may now be seen in the Netherlands.

As for Debord, he too engaged in a particular kind of artistic activity, collaborating with Jorn on two books of collages, which the authors called "essais d'écriture détournée"—experimental writing using *détournement*. Published in limited editions, these were *Fin de Copenhague* (1957) and *Mémoires* (1959). This last work, in which "each page may be read in any direction, and the reciprocal relationships between phrases are invariably incomplete" (*IS* 3/11; *SIA,* 56), relies exclusively on "prefabricated elements" to recount the years of existence of the Letterist International. Around the same time, Debord made the medium-length film *On the Passage of a Few Persons through a Rather Brief Period of Time* (1959). In this instance the text of the film conformed to a "framework" evoking the Letterist years, with as accompaniment images largely borrowed from elsewhere and subjected to *détournement*.

The SI published a number of monographs on its artists and agreed to construct a labyrinth suitable for *dérives* at the Amsterdam Communal Museum, although in the end this project was never realized. The Situationists were out to seize control of the cultural sphere and transform it: indeed, in the first issue of the group's journal, Debord asserted that the SI "should be looked upon . . . as an attempt to build an organization of professional revolutionaries in the realm of culture" (*IS* 1/21).[33]

It was nevertheless not very long before an irreparable split opened up within the SI over the relationship between "culture" and "revolution." For a fraction of the group, with Debord at its head, the sphere of artistic expression was truly superseded: the liberation of art had been "the destruction of [that] expression itself" (*IS* 3/6; *Oct.*, 106). (By 1961 Debord and Bernstein were the only survivors of the original Letterist group, though Debord's positions soon found new supporters in the persons of the Belgian Raoul Vaneigem and the Hungarian exile Attila Ko-

---

33. When the Situationists acknowledge, in 1967, that in the early days they had occasionally, "in a still non-critical manner employed . . . certain concepts of the old (Trotskyist) far Left" (*IS* 11/58), or when Jean-François Martos, in his orthodox *Histoire de l'Internationale Situationniste* (Paris: Gérard Lebovici, 1989), concedes that it was only in 1961 that the SI "eliminated its last traces of Trotskyist influence" (143), the allusion is probably to assertions of this kind; other examples might be Debord's reference in 1957 to a few "local half-successes" achieved by revolutionary movements that, "especially in the case of the Chinese revolution, favor a renewal of the revolutionary movement as a whole" (*Rapp.*, 689) or, again, his statement that the Situationists had "clearly megalomaniacal ambitions, albeit ambitions that might not be measurable by the prevailing criteria of success," in that "they would be content to work anonymously, at the Ministry of Leisure, for any government which at last took it upon itself to change life, for a salary commensurate with that of skilled workers" (*Pot.*, 277).

tanyi.) On the Debordian view, works such as *Finnegans Wake* had already written finis to pseudo-communication, and the task ahead was to discover a new kind of communication (see *IS* 3/3–7; *Oct.*, 102–8) and to realize art qua "revolutionary praxis" (*IS* 4/5). "Our time no longer needs to *draft poetic agendas;* rather, it needs to execute them" (*IS* 8/33; *SIA*, 117). There were other Situationists, however, who were willing neither to jettison a traditional view of the artist nor really to accept the discipline demanded. Constant did not judge it opportune to postpone all attempts at realizing "unitary urbanism," and indeed to defer all practical experimentation in this area, until "after the revolution." Practically all the SI artists voiced skepticism regarding the revolutionary vocation of the proletariat, preferring to entrust the task of challenging modern culture to the intellectuals and creators and adopting the perspective of a "gradual evolution" rather than that of a revolution they deemed far distant. For Debord, by contrast, *new conditions* for revolution had now come into play (see *IS* 3/22–24). The SI's annual conferences, which generally brought together a dozen or so participants, sought to coordinate the movement's activities, but in the end the divergence of views turned out to be insurmountable. In June 1960, Constant was obliged to resign from the SI before he became a polemical target; the epithet "technocratic" would still be leveled at him by the Situationists years later, after he had sought a leading role in the "Provo" movement in Amsterdam (*IS* 11/66). Gallizio had been expelled in the same month (though in more honorable circumstances) on account of his inability to resist the appeal of a personal career in the art world (see *IS* 5/10). As for Jorn, who had little inclination to submit to the dictates of an organization, he parted company with the SI on friendly terms in 1961.[34] By contrast, the SI's expulsion of the German section, and its split with nearly all of its Scandinavian membership (the "Nashist" tendency) in the spring of 1962, took place in an atmosphere of reciprocal sectarianism and hate. As early as August 1961, at the Fifth SI Conference in Gothenburg, Sweden, a resolution had been passed defining the production of any work of art as "anti-Situationist," thus in effect halting the earlier program, which had envisaged contesting culture from within. By 1962 the SI had achieved a measure of unity, but the price paid had been the reduction of the group's size to a bare minimum.

34. Debord and Jorn always held each other in high esteem (Jorn died in 1973), as witness Debord's preface, written in 1972, to *Jorn/Le Jardin d'Albisola* (see Bibliography 1).

For the next four years, roughly speaking, rather less was heard from the Situationist International, while Debord and Vaneigem worked on their respective books.

At any rate until 1963, the question of art took up a good many pages in *Internationale Situationniste*, not a few of them reporting internal debates on the subject. To begin with, the Situationists strove to champion a radical modernism holding all existing artistic forms in contempt on the grounds that they did not come to terms with the new situation created by advances in humanity's domination of nature. Michèle Bernstein praised Gallizio's "industrial painting" precisely because it represented progress relative to artisanal production (*IS* 2/27; Oct., 94–95). It is telling that, even though they had by this time much attenuated their attacks on Surrealism, the Situationists continued to rebuke the Surrealists for their "refusal to envisage a liberatory use for the superior technological means of our time" (*IS* 2/33). On the one hand, the historical conjuncture offered the artist the objective possibility of mobilizing these means in such a way as to give life meaning; but at the same time society, while according him the abstract right to do so, in reality made it impossible. This contradiction meant that the liberation of modern art had entailed its self-destruction and that artists were forced to reject their vocation as ever more limited (*IS* 3/4; Oct., 103). On the basis of an antagonism characteristic of its thinking, the SI concluded that only two courses now remained open: either to pursue the destructive process, but to envisage it as a beautification and adoration of nothingness, or else, for the first time in history, to actualize artistic values directly in everyday life as an art that was anonymous and collective, an "art of dialogue" (*IS* 4/37). Consequently, any "work" intended to endure or to be preserved as an exchangeable commodity must now be abandoned, and superseded, not by some workless art, not by "happenings" or "performance," but in such a way as to transcend the dichotomy between artistic moments and moments of banality. Traditional artistic activities had value only inasmuch as they contributed to the construction of situations, and it was quite possible to be a Situationist without "creating," for human behavior in itself partook of unitary urbanism and indeed constituted its true goal. Such creation would nevertheless be restricted to mere preliminaries until such time as the complete control of a town, at the very least, made it possible to construct an experimental life. If the Situationists considered themselves to be the real heirs of the avant-garde movements of the 1910–25 period, it was precisely inasmuch as they

were *no longer* artists but constituted "the only movement able, by incorporating the survival of art into the art of living, to speak to the project of the authentic artist" (*IS* 9/25; *SIA*, 139); right up until the end,
the SI conceived of all of its activity as a sort of avant-garde art. By contrast, the many spurious heirs of earlier avant-gardes could in the Situationist view no longer lay claim even to aesthetic merit, for they were
nothing but shopkeepers. The SI called itself an "avant-garde of presence" (*IS* 8/14; *SIA*, 109) as opposed to the "avant-garde of absence"
of the Ionescos or Durases, basking in acclaim for the supposed auda-
ciousness with which, half a century after the fact, they wheeled out the
Dadaists' purely negative critique. The SI described almost all the artistic
tendencies of its time as "neo-Dadaist," and emphasized that the Situationists were proposing something new and positive, being of the view
that the unification of life and art, which so many other movements,
even the most progressive, deemed desirable but far distant, was in fact
attainable and imminent. What distinguished them from the artists of
"decay" was perfectly summed up in the formulation, "We want to work,
not on the spectacle of the end of a world, but on the end of the world
of the spectacle" (*IS* 3/8; *Oct.*, 108). Perhaps overstating the significance
of the phenomenon, the SI observed elsewhere that art in the postwar
period had lost its status as a "privilege of the ruling class" and become
a product for mass consumption and a leading form of alienation (*IS*
9/40–41; *SIA,* 143).

It is important to bear in mind just how far removed the SI's position
was from an anticultural stance. We need only recall the following passage, from 1963: "We are against the conventional form of culture, even
in its most modern manifestation, but this is not to say that we prefer
ignorance, the petty-bourgeois common sense of the shopkeeper, or neo-
primitivism. . . . We place ourselves beyond culture. Not before it, but
after. We say it is necessary to *realize* culture by transcending it as a
separate sphere" (*IS* 8/21; *Oct.*, 137). As early as 1956 the young Letterists had scorned the abandonment of art as a kind of "religious conversion" on the part of artists who were in any case failures; the proper
aim, for the Letterists, was "the invention of a higher form of activity"
(*Pot.*, 228). Unlike the Surrealists of the thirties, who wanted to "put
poetry at the service of the revolution," the Situationists wanted to "put
revolution at the service of poetry"—but the poetry they had in mind
was not the "poetry without poems if necessary" of the Surrealists but
rather "a poetry *necessarily* without poems" (*IS* 8/31; *SIA*, 115). The
art of the past was by no means condemned, for it had often represented

the only testimony, albeit distorted, to the "clandestine problems of everyday life" (*IS* 6/25; *SIA*,73); and only in the ambit of past artistic activity could one find attractive forms of conduct. In non-revolutionary periods, it was in poetic circles that the notion of the totality survived (*IS* 8/31; *SIA*, 115). In short, modern art as a whole was anti-bourgeois (*IS* 9/40; *SIA*, 143). The art of the past should be judged historically and soberly, neither rejected in toto nor accepted in toto (*IS* 7/24). "We think that modern art, wherever it has turned out to be genuinely critical and innovative by virtue of the very conditions of its emergence, has performed its role, which was a great one, very well" (*IS* 7/24; *Oct.*, 137).

All the same, the Situationist criticism of the work of art is curiously reminiscent of the psychoanalytical account, according to which such productions are the sublimation of unfulfilled wishes. For the Situationists, inasmuch as progress had removed all obstacles to the realization of desires, art had lost its function, which was in any case subordinate to desires themselves. This is certainly one of the most debatable aspects of the Situationist theory of art.

In *The Society of the Spectacle* explicit discussion of the cultural sphere is limited, but Debord does offer a theoretical foundation going beyond the mere assertion that an independent art is an impossibility in the present era. He argues that the unity of life was lost when the original myth-based society disintegrated as a consequence of the increasing division of labor. Several separate spheres, each independent of the others, then came into being. To one of these spheres, namely culture, fell the task of representing the very unity that had disappeared, whether in the field of knowledge and learning or in that of direct experience and communication (*SS* §180)—in the fields, in other words, of science on the one hand and art on the other. But since the notion of a part replacing the whole is contradictory, so too is the idea of culture as an independent realm. No sooner, therefore, had culture achieved its independence (an occurrence whose date Debord does not specify) than a mechanism was set in motion by virtue of which the further culture advanced, the more doubt it was obliged to cast on its own social role. Precisely because it represented what was lacking in society, namely communication, and any unity in the different moments of life, culture had to refuse to be merely the *image* of that lack.[35]

---

35. The demand that the content of art be actualized had already been raised by a good number of Romantics. In 1794 Hölderlin wrote to his friend C. L. Neuffer as follows: "So much the worse! If we must, we shall break our wretched lyres and *do* what the artists have only *dreamed* of doing!" This interesting quotation, and others equally perti-

The "sudden expansion of knowledge" brought culture to an awareness that history was its heart (*SS* §182), just as it was the heart of society as a whole. Finding itself in a partially historical society, and knowing it, culture could only balk at *representing* a "meaning" that in a truly historical society would be *lived* by all. The rationality that a divided society had relegated to the domain of culture inevitably discovered that, so long as it remained cut off from the totality of life, it was in fact but partly rational (*SS* §183).

If it was to keep faith with its historical "heart," culture had to dissolve all ontological or static qualities; within it, innovation would invariably prevail over conservative tendencies (*SS* §18). As culture's autonomy grew, so too did its awareness that its newfound autonomy was at odds with its task. The climax of the history of culture would also be its eclipse as a separate sphere. Debord notes that this turning point occurred for philosophy with Hegel, Feuerbach, and Marx, whereas in the case of art it was reached only a century or so later.

Art was supposed to be "the language of communication" (*SS* §187), but the gradual evaporation of all the prerequisites of real communication had led language—whether the language of literature or that of the figurative arts—to bear witness, precisely, to the impossibility of communication (*SS* §189). In the course of the destruction of all formal values, as this unfolded from Baudelaire to Joyce and Malevich, art became ever more vigorous in its refusal to be the fictive language of a nonexistent community. Simultaneously, the self-destruction of art voiced the necessity of *rediscovering* a common language that would be the true language "of dialogue" (*SS* §187); and the more clearly art expressed the urgent need for change, the more it had likewise to proclaim the impossibility of achieving it on the purely artistic plane. "This is an art that is necessarily *avant-garde;* and it is an art that *is not.* Its vanguard is its own disappearance" (*SS* §190). Modern art ended with Dada and the Surrealists, movements that, albeit in a flawed way, sought to abolish independent art while realizing its content. They set themselves this task just as (and this is no coincidence) the world was witnessing "the proletarian revolutionary movement's last great offensive" (*SS* §191). The "active" phase of the process of decay ended in the interwar years, with the twin defeat of the political and aesthetic vanguards. From that point on no authentic art was possible: anyone who wished to remain true to the

---

nent, are to be found in Martos's *Histoire de l'Internationale Situationniste* (see pp. 84–100).

meaning of culture could do so only by *negating* culture as a separate sphere and *realizing* it through the theory and practice of the critique of society (*SS* §210–11).

Thenceforward the decay of culture assumed a different meaning, becoming itself part of the armamentarium by whose means the bourgeoisie strove to maintain art as a dead object of contemplation. Once detached from the necessity of rediscovering a new language in practice, the self-destruction of language was now "co-opted" and enlisted in "the defense of class power" (*SS* §184). The continual destruction of forms, as for example in the Theater of the Absurd, in the *nouveau roman*, in the new abstract painting, or in Pop Art, so far from expressing history's dismantling of the existing social order, was nothing but a trite copy of what existed made from an objectively affirmative standpoint: "the unadorned claim that the dissolution of the communicable has a beauty all its own" (*SS* §192). The end of an independent art, understood as a succession of different styles, renders the entire history of art readily accessible to the consumer: with the detritus of all periods, all past civilizations, the society of the spectacle sets out to build a kind of baroque edifice perfectly embodying that negation of the historical which is so essential to its culture of decay.[36]

The Critique of Everyday Life

The other main preoccupation of the Situationists during the first years of the SI was the realm of *everyday life*, its critique and its revolutionary transformation. The "historic" avant-gardes had already sought a change that took account of this "banal" reality, which had hitherto barely ever been reflected upon. During the same period, philosophy had likewise opened the door to it, as witness the work of Georg Simmel, the young Lukács's *Soul and Form*, or, later, the proponents of phenomenology and existentialism. Philosophical thought tended, however, merely to transform "everydayness" into another abstract category and to treat the quotidian as the locus of banality par excellence; banality was thus invested by philosophy with an eternal character, and everyday life was considered to be unchanging, no matter what transformations might take place in life's "higher" spheres.

Beginning with Rimbaud's injunction to "change life," the artistic

36. It is rather striking that this analysis should have been made some fifteen years before the "postmodernism" fad, explicitly promoting just such a relationship with culture, was launched in the intellectual marketplace.

avant-gardes had chosen the opposite path, embracing the notion that everyday life can and must change, and indeed that such change is the yardstick by which all promised or effective transformations ought to be gauged. The first criticisms leveled at the Soviet Union by the Surrealists concerned not that country's economic or social structure but rather the survival in it of numerous characteristics of bourgeois morality, among them respect for one's parents.[37] To ask the simple question "Will individuals be happier in their everyday lives?" was the easiest and indeed the most appropriate way of criticizing many supposedly Marxist conceptions according to which the benefits of the revolution were largely reduced to an increase in productivity.

The young Letterists also concerned themselves initially with the search for another life style, for a different everyday life; they even went so far as to reverse the traditional relationship between art and life, seeking to enlist artistic works in the "construction of situations." They held the view that whatever detached itself from the everyday plane was a form of alienation and that the quest for "superior moments" meant devaluing the reality of everyday experience. Needless to say, the everyday life to which they were referring was as yet to be constructed in its entirety, nor was their intent in any way to reduce privileged moments of life to the level of everyday life as it actually existed. But the fact that the actual everyday realm was a realm of privation was attributable not to some immutable destiny but to the effects of a specific social order.

The writings of the Letterist International already clearly outline a critique of the new conditions that were being imposed on everyday life precisely when it was becoming objectively possible to remove so many obstacles to its liberation. Later, when the young Letterists moved beyond spontaneous refusal and sought a deeper theoretical understanding, they came upon the work of Henri Lefebvre. Lefebvre's influence on the future theories of the Situationists was very great. In 1947 Lefebvre asserted that "Marxism, as a whole, really is a critical knowledge of everyday life" (CEL I, 160; Eng., 148); twenty years later the Situationists published a comic strip, "The Return of the Durutti [sic] Column," incorporating a détournement of Delacroix's Death of Sardanapalus in which the king is made to say, "Yes, Marx's thought really is a critique of everyday life" (see IS 11/33).

A philosopher and sociologist, Henri Lefebvre had a significant part,

---

37. See "On the Time When the Surrealists Were Right" (1935), in André Breton, *Manifestoes of Surrealism*, trans. Richard Seaver and Helen R. Lane (Ann Arbor: University of Michigan Press, 1969), 251–52.

during his long life, in many decisive stages in French culture. He published some seventy books. In the twenties he was a prime mover in the "Philosophies" group, one of the rare attempts in France to develop an independent Marxist theory. This group found itself at times in concert, at times in competition with the Surrealists. In the wake of this experience Lefebvre joined the French Communist Party, in which he remained active for some thirty years, seeking, sometimes with grotesque results, to reconcile his research with the party line.[38] In the thirties he was the first author in France to make known the young Marx's economic and philosophical manuscripts, and in his *La Conscience mystifiée* [The Mystification of Consciousness] of 1936, he explored the theme of alienation, until then largely ignored by the French.[39] During the period of "de-Stalinization," Lefebvre was for a time considered "the most important of contemporary Marxist philosophers,"[40] although his thinking was in fact highly eclectic (even, according to some critics, dilettantish), drawing upon Nietzsche, Husserl, or Heidegger as well as upon Marx. Lefebvre's renown in the fifties doubtless stemmed from his many popularizing accounts of Marxism, but his most significant contributions to theory are to be found above all in Volumes I and II of of his *Critique of Everyday Life*. The first volume was written in 1945 and published in 1947, and it is marked by the climate of enthusiasm that followed the liberation of France. Lefebvre's long foreword to the second edition (1958) and the second volume of the work, published in 1961, take up the study from a substantially different point of view.[41]

When Debord and Lefebvre met each other at the end of the fifties, each had arrived independently at similar conclusions, though it is a reasonable assumption that Debord was acquainted with the first volume of Lefebvre's *Critique*. An intense and personal intellectual relationship grew up between the two and endured for several years; according to Lefebvre, this was "a love story that did not end well."[42] Out of this fruit-

38. As recounted by Lefebvre in his *Le Temps des méprises* (Paris: Stock, 1975) and *La Somme et le reste* (Paris: La Nef de Paris, 1959).

39. Lefebvre nevertheless frequently stressed his misgivings about Lukács, and he criticized *History and Class Consciousness* and Lukács's earliest works as readily as he did the later works; there were, however, some aspects of Lukács's thought of which he approved.

40. To quote the jacket copy of *La Somme et le reste*.

41. Henri Lefebvre, *Critique de la vie quotidienne I: Introduction* (Paris: Grasset, 1947); 2d ed. (Paris: L'Arche, 1958); Eng. trans. by John Moore: *Critique of Everyday Life I: Introduction* (London: Verso, 1991). *Critique de la vie quotidienne II: Fondements d'une sociologie de la quotidienneté* [Foundations of a Sociology of Everydayness] (Paris: L'Arche, 1961). A third volume (Paris: L'Arche, 1981) is subtitled *De la Modernité au modernisme (Pour une métaphilosophie du quotidien)* [From Modernity to Modernism: Toward a Metaphilosophy of the Everyday].

42. Lefebvre, *Le Temps des méprises*, 109.

ful encounter came, on the one hand, "Perspectives for Conscious Alterations of Everyday Life," a talk delivered by Debord in May 1961 to
a study group convened by Lefebvre (*IS* 6/20–27; *SIA*, 68–75), and, on
the other hand, the second volume of Lefebvre's work, published at the
end of the same year.[43] At certain points, these two texts correspond almost word for word.

Henri Lefebvre was the only person with an institutional position in
the cultural world with whom the Situationists ever worked closely. He
had a reputation as a heretic, but he was nevertheless a signed-up academic and intellectual and indeed until 1958 had been an eminent member of the Communist Party. The Situationists were no doubt attracted
by his conviction that real life had to be transformed. Lefebvre had come
by this aspiration in the days of his collaboration with the Surrealists in
the nineteen-twenties, and it had retained its power over him despite his
subsequent and at times violent polemics with them. As he himself put
it, "this metamorphosis of everyday life was the reason for my commu-
nicating with Surrealism through Éluard. It was a message that, very
much later, I conveyed in turn to the Situationists"; needless to say, the
Situationists themselves would certainly have taken issue with the implication that they had to wait for Lefebvre before discovering the need
for such a change.[44] In any case, even after his break with the SI, Lefebvre acknowledged that "there has been no avant-garde since the Surrealists, except for the Situationists."[45]

Volume I of the *Critique of Everyday Life*, which is subtitled *Introduction*, proclaims the importance of everyday life as a dimension of human
existence that is quite fundamental, and quite misunderstood. Later, Lefebvre would make the claim that this discovery was on a par with the
Freudian analysis of sexuality or the Marxian analysis of labor (*CEL II*,
30). Certainly this was the first time that the everyday dimension had
been placed in a critical, Marxist perspective. Lefebvre's approach to the
subject is quite far removed, however, from that adopted later by the
Situationists. Lefebvre champions the fecundity (or at least the potential
fecundity) of everyday life, and he sees this realm as a whole—not just
"exceptional moments" within it—as the site of human self-realization.

43. Characteristically for the SI, Debord's address was not delivered live but via a
tape recorder. Here is a good example of a now commonplace device—witness the frequent replacement of speakers at conferences by video recordings—being invented by an
avant-garde group with a quite different purpose in mind.
44. Lefebvre, *Le Temps des méprises*, 52.
45. Ibid., 166.

He thus defends the everyday against all attempts to describe it as irremediably banal, judging these attempts "bourgeois" in that they fail to distinguish between everyday life as such and everyday life as circumscribed by bourgeois society (*CEL I*, 124–25; Eng., 112). Literary modernism from Baudelaire and Rimbaud to the Surrealists was guilty, in Lefebvre's view, of fostering flight from everyday realities into the realm of the fantastic and bizarre (*CEL I*, 118–42; Eng., 106–29). This sharply critical attitude, like his rebuke to the effect that these modernist tendencies detested work, was rooted in the "communist" mentality of the time and surely would have had scant appeal to a Debord. (Ten years later, however, Lefebvre's ideas in this connection had changed significantly: his extreme assessment of Surrealism was toned down [*CEL I*, 37; Eng., 29], and he was even proposing a form of "revolutionary romanticism.") Similarly anchored in the atmosphere of the immediate postwar period is Lefebvre's emphasis on the idea that private life, strongly suspect as an expression of "bourgeois" individualism, would be overwhelmed by the political and collective sphere.

The idea of Lefebvre's that brings him closest at this time to the future theses of the Situationists is that the everyday constitutes the only reality in face of the *unreality* produced by alienation, which seems "more real than anything authentically human"; Lefebvre cites "great ideas" as an example of such unreality (*CEL I*, 182; Eng., 169). In the renewal of Marxism for which Lefebvre argues (*CEL I*, 191; Eng., 178), an important role is assigned to the critique of the alienation of everyday life and of its scandalous impoverishment relative to what science and technology are now capable of delivering. Lefebvre breaks here with the Stalinist notion according to which the economic base of society mechanically determines the superstructure, including among other things modes of life. He maintains that "objective conditions" do not suffice to produce a revolution and that revolution will not occur until the masses "are no longer able or willing to live as before" (*CEL I*, 195; Eng., 182). Such claims, like Lefebvre's thesis that philosophy is also a form of alienation, one that must be not simply abolished but transcended in the Hegelian sense, that is to say realized on the everyday plane (*CEL I*, 265; Eng., 250), clearly foreshadow a number of the principal themes of the Situationist theory of the nineteen-sixties.[46] The true content of philosophy lies in the idea of the "total man," the realization of which would en-

---

46. Paradoxically, in claiming that philosophy is a form of alienation, Lefebvre was simultaneously offering a *defense* of philosophy, which in the Stalinist view had been rendered obsolete by science.

tail the disappearance of the divisions between superior and inferior moments of life (*CEL I*, 213–14; Eng., 199–200); between the rational and
the irrational (*CEL I*, 201; Eng., 188); and between public and private—
after the fashion, roughly speaking, of the traditional festival (*CEL I*,
221; Eng., 207). Lefebvre foresees a new "art of living" (*CEL I*, 213;
Eng., 199) and a "new wisdom" (*CEL I*, 263; Eng., 248) commensurate
with the level already reached in the human domination of nature; and
he expresses the hope that a kind of progress may soon be achieved that
has no negative aspect (*CEL I*, 244; Eng., 229). Lefebvre nevertheless
conceives the delay affecting everyday life in essentially material terms:
the proletarian still often lives in a hovel, while the power of society is
deployed at the level of the state or of industry (*CEL I*, 245–46; Eng.,
230–31).

The long foreword to the second edition of the first volume of Lefebvre's *Critique of Everyday Life* dates from 1958; it is thus able to
take account of the dramatic eruption of "modernity" into French everyday life discussed earlier. First and foremost, Lefebvre notes a distinct *deterioration* in everyday life, which now represents a backward
sector relative to the development of technology, and he speaks in terms
of "uneven development" (*CEL I*, 15; Eng., 8). This backwardness is
rendered all the more pertinent by the fact that technology has itself
greatly widened that gulf between the possible and the real to which
Lefebvre attributes such great motor power. In this sense, it may be said
that technology levels a more telling critique at everyday life than does
poetry, for it is able to challenge current everyday experience with realizable possibilities, not with mere reveries (*CEL I*, 16; Eng., 9). The
organization of leisure, too, in a sense constitutes a critique of everyday life, for it implies the idea of a free use of available means; at the
same time, of course, under existing conditions it also constitutes a new
kind of alienation (*CEL I*, 49; Eng., 40)—and this is particularly true
when man in his "free" time becomes a mere spectator living by proxy
(*CEL I*, 41–45; Eng., 32–35).[47] Lefebvre's deviation from Stalinism is
quite clear here.[48] And the common ground that he was to find with Debord may be glimpsed in a number of the analyses that follow: thus he

47. Lefebvre notes this in a very specific context, that of sport and sports fans (*CEL I*,
45; Eng., 36). Here as elsewhere, the Situationists were able to derive a general principle
from the conclusions of an observer content to limit himself to a narrowly circumscribed
area. This particular kind of *détournement* of the findings of so-called specialized knowledge was undoubtedly one of the SI's strong points.

48. Which is not to say that he was not still engaged in mental acrobatics with respect
to the positive and negative aspects of the Soviet Union.

contests the idea that man is fulfilled through work, arguing that labor in its present fragmented forms renders any such fulfillment impossible (*CEL I*, 48; Eng., 38); he notes that economic alienation is not the only form of alienation (*CEL I*, 72; Eng., 61–62); he rejects the idea that the state can be agent of socialization, observing that the state seems, on the contrary, to be "the only link between . . . social atoms" (*CEL I*, 102; Eng., 91); he maintains that everyday life and the level of happiness achieved therein are an appropriate measuring rod of social progress, even in the so-called socialist countries (*CEL I*, 58; Eng., 49); and he subscribes to the Hegelian view that "things progress (in other words, certain things disappear) with their bad side forward" (*CEL I*, 82; Eng., 71). Lefebvre's view that the everyday is the frontier between the dominated and the non-dominated, the source of both alienation and disalienation (*CEL I*, 97; Eng., 86), is also part of the theory of the Situationists. It nevertheless contains an unresolved ambiguity: is everyday life today, despite everything, the site of hidden riches and the starting-point of a general movement of refusal, or, alternatively, is it an impoverished zone to which the construction of real life can only be opposed? Lefebvre himself seems to take the first view in Volume I and the second in Volume II of his *Critique*.

In 1957 Lefebvre had published an article on "Le Romantisme révolutionnaire," offering a theoretical justification for a new romanticism that would criticize reality, not in the name of the past or of pure revery, but instead from the standpoint of the possible, of the future; this attitude would maintain the discordance between the progressive individual and the world without reinstating some suprahistorical antagonism between individual and society as such.[49] It was precisely the now real possibility of a new totality that was in Lefebvre's view responsible for the existing cultural vacuum, and the romanticism he envisioned, by taking as its theme the possible uses of humanity's means of controlling nature, would be an expression of modernity in the best conceivable sense.

In the first issue of *Internationale Situationniste*, Debord endorsed this project in broad outline but reproached Lefebvre for restricting himself to "the simple expression of [a] discordance" and failing to envisage practical experiments for exploring new uses of life (*IS* 1/21; *Oct.*, 91). Lefebvre's "consciousness of the possible/impossible" was too vague a notion, according to Debord, and it was a mistake to continue rely-

49. Reprinted in Henri Lefebvre, *Au-delà du structuralisme* (Paris: Anthropos, 1971), 27–50.

ing, like Lefebvre, solely on the "expression" of society's contradictions, which "have already been expressed by all modern art *up to and including the destruction of the expression itself*" (*IS* 3/6; *Oct.*, 106). Henceforth, "art can cease to be a report on sensations and become a direct organization of higher sensations" (*IS* 1/21; *Oct.*, 90).

In the second volume of his *Critique* (1961), Lefebvre cites with approval Debord's observation that everyday life "is literally 'colonized'" (*CEL II*, 17; cf. *IS* 6/220; *SIA,* 70), and the collaboration between the two is discernible in a number of ideas to which they both subscribed. Thus Lefebvre acknowledges that a social transformation could be precipitated not by poverty but by needs and desires in their richness and complexity (*CEL II*, 37), as too by a reaction against the manipulation of needs divorced from desires (*CEL II*, 16–17, 91–92). He describes urbanism as one of the sectors of life that have remained "backward" relative to the overall technological development of production (*CEL II*, 149), especially in view of the fact that "new towns" testify only to a degradation of everyday life (*CEL II*, 82). Here we see the beginnings of Lefebvre's later passionate interest in the issues of town planning and space, to which he was later to devote a long series of publications.[50]

At the time of his friendship with Debord, Michèle Bernstein, and Raoul Vaneigem, Lefebvre was becoming ever more firm in his belief that philosophy was dead, and destined to be superseded in the sense of philosophy-becoming-the-world rather than in that of the-world-becoming-philosophy (*CEL II*, 29, 187). The SI had reminded him that, in his talk of the end of philosophy (in *La Somme et le reste*), he was "forgetting that this idea has been the basis of revolutionary thought since the eleventh of the *Theses on Feuerbach*" (*IS* 3/5; *Oct.*, 105). Lefebvre also considered the end of art, arguing that Marx's program needed extending to cover the "becoming-world" not just of philosophy, the state, and the economy but also of art and ethics, for these too were "ways of fictively transforming everyday reality" (*CEL II*, 188). Further, the second volume of the *Critique* contains frequent references to "non-participation" and "passivity" being reinforced by new technological advances, such as television, which present the world as a "spectacle" (*CEL II*, 78, 225–26). Lefebvre emphasizes that everyday life and

50. These include *Le Droit à la ville* (Paris: Anthropos, 1968); *Du Rural à l'urbain* (Paris: Anthropos, 1970); *La Révolution urbaine* (Paris: Gallimard, 1970); *Espace et politique (Le Droit à la ville II)* (Paris: Anthropos, 1972); and *La Pensée marxiste de la ville* (Paris/Tournai: Casterman, 1972). The culmination of the series is *La Production de l'espace* (Paris: Anthropos, 1974); English translation by Donald Nicholson-Smith entitled *The Production of Space* (Oxford: Blackwell, 1991).

history have over time become further and further detached from one another (*CEL II*, 26), while Debord, in his talk on "Conscious Alterations of Everyday Life," treats the everyday dimension as a sector following along rather tardily in the wake of historical development—as, precisely, an underdeveloped and colonized realm. The everyday is the locus of the production of history, but this production is unconscious, and history soon separates itself off and sets itself up as an independent force. And, inasmuch as everyday life is separate from history, it also resists the upheavals brought about in other social realms by the development of the forces of production. And it is indeed from the standpoint of everyday life that everything that claims to be superior to it can and must be rejected, and this even within the sphere of revolutionary politics: "great" leaders, "historic" acts, appeals to the eternal, and so on (*IS* 6/26–27; *SIA*, 74–75).[51]

The distinction between everyday life, at present cyclical and subjected to the quantitative principle, and history, as locus of unique and qualitative events, would be considered by Debord only later on, in *The Society of the Spectacle*. But already in the *Critique of Everyday Life* we find mention made (though this was not Lefebvre's discovery either) of the contrast between, on the one hand, societies founded on simple reproduction, which are cyclical, stable, non-accumulative, and expend their surplus on construction and celebration, and, on the other hand, those founded on expanded reproduction, in which the cyclical aspect, though it does not disappear completely, serves merely as a "base" (*CEL II*, 317–28, 336–37). This distinction, which corresponds to Marx's schema of the simple and expanded reproduction of capital, is applied by Lefebvre to the whole of social life: "This accumulative process brings society . . . into *history*," he writes, with the result that "the economic principle becomes predominant and determinant, as it was not in ancient societies. . . . Individuals and groups make this history, but they do so blindly" (*CEL II*, 324). Human activities themselves now fall into two categories, accumulative and non-accumulative, while everyday life, which remains bound to the cyclical but which is at the same time subordinated to accumulation, lies at the intersection of the two (*CEL II*, 335–36). A genuine personal life ought to be created as a work, as conscious history, and thus rescued from the impervious mechanisms that at present govern everyday life (*CEL II*, 337).

After a few years, Lefebvre and the Situationists parted company

---

51. Not that Debord himself ever rejected a certain kind of *gloire*.

amidst reciprocal accusations of plagiarism concerning in particular a text on the Paris Commune.[52] Lefebvre carried on with his research, deepening its anthropological resonance, and trying without much success to promote his views as a counter to structuralism. The Situationists proceeded along their own path, and when the big moment of 1968 arrived, Lefebvre was one of their favorite targets as a "recuperator" busily assimilating revolutionary themes into the perspective of the existing society.

All in all, it is fair to say that Lefebvre took at least as much from the Situationists as they took from him. To be convinced of this, one needs merely to look at a lecture of his from 1967 on "literature and modern art as forms of the destruction and self-destruction of art."[53]

The Situationists and the Sixties

After 1962, the history of the SI unfolded for the most part in France. With a membership never exceeding twenty, and generally standing at much less than that, the group sustained an often underground agitation whose significance has now been widely acknowledged in studies of the period.[54] The very least one can say is that no one anticipated the liberatory content of the events of 1968 as well as the Situationists, and this must be granted quite independently of the questions of the extent to which they may have "influenced" the protagonists of those events and the extent to which those protagonists may have been conscious of such an influence. Thirty years later, now that Althusserianism, Maoism, workerism, and Freudo-Marxism have all disappeared into historical oblivion, it is clear that the Situationists were the only people at that time to develop a theory, and to a lesser extent a practice, whose interest is not merely historiographical but retains a potential relevance today.

52. See *IS* 12/108–111 and Lefebvre, *Le Temps des méprises*, 160.
53. Henri Lefebvre, "De la Littérature et de l'art moderne considérés comme processus de destruction et d'auto-destruction de l'art," in *Au-delà du structuralisme*, 241–59.
54. See for example Gombin, *Origines du gauchisme;* M. Demonet and others, *Des Tracts en mai 68* (Paris: Champ Libre, 1978); Pascal Dumontier, *Les Situationnistes et mai 68: Théorie et pratique de la révolution (1966–1972)* (Paris: Gérard Lebovici, 1990); Christine Fauré, *Mai 68 jour et nuit* (Paris: Gallimard, Collection Découvertes, 1998); and Marie-Louise Syring, ed., *Um 1968: Konkrete Utopien in Kunst und Gesellschaft* (Cologne: Du-Mont Verlag, 1990), catalog of an exhibition mounted at the Städtische Kunstalle, Düsseldorf, from 27 May to 8 July 1990. This last publication pays the SI this somewhat ambiguous compliment: "By far the greatest influence that the theory of art and aesthetics exercised upon the protest movement of students and left-wing intellectuals was in all likelihood that of the Situationists, something which practically nobody recalls today."

Apart from publication—the journal *Internationale Situationniste* in France, one issue of a Situationist journal in Germany and one in Scandinavia, and various lesser productions—the SI did not have a very visible public existence between 1962 and 1966. By around 1965, the working out of the Situationist analysis was essentially complete, and the group turned its attention to the search for ways of putting it into practice. This is apparent from the circulation, at the end of 1965, of a pamphlet in English on the black uprising in Watts, in which the SI contended that the spectacle designed for blacks was simply a more impoverished version of the one intended for whites; in consequence blacks grasped the deception more quickly and, since they possessed less than whites, proceeded to demand everything.[55] But it was not until late in 1966 that the SI's practical activity entered its decisive phase with the famous "Strasbourg scandal." This event may in hindsight seem a little tame, and it would doubtless have aroused but scant attention had it occurred two years later than it did. At the time, however, all it took to precipitate a major outcry in the press and unleash legal reprisals was for a few SI sympathizers to get themselves elected to the leadership of the campus chapter of the national student union, use that organization's funds to print up a Situationist pamphlet, and then propose the self-dissolution of the union on the grounds that it was nothing but a mechanism for integrating students into an unacceptable society. Some weeks earlier a few Strasbourg students in agreement with the SI had bombarded the "cybernetician" Professor Abraham Moles—an old Situationist target (*IS* 9/44–48)—with tomatoes; such gestures, soon to become commonplace in French universities, were also still a novelty. Scandal broke out when such signs of a growing student rebellion, disdainful of all traditional channels of dissent, were backed up by the *content* of the "Strasbourg pamphlet," an SI text written for the most part by the Situationist Mustapha Khayati and entitled *Of Student Poverty, Considered in Its Economic, Political, Psychological, Sexual, and, Particularly, Intellectual Aspects, and a Modest Proposal for Its Remedy.*[56] This text, whose cir-

---

55. *The Decline and the Fall of the "Spectacular" Commodity-Economy* (Paris: Internationale Situationniste, 1965). Debord's (unattributed) French text appeared for the first time in *IS* 10 (March 1966). (See Bibliography 1.)

56. *De la Misère en milieu étudiant, considérée sous ses aspects économique, politique, psychologique, sexuel et notamment intellectuel et de quelques moyens pour y remédier* (Strasbourg: Union Nationale des Étudiants de France/Association Fédérative Générale des Étudiants de Strasbourg, 1966); reprinted in book form (Paris: Champ Libre, 1976); and in another edition (Aix-en-Provence: Sulliver, 1995). English version, with introduction and "Postscript," published as *Ten Days That Shook the University* (London: Situationist International [1967]). Another English translation is in *SIA*, 319–37. Chinese/

culation in France and then abroad quickly reached tens of thousands of copies, makes no concessions to students satisfied with their status and eager merely to improve it. "We might very well say," it begins, "and no one would disagree with us, that the student is the most universally despised creature in France, apart from the priest and the policeman." There follows a brilliantly mordant and satirical account of student life, along with a synopsis of Situationist ideas. Khayati ends with an exhortation to conceive of revolution as a festival and a game—"to live instead of devising a lingering death, and to indulge untrammeled desire." Such sentiments, summed up in the words "Vivre sans temps morts et jouir sans entraves," were soon to appear as graffiti on many a wall.[57]

Late in 1967 the two major accounts of Situationist theory were published: Debord's *La Société du spectacle* and Vaneigem's *Traité de savoir-vivre l'usage des jeunes générations*.[58] At the same time, the Situationists were continuing to produce posters and pamphlets in comic-strip format, some of them "*détournés*," others "directly created," which effectively promoted their theses—their rejection of all "partial," single-issue demands, their even stronger denunciation of a militantism justified in terms of "serving the people," and their championing of a revolution that would be founded on pleasure without, however, scorning the theoretical dimension. The deepest impulses of May 1968, that brief moment when an upside-down world was indeed set back on its feet, were far more in tune with the SI than with "Vietnam Committees" and calls for university reform.

How did the Situationists manage this? In the first place, no doubt, thanks to their rigor, their intransigence, and their refusal of all eclecticism. They believed themselves to be the sole voice, at least in France,

---

French/English edition published in René Viénet's "Bibliothèque Asiatique" (Paris: "Champ Libre," 1973).

57. The SI's refusal to admit the organizers of the Strasbourg scandal to membership of the group caused them to feel manipulated, occasioning furious salvoes of mutual recrimination and leading eventually to the expulsion of all the Strasbourg Situationists. Polemics of this sort arose several times during this period, often characterized by denunciations of Debord for his alleged dictatorial control over the SI.

58. Raoul Vaneigem, *Traité de savoir-vivré l'usage des jeunes générations* (Paris: Gallimard, 1967); paperback edition, with a new preface by the author (Paris: Gallimard, Collection Folio, 1992). English translation by Donald Nicholson-Smith: *The Revolution of Everyday Life* (London: Rebel Press/Seattle: Left Bank Books, 1983); rev. ed., with Vaneigem's 1992 preface (London: Rebel Press/Seattle: Left Bank Books, 1994). Vaneigem's book was at least as well received as Debord's in 1967, and at that time it was widely thought that the two works said much the same thing. Today the differences are more apparent; indeed, as early as the seventies there was a good deal of bitter infighting between "Vaneigemists" and "Debordists."

of a revolutionary theory adequate to the new era, all others claiming
to defend such a theory having in reality abdicated their role. "What
thought has lacked above all over the last few decades is . . . trenchancy"
(*IS* 9/25; *SIA,* 140): this sentiment was central to the development of the
SI's rejection of the prevailing ecumenism. "The fact is that we want
ideas to become *dangerous* once again. We cannot allow people to support us on the basis of a wishy-washy, fake eclecticism, along with the
Sartres, the Althussers, the Aragons and the Godards" (*IS* 11/30; *SIA,*
212). Too many revolutionary groups had been co-opted on account of
their inability to distinguish clearly between partisans and adversaries of
the society to which they were opposed. This explains the importance
the SI accorded to the breaking off of relations with any member who
could not handle the group's requirements, as likewise with anyone who
persisted in mixing with people judged by the group to be in some way
dubious (the Situationists called this last practice "la rupture en chaîne,"
or "serial breaks" [*IS* 9/25; *SIA,* 140]). Similarly, public and unequivocal statements of position were expected from anyone wishing to col-
laborate with the SI.

Combating all fake social critics and pseudo-revolutionaries was in
the Situationist view one of the most urgent of tasks, and the SI had no
qualms about launching ad hominem attacks on this front. They simply
refused to treat with anyone who was already compromised (with Stalinism, for example), and they explicitly asserted that, "even if we may
be momentarily mistaken on many minor points, we shall never be able
to accept that we might have been wrong in a *negative* judgment of persons" (*IS* 9/4–5; *SIA,* 137). The endless polemics conducted amongst
themselves by the representatives of various "semi-critical" factions posed
no real obstacle to their supporting one another in their participation in
the world as it was (*IS* 10/78ff.). The Situationists had absolutely no
part in this universe. They had no relationship with academia, participated in no round-table discussions and attended no cultural meetings,
wrote articles in no periodicals other than their own, and were never
heard on radio or television. They were distinct from all the other leading figures in the May 1968 events in that they did not belong to the
university either as students, like Daniel Cohn-Bendit, or as teachers, like
Althusser; they hailed neither from the literary world, as Sartre did, nor,
indeed even less, from the variegated milieu of left-wing militantism.
Their artistic and bohemian origins were in fact plain to see not only in
their goals but also in their means of pursuing them. The Situationists
nevertheless emphasized that the artistic bohemianism of old must be

abandoned, because it invariably produced works of art that were quite saleable after a generation or so.[59] A better model, according to the Situationists, was that offered by a "saboteur" like Arthur Cravan (*IS* 8/11).

The SI was never at a loss for a good reason to disapprove of anyone. Thus many people were rebuked for making theoretical accommodations with the existing state of things, or simply for abandoning revolutionary positions espoused earlier; others were taken to task for possessing no theory at all, even though they might have a sincere interest in revolution, or, worse, for holding the utility of theory in contempt, or again for condemning themselves to inactivity out of exaggerated suspicion of any type of organization; as for those who spoke in very abstract or distant terms of the social revolution, of the end of art, or of upheaval in everyday life, the Situationists reprimanded them for failing to grasp that all this was either already under way or very high on the agenda. The most pressing task, in the Situationist view, was to analyze the new conditions and the new subjects of revolution, whereas so many revolutionaries had their sights fixed firmly on the revolutions of the past, and so many others were gazing into a distant future, instead of seeing the revolution in the present. But even individuals who had steered clear of all these reefs were not always immune from the reproach that they spoke the truth in a purely abstract way, "without any echo, without any possibility of intervention" (*IS* 12/4; *SIA*, 227). On the question of the impact of its own ideas, the SI had an irrefutable answer: when these ideas reached a large audience and were openly discussed in the bourgeois press, the reason was that it had become impossible to ignore them; on the other hand, when no one paid any attention to them, it was because they contained truths too scandalous to be confronted.

Now that the "ludic" critique of urban planning and the construction of situations had faded into the background, the chief preoccupation of the SI became that "second proletarian onslaught on class society" (*SS* §115) for which the Situationists' ideas were supposed to supply the theory. We have already noted that Debord extends the notion of the proletariat to cover "the vast mass of workers who have lost all power over the use of their own lives" (*SS* §114). Having reached the conclusion that "in our time the cards of the class struggle are being *redealt*— which is in no way to say that the struggle is over, but merely that it is

---

59. Even harder to defend was the bohemianism affected by people who were unwilling even to abandon their student status (see *De la Misère*, 7–8; *SIA*, 322–23).

not continuing in strict accordance with the old schema" (*IS* 8/13), the
SI was impelled to pay particular attention to new forms of social rebellion, from wildcat strikes to such seemingly "apolitical" phenomena
as the vandalism of youth gangs and the looting and destruction characteristic of black riots in the United States. Debord saw such acts as implicit rejections of the commodity and of forced consumption, and he
drew a parallel between a first proletarian assault, which had challenged
the organization of production, and a second, which was about to be
mounted against capitalist "affluence." Just as the rise of the traditional
workers' movement had been announced by "Luddite" attacks on machines, so now such "criminal" acts were harbingers of the destruction
of "the machinery of permitted consumption" (*SS* §115).

The Situationists certainly had no monopoly when it came to moni-
toring all the signs of discontent and refusal that the society of the sixties provoked; they themselves acknowledged the historical pertinence
of some sociological research, notably in the United States (*IS* 7/16; *SIA,*
87). But they were indeed alone in perceiving a new kind of revolutionary potential in those signs. When 1968 proved them right, at any rate
for a while, they could proudly proclaim that they were the only ones
"to have recognized and pointed out the new focuses of revolt in modern society (focuses which do not at all exclude the old ones, but on the
contrary bring them back to light): urbanism, spectacle, ideology, etc."
(*IS* 12/14; *SIA,* 227).

The critique of urbanism was one of the main themes in the Situationist analysis of the degradation of life, and the tones used sometimes
bespoke extreme outrage. This was a time when France was being covered by modern houses and entire new towns of hitherto unimaginable
ugliness, and the Situationists evoked "concentration camps" in this regard (*IS* 6/33–34; *Oct.,* 123–24; *Dérive,* 119). Describing city planning
as a "geology of lies" (*IS* 6/18; *SIA,* 67), as a materialization of social
hierarchies, they observed that modern architecture had about as much
to do with places to live as Coca-Cola had to do with a satisfying drink.

Supermarkets, high-rises, and holiday resorts in the manner of the
Club Méditerrannée clearly demonstrated that the real modern dichotomy was between *organizers* and *organized.* This was of course exactly
the same distinction as the one—so crucial to the spectacle—between actors and spectators.

The rejection, not just of all aspects of existing society, but also of
practically all attempts to change it, frequently generated a tendency in

proximity to Debord, from the Letterists to the "pro-Situationists" of the seventies, toward a nihilism based on the firm conviction that all practical action was already a betrayal of the purity of refusal. On several occasions, Debord felt obliged to combat this purely abstract radicalism, which was usually a cover for the shortcomings of its proponents with respect to any kind of practical activity and sometimes served purely and simply as a way of attacking the SI for its "arrivisme" whenever it met with some kind of success in the outside world (see for example *IS* 9/3: *SIA*, 135; *IS* 10/72; *IS* 11/58). The Situationists were not interested in basking in any kind of purity, however, nor did they wish to limit themselves to "refining dialectical discourse *within the pages of [a] book*" while failing to engage "the totality to be transformed in reality" (*IS* 10/73).

Their pitiless analysis of the power of totalitarian conditioning in the society of the spectacle did not blind the Situationists to the fact that countervailing forces were at work too. The system embodied insurmountable contradictions, among them its inability to alienate its subjects absolutely, to do entirely without "their participation" (*IS* 7/9; *SIA*, 81). And, as Debord pointed out at the Situationists' seventh congress, "despite the alienation of everyday life, the opportunities for passion and playfulness to find expression are still very real, and it seems to me that the SI would be seriously in error were it to suggest that all life outside Situationist activity was completely reified" (*VS*, 136; Eng., 120).

According to the SI, a new revolutionary movement would lack neither for dissatisfaction as its motive, nor for a revolutionary subject, but rather for any clear vision of the goals and methods of struggle. The emancipation of the proletariat had no worse enemy than that class's persistent illusions concerning itself. By failing to distinguish its conception of the historical struggle clearly enough from that of the bourgeoisie, the proletariat had allowed internal hierarchies, "representatives" who rapidly became uncontrollable, authoritarian structures, and an uncritical attitude toward the state-form to transform workers' organizations—and even entire states, in cases where those organizations had seized power—into the greatest of obstacles to the revolutionary project.

The longest chapter of *The Society of the Spectacle*, "The Proletariat as Subject and Representation," is concerned with the history of the modern revolutionary movement. As we have seen, Debord locates the source of this movement's problems in Marx's thought itself, in the excessive faith that Marx placed in economic mechanisms to the detriment

of conscious practice. The authoritarianism that both Marx and Bakunin displayed within the First International was a symptom of the degeneration of revolutionary theory into an *ideology*, and it arose from
an unfortunate assimilation of their project with the methods of the bourgeois revolution. The anarchists, despite several positive contributions,
eventually fell victim to their own idealist and antihistorical *ideology* of
freedom, while the social democracy of the Second International uni-
versalized the split between the proletariat and the autonomous representation of the proletariat and was thus a precursor of Bolshevism.[60]
The October Revolution, once the radical minorities had been eliminated,
led to the rule of a bureaucracy that merely substituted for the bourgeoisie as manager of the commodity economy. Trotsky himself subscribed to Bolshevik authoritarianism, and neither he nor his followers
ever acknowledged that the bureaucracy in Russia was a genuine ruling
class and not just, as they said, a "parasitic caste."

Debord offers a well-honed analysis of how the absolute rule of ideology and lies induced a complete absence of realism in bureaucratic
regimes, keeping them in an inferior position relative to "free-market"
economies. Nor was it possible for these regimes to reform themselves,
for the bureaucratic class controlled the means of production only by
virtue of its control of ideology and consequently could never acknowledge the falsehood upon which it was founded, namely, that it was not
an expression of proletarian power but, indeed, a bureaucracy exercis-
ing power in its own interest.

Debord's account is doubly significant today. Scarcely anyone, friend
or enemy, would have believed the foundation of the Soviet system to be
so fragile and absurd that the whole edifice would collapse at the first
serious attempt to reform it. In the nineteen-sixties, the counterrevolutionary character of that system was certainly not apparent to many
in France: despite widespread condemnation of Stalinism and defection
from the French Communist Party, virtually no Left thinkers dared so
much as describe the Soviet Union in plain language as a class society,

60. Debord describes Lenin as "a faithful and consistent Kautskyist" (*SS* §98), and
here he is following Karl Korsch—the other great Marxist heretic (with Lukács) of the
twenties—almost word for word. Korsch's classic work of 1923 was translated into
French in 1964 as *Marxisme et philosophie* (Paris: Minuit, Collection "Arguments"),
and Debord owes several important insights to him, notably the idea that philosophy
must be realized before it can be abolished. See Karl Korsch, *Marxism and Philosophy*,
trans. Fred Halliday (London: New Left Books, 1970), especially the criticism of Lenin in
"The Present State of the Problem of 'Marxism and Philosophy'—An Anti-Critique,"
which is Korsch's preface to the second edition of his book (1930).

much less renounce their allegiance to the Leninist tradition. At most, their revolutionary hopes would simply be shifted to some other *state* or other—to Yugoslavia or Cuba, to Vietnam, Albania or Algeria, or, and above all, to China.

The task of illusorily representing the revolutionary option in the world had hitherto fallen to the Stalinist countries and their proxies, the so-called communist parties of the West. The conflict between the Soviet Union and China, however, along with a succession of splits between various bureaucratic powers, finally shattered any monopoly on this supposed option, thus marking the beginning of the end of these regimes. As Debord wrote, "this crumbling of the worldwide alliance based on bureaucratic mystification is in the last analysis the most unfavorable portent for the future development of capitalist society. For the bourgeoisie is now in danger of losing an adversary that has objectively supported it by investing all opposition to its order with a purely illusory unity" (SS §111). Today it is plain to see that the Soviet Union was relieved of its functions simultaneously with the almost complete disappearance of those revolutionary tendencies that the spectacle had sought in this way to siphon off into bureaucratic forms. When the "Prague Spring" occurred, by contrast—an event to which the SI assigned great importance (IS 12/35–43; SIA, 256–65)—the West in effect backed Soviet intervention.

In Debord's view, the end result of these developments was positive: the proletariat had "lost its *illusions*. But it [had] not lost its being" (SS §114). The next revolutionary upsurge would free it from the enemies that had betrayed it from within; meanwhile, it could and must stop "combating alienation by means of alienated forms of struggle" (SS §122). Thanks to workers' councils, which the SI had begun evoking in 1961 (IS 6/3; SIA, 63), the participation of everyone would eliminate all specialization and all independent authorities. Such councils would constitute both the means for conducting the struggle and the principle of organization of the future liberated society.

The failure of the revolutionary activity of the proletariat is of course readily accounted for in terms of the influence of those "working-class bureaucracies," the trade unions and political parties. Specifically, the Situationists held these organizations responsible for the fact that the factory occupations of 1968 did not lead to full-scale revolution. All the same, one might well wonder how it is that a proletariat which according to the SI, is revolutionary *in itself* could have so consistently, and for decades on end, been led down the garden path by bureaucrats.

Their concern that the next social explosion too might be defused by these bureaucratic organizations led the Situationists to sustain a sharply polemical relationship with all the neo-Leninist *groupuscules* that began to proliferate after 1965. "Militantism" was in any case unacceptable to the Situationists, especially when grounded in a logic of self-sacrifice in accordance with which a political activity acknowledged by its own practitioners to be unsatisfying, albeit morally necessary, went hand in hand with a thoroughly conformist life style. "Boredom," ran a Situationist slogan, "is always counterrevolutionary." The SI was just as disinclined, however, to endorse hippiedom and "youth culture" if these sought to change but a small, isolated portion of life.[61] The realization of one's own desires and revolutionary action had to be one and the same thing.

With respect to the break with Leninism, to the transcendence of economistic Marxism, and in a general way to the opening up of new horizons, Debord was much in debt to the Socialisme ou Barbarie group and its eponymous journal.[62] Founded in 1949 in Paris, "S. ou B." evolved largely on the basis of the collaboration-*cum*-conflict between Cornelius Castoriadis, who used various pen names (Chaulieu, Coudray, Delvaux, Cardan), and Claude Lefort, who sometimes signed "Claude Montal." Forty issues of the journal appeared before the group disbanded in 1965.[63] The starting point had been a break with Trotskyism centered on Trotsky's definition of the Soviet Union as a workers' state in essence, but a workers' state that had been "deformed" by the contingent rise within it of a "parasitic stratum." From the outset *Socialisme ou Barbarie* argued, to the contrary, that the Soviet system was "worse than feudalism." It offered a sober analysis of the relations between accumulation, bureaucracy, and exploitation and explained that in the case

61. The SI rejected all attempts—such as Henri Lefebvre's in 1962—to reduce it to a youth-related phenomenon (*IS* 8/61).

62. In 1976, Champ Libre brought out a new edition of *L'URSS: Collectivisme bureaucratique*, by the Italian Trotskyist Bruno Rizzi, first published at the author's expense in Paris in 1939 and then almost entirely forgotten. According to Champ Libre's jacket copy, Socialisme ou Barbarie drew extensively from this source without ever acknowledging the fact. An English translation is Rizzi, *The Bureaucratization of the World* (London: Tavistock/New York: Free Press, 1985).

63. Issues for the years 1953–57 only have been reprinted in book form (Paris: Alcratie, 1985). Most of Castoriadis's articles from *Socialisme ou Barbarie* were reissued in a series of paperback volumes (Paris: Union Générale d'Éditions, Collection 10/18, 1973–79), and many have been translated into English in Castoriadis, *Political and Social Writings*, ed. and trans. David Ames Curtis, 3 vols. (Minneapolis: University of Minnesota Press, 1988–93). In this connection, see Philippe Gottraux, "*Socialisme ou Barbarie*": *Un Engagement politique et intellectuel dans la France de l'après-guerre* (Lausanne: Payot, 1997), where some attention is also paid to the SI (pp. 221–27).

of Russian underdevelopment the bureaucracy played a part similar—
though not identical—to that of the bourgeoisie in Western capitalism.
Sartre, Althusser, and innumerable others would continue wondering
until the mid-sixties how a system whose economic base was in their
view unquestionably socialist could support a superstructure that was un-
deniably repressive. In contrast, *Socialisme ou Barbarie* demonstrated as
early as 1949, with ample statistical evidence, that Soviet society was in
fact a class system founded on exploitation of the most brutal sort.[64]
Later on, the journal would publish similar analyses of China.[65] The basis
of such new analytical insight was the realization that in modern societies the *legal* ownership of the means of production—which in Eastern
European countries could even belong formally to the workers—was in
actuality ever more separate from the actual management of those means.
Thus the oppression and exploitation of the proletariat was the job of
bureaucratic managers, not only in the East but also in the West: the real
antagonism everywhere was that between the organizers and the organized, between those who gave orders and those who followed them. This
meant rejecting—and here was another departure from Trotskyism—the
idea of a vanguard party, which clearly only reinforced that antagonism.
It was thus that Socialisme ou Barbarie came to rediscover the idea of
workers' councils. But then the group got mired in an interminable debate over whether to confine their role strictly to that of a class *instrument*, disseminating information to the workers while refusing anything
resembling party building, or whether on the contrary to accept the view
that such a course would mean dooming themselves to hopeless ineffec-
tiveness and therefore that some form of organized vanguard activity
was indispensable.

Before considering the Situationist response to this problem, which
confronted all the French groups positioned between anarchism and
communism, it is worth pausing to note a number of contributions made
by Socialisme ou Barbarie, especially during the later fifties. The economic and social analyses presented in the journal were buttressed by
empirical detail to a degree quite untypical of the French debate of the
time, which tended to be abstract and rhetorical. Very early on, the group
pointed out how the fragmentation of production, and of social life as a
whole, had reached the point where their meaning could be explained

64. See "Les Relations de production en Russie," *Socialisme ou Barbarie* 2 (May
1949); reprinted in Castoriadis, *La Société bureaucratique*, vol. 1 (Paris: Union Générale
d'Éditions, Collection 10/18, 1973). English translation: "The Relations of Production in
Russia," in Castoriadis, *Political and Social Writings*, 1:107–57.
65. See the articles by P. Brune in nos. 24 and 29.

only by specialists, and it evoked the disappearance of the factory as an agent of socialization; it also pointed up the basic contradiction that arose in consequence, inherent to a system that sought to deprive individuals of all power of decision, even over their own lives, without for all that being able to dispense with their collaboration. Socialisme ou Barbarie argued that the true content of socialism was neither a planned economy, nor simply an increase in the material standard of living, but rather the prospect of giving meaning to life and work, releasing creativity and reconciling man and nature.[66] Thus the traditional Left was attacked for always restricting itself to demands for more production, more education, etc., of the kind that already existed. Reducing working hours was not a sufficient remedy if work itself remained a servitude, if work were not rendered "poetic." The theme of generalized self-management, which was to have so much success in 1968 and its aftermath, appeared here perhaps for the first time. In contrast to the "orthodox" Marxists, members of Socialisme ou Barbarie were convinced that capitalism was quite capable of providing workers with adequate economic security, even in the long term, and since high wages and increasing free time contributed to the stability of the system, they felt that these would continue to be conceded. What had formerly been considered insoluble contradictions in capitalism, as for instance crises of overproduction, were in reality indicative merely of a capitalism that had not yet been perfected. On the other hand, the true basic contradiction of capitalism was now becoming visible, namely the system's need to stimulate participation from its workers while at the same time barring it. The class struggle of the future ought therefore to be grounded in "subjective" factors, first and foremost the desire to reject an imposed passivity and create another kind of life.

In 1957, Edgar Morin, then an editor of the journal *Arguments*, voiced criticisms of *Socialisme ou Barbarie* that closely resemble those that would often later be directed from various quarters at the SI: *Socialisme ou Barbarie* failed to take into account the bureaucracy's internal contradictions, its different strata, and consequently the journal's schematic analyses were merely prophecies that could not inform any strategy designed to take advantage of the enemy's inner rifts. True to its name, said Morin, *Socialisme ou Barbarie* was millenarian: the choice was absolute

---

66. See especially Castoriadis, "Sur le Contenu du socialisme, II," *Socialisme ou Barbarie* 22 (July 1957); reprinted in *Le Contenu du socialisme* (Paris: Union Générale d'Éditions, Collection 10/18, 1979). English translation: "On the Content of Socialism, II," in Castoriadis, *Political and Social Writings*, 2:90–154.

as between socialism and barbarism. Reducing everything to the single proletariat/bureaucracy opposition, "*Socialisme ou Barbarie* goes straight to the crux of the matter, but only to isolate and hypostasize it."[67]

Beginning in 1958, *Socialisme ou Barbarie* began to take an interest in certain aspects of the social totality that had hitherto been neglected by Marxist analysis, and this new interest became the basis of a reciprocal influence between the group and the Situationists. In 1960 Debord collaborated with "P. Canjuers" (Daniel Blanchard), a member of Socialisme ou Barbarie, on a short but important pamphlet, *Preliminaries Toward Defining a Unitary Revolutionary Program*. Shortly afterwards, however, *Socialisme ou Barbarie* shifted from its critique of economistic Marxism to a critique of Marxism *tout court*, and its new horizons faded, as the Situationists saw it, into a hodgepodge of psychology, anthropology, and so on containing anything but the totality. The SI proceeded to deluge Socialisme ou Barbarie with criticism, primarily on the grounds that it sought to harmonize and humanize existing production relations (*IS* 6/4: *SIA*, 64; *IS* 8/4: *SIA*, 102), but also because it represented "the furthest left and the most deluded fringe of those managers and mid-level functionaries of the Left who want to have a revolutionary theory of their own actual career in society" (*IS* 9/34).[68] When *Socialisme ou Barbarie* eventually disappeared, the SI recorded its demise with satisfaction (*IS* 12/47; *SIA*, 265). The fact remains that some of Castoriadis's criticisms of Marxism may equally well be found in Debord— witness the refusal of both to treat the revolt of the proletariat as a kind of chemical reaction catalyzed by poverty instead of placing consciousness and the historical struggle at its center. The difference, however, is that these ideas led Castoriadis to mutate within a few years into a garden-variety champion of "Western democracy," whereas they led Debord to locate the pressure points of a possible new revolt.

Unlike some anarchistically inclined groups, the SI did not believe that the concept of a vanguard had to be exorcised utterly as being absolutely inextricable from "the Leninist notion of the 'vanguard' party, whose task it was to represent—and above all to *direct*—the working class" (*IS* 11/64). The Situationists chose a third path, aspiring to be nothing more than a "Conspiracy of Equals, a general staff that *does not want troops*," and declaring that "*the only thing we organize is the*

---

67. *Arguments* 4 (September 1957).
68. A charge that is hard to rebut in view of the academic stardom later attained by Castoriadis and Lefort.

detonator; the explosion must be free, escaping permanently from our control just as it does from anyone else's" (*IS* 8/27–28; *SIA,* 113). The point was made quite clearly: "The SI does not want disciples" (*IS* 8/59; *SIA,* 134). What was sought was an intentionally very small group— "the purest form of an anti-hierarchical body of anti-specialists" (*IS* 5/7; *Dérive,* 106). The purpose was threefold: to ensure participation "only at the highest level" (*IS* 9/25; *SIA,* 140); to maintain internal coherence; and to establish relations of equality between all members. The third aim, at any rate, as the SI admitted, was in fact never achieved (*VS,* 75–76; Eng., 71). In sharp contrast to organizations of "militants," the SI not only refused to proselytize, it also made entry into the group particularly difficult: one of the conditions required was to be "possessed of genius" (*IS,* 9/43; *SIA, 146*)! Over the years, more than two-thirds of the members were expelled and several others forced to resign. The Situationists consistently refused to allow followers to rally around them and would meet only with groups or individuals acting on their own account, because they believed in "letting autonomous people make their own way in the world" (*IS* 9/25; *SIA,* 140)—although it has to be said that in reality such people were a tiny bit hard to find.

The SI felt that its task lay in a revolutionary movement that "had to be reinvented" (*IS* 6/3; *SIA,* 63). As part of the process, all illusions had to be stripped away, and the first step in that direction was to recognize that the old movement had failed irrevocably and that no new one yet existed (*IS* 9/26; *SIA,* 141). Any attempt at reconstitution would have to draw upon four traditions: "the workers' movement, modern poetry and art in the West (viewed as preliminaries to the experimental search for a way forward to the free construction of everyday life), the thought of the period of the transcendence of philosophy (Hegel, Feuerbach, Marx), and emancipatory struggles from the Mexico of 1910 to the Congo of today" (*IS* 10/45–46; *SIA,* 149).

Even after May 1968, the Situationists refused to assume leadership over all those, now numbering in the thousands, who espoused their ideas. This militated against their emergence as an independent vanguard, with its threat of incipient bureaucratization; it also obviated the kind of tactical maneuvering and the semi-travestying of their ideas that other groups accepted for the sake of attracting as many members as possible. From 1966 on, many individuals and groups had started making independent use of Situationist ideas, techniques, slogans, and language. This helped lend the SI an aura of mystery: the organization seemed like the invisible and impenetrable eye of a whirlwind, for the Situationists had no headquarters, they never talked to journalists, they held no public meetings, and nobody knew exactly who or how many exactly they were. Indeed, after May 1968 the SI's hand was seen in a multitude of oppositional actions with which in reality it had no direct involvement.

In his book on the Enragés and Situationists in the occupations movement of May 1968, the Situationist René Viénet writes: "the agitation launched at Nanterre by four or five revolutionaries, who would later constitute the Enragés, was to lead in less than five months to the near liquidation of the State. . . . Never has a campaign undertaken by so few individuals resulted in so short a time in such consequences."[69] The hyperbole notwithstanding—what the Enragés really did was start a chain reaction—it is certainly true that Debord and his friends had developed to an unheard-of degree the ability to obtain enormous results from few actions carried out by few people. In this way too the lie was given on the practical level to the thesis, so fashionable in the sixties, of the death of the subject and of the individual. The Situationists indeed called for "masters without slaves" (IS 12/81; SIA, 292) in a society that had lost all "mastery" over its means and where "the masters come from the negative; they are the bearers of the anti-hierarchical principle" (IS 8/13; SIA, 103).

For the SI, then, the task of the avant-garde was not to bring revolutionary movements into being but rather to offer theoretical support to already existing movements. Capitalist society was already foundering on its own; alternatives were what was lacking. Nor was it a matter of "utopian" alternatives: whereas the old Utopians had been theoreticians in search of a praxis, in 1962, according to the SI, there was "a host of new practices in search of their theory" (IS 8/10). Apart from revolutionary practice, moreover, all the technical means and all the other material conditions required for the building of a new society were now present. This was therefore an "immanent critique" of society, after the fashion of Marx, or in other words a critique that did not outline some abstract utopia but instead confronted the reality of society with its promises and pretensions. This was why the Situationists firmly rejected the suggestion that their ideas were utopian (IS 9/25; SIA, 140); those ideas were not only realizable, they were above all "popular" (IS 7/17) and in everyone's head (IS 7/30; SIA, 93), because the SI "identified with the deepest desire present in everyone" (IS 7/20). An avant-garde

69. Enragés et situationnistes dans le mouvement des occupations (Paris: Gallimard, 1968), 25. Partial English translation: Enragés and Situationists in the Occupation Movement, France, May '68 (New York: Autonomedia/London: Rebel Press, 1992), 19.

that merely explains to the proletariat what it can do, and incites it to do it, was in no danger of becoming manipulative. The Situationists believed, therefore, that they had no need to go out and sell their theory and that on the contrary the real struggle of the workers would surely bring *them* to the SI's door, at which time the SI would place itself at their disposal (*IS* 11/64).

The Situationists were nonetheless masters of the art of self-advertisement. From the Letterist period on, they always made quite sure that the name of their organization was associated with each of their public actions. But their real strength in this regard was their incomparable style, founded for the most part on the combination of a highly worked intellectual content—frequently denounced as "hermetic"—with a transgression of established forms quite unusual for the time, indeed in many ways something genuinely new: the systematic use of insult; the reliance on "low" cultural forms such as comic strips, graffiti, and satirical songs; the ostentatious lack of respect for authorities and conventions (a respect that was traditionally stronger in France than elsewhere); the refusal to care whether adversaries saw one as "reasonable" or "acceptable"; the mockery of things that other people felt were already very daring or innovative. So far from pandering to their audience, the Situationists would often insult them, sticking people's noses in their own misery and pouring scorn on anyone who did not try to do something about it. To describe art, including its "avant-garde" varieties, as a corpse every bit as rotten as the church, was apt in those days to scandalize even the most "radical." Already in the early sixties, the SI was asserting that Dada's true heir was not American Pop Art but the spontaneous revolt of the Congolese people (*IS* 7/23).

It was *communication*, the legacy of authentic modern art to the new revolutionary movements, that now had to be established (*VS*, 134; Eng., 121). Some of the observations on art and language in *Internationale Situationniste* are among the most interesting things to be found there. The Situationists contrasted "information" as dispensed by power with "communication" and "dialogue"—a basic distinction that in their view had not been adequately addressed. As early as 1958, Debord declared that "all forms of pseudo-communication must be consigned to utter destruction, so that one day we may achieve real, direct communication" (*IS* 1/21; *Oct.*, 92). On the terrain of the "insubordination of words" (*IS* 8/29; *SIA*, 114) the SI enjoyed some of its greatest successes: in "the wars of decolonization of everyday life" (*IS* 8/28) the liberation of language had a central role, and it is not surprising that the Situationists should have devoted far more attention than any other revolutionary group to the development of their own particular style. Debord went so far as to seek a theoretical basis for an "insurrectional style" (*SS* §206) which, as the free appropriation of the past's positive contributions, he identified with *détournement*. The examples he offers, however, are limited to inversions of the genitive after the fashion of the "philosophy of poverty" versus the "poverty of philosophy," as practiced by Feuerbach and Marx. If such inversions became almost a trademark of Situationist writing, this was not merely out of literary coquettishness: the device was intended to express the "fluidity" (*SS* §205) of concepts, the fact that relationships between things are not set in stone and are indeed subject, for example, to inversions.

All the same, the stress continually laid by the Situationists on "communication" is in a way belied when they assert, for instance, that "people must take us or leave us as a whole. There can be no picking and choosing" (*IS* 7/19).[70] As justifiable as it might be to reject the bourgeois cult of "tolerance," it is hard to overcome the suspicion that "communication" for the SI meant the exchange of ideas between people who were already thinking the same way. More seriously, the Situationists undoubtedly embraced the Leninist sentiment that their own revolutionary organization embodied the rationality of history. It is no coincidence that despite their extreme minority status they frequently proclaimed that they represented the real "essence," the true "in-itself," of revolutionary moments. The SI distinguished on occasion between revolutionary theory and "propaganda"; in practice, however, this proved to be a very fine line indeed.

The Situationists' criticisms of leftist organizations—of a "Left that talks only about the things that the television talks about" (*IS* 10/32)—have a perspicuity that continues to astonish, even if their polemics sometimes bore traces of a desire to maintain a monopoly on the radical, or trailed off into pettifoggery. A bubble that the SI found easy to burst was the excessive enthusiasm for revolutionary movements in the Third World, which tended to be contemplated passively in Europe by "consumers of illusory participation" striving to cover up their own ineffectuality. The

70. The concept of communication was taken by the Situationists in a broad sense that included conveying the idea of the impossibility of all communication. Conveying that idea was a typical feature of modern art, part of its destruction of all traditional languages, and it naturally caused many to reject it as "incomprehensible" and thus hardly communicative.

SI (like Socialisme ou Barbarie) believed that "the revolutionary project must be realized in the industrially advanced countries" (*IS* 7/13; *SIA*, 85) and that the prospects for social revolution were far better in the Soviet Union—as in England—than in, say, Mauritania (*IS* 8/62).[71] A bit of mockery of Third-Worldism is no doubt to be detected in the SI's use of such terms as "backward sector," "underdevelopment," and "war of liberation" in connection with the issue of everyday life.

On another front, the Situationists were far from convinced that the students could constitute a revolutionary subject, nor did "the young" per se, or the various "marginal" groups, inspire any confidence in them in this regard.[72] This was another thing that radically distinguished the SI from other left-wing currents that it might be said to resemble in some respects. Only the proletariat, on the Situationist view, occupied the crucial position that would allow it to overthrow the entire social order. It has frequently been remarked that this view is somewhat paradoxical for a group that, doubtless before others, had abandoned any positive notion of work.[73] The whole of the Left, including the anarchists, had always thought in terms of liberating work and based the proletariat's entitlement to rule society on the fact that it was the proletariat that labored. The programmatic demand for a liberation *from* work, as a way of asserting the rights of the individual under the banner of subjectivity and play, had precedents only in the artistic avant-gardes—as witness Rimbaud's "I will never work" (in the poem "Qu'est-ce pour nous"), or the cover of the fourth issue of *La Révolution Surréaliste* (July 1925), which declared "War on Work!" In 1960 Debord and Canjuers asserted that working toward making productive activity passionate by means of "a general and permanent conversion of not just the means but also the ends of industrial labor will in any case be the minimum passion of a free society" (*Prelims.*, 346; *SIA*, 309). One of the greatest joys of the Situationists during the general wildcat strike of 1968 was seeing the reappearance on walls of a graffito that Debord had famously put up back in 1953: "Never Work!" (see illustrations, *IS* 8/42 and *IS* 12/14). To the reproach that they had failed to address the reality of work, the Situationists' reply was that they "had scarcely ever

71. See for example the first installment of "Le Mouvement révolutionnaire sous le capitalisme moderne," *Socialisme ou Barbarie* 31 (December 1960); reprinted in Castoriadis, *Capitalisme moderne et révolution*, vol. 2 (Paris: Union Générale d'Éditions, Collection 10/18, 1979). English translation: "Modern Capitalism and Revolution," in Castoriadis, *Political and Social Writings*, 2:226–58.

72. They had already taken this view in their Letterist days (see *Pot.*, 92–94).

73. See Gombin, *Origines du gauchisme*, 96–97; Eng. trans., 75–76.

addressed any problem other than that of work in our time—its conditions, its contradictions, its consequences" (*IS* 10/67). And it is quite true
that, although they never produced detailed analyses of the work world
after the fashion of *Socialisme ou Barbarie*, they clearly showed how the
logic of work had been extended to all social life and especially to the
consumption of leisure time. The Situationist thesis was that society's
source of meaning and self-justification, the point of reference whence
individuals derived their identity, was in the process of shifting from
work to so-called leisure activities (see for example *IS* 6/25; *SIA*, 73).

Especially during the early years, the Situationists looked upon themselves as bearers of "the modern"—and this sometimes in the tritest
sense, as when they proposed destroying old buildings to make way for
new (*Pot.*, 206: *Dérive*, 57; *IS* 3/16). At the same time, their most dangerous enemies, as they saw it, were those *modernists* who sought to
use the results of progress, and especially of revolutionary progress, as
means for improving the prevailing organization of society. This applied
above all to "cybernetics"—very much in vogue in the sixties as a supposed answer to all problems—but also to semiotics, structuralism, information technology, industrial psychology, and so forth. The Situationists were well aware, however, that they were "necessarily on the same
road" as those who were at the opposite pole from them as judged by intentions and outcomes (*IS* 9/4; *SIA*, 136); consider, for a good example,
the Situationists' contempt for Jean-Luc Godard, whom they accused of
appropriating many *trouvailles* from the avant-garde, and notably from
the cinema of Guy Debord, without the slightest understanding of any
of them (*IS* 10/58–59; *SIA*, 175–76).

The SI was thus also well in advance in its grasp of another idea that
became very fashionable after 1968, namely the idea of co-optation, or
récupération; later, the Situationists would go so far as to comment sar-
donically on "people who . . . have little to worry about on that score
since they generally don't possess much that could arouse the rapacity
of recuperators" (*IS* 12/18; *SIA*, 240).

May 1968 and After

The role in May 1968 of the SI and of a kindred group, the Enragés of
Nanterre, is well known, and the Situationist account of what transpired
is set forth in the abovementioned book by René Viénet and in the twelfth

issue of *Internationale Situationniste*. Here we shall merely recall the SI's struggle against the influence on the student rebellion of various "bu-reaucratic" groups, from the Maoists to Daniel Cohn-Bendit's Mouve-ment du 22 Mars, and likewise against the influence of the big trade unions on the workers. The Situationists strove to generalize the occu-pations movement and called from the outset for the formation of work-ers' councils, but at the same time they cautioned continually against an excessively triumphant attitude. Their influence is particularly evident in the poetic graffiti that covered the walls of Paris. Despite the often very traditional tones of their rhetoric, the Situationists were nonetheless thor-oughly aware that the significance of the moment lay not in the throw-ing up of a few barricades, but rather in the fact that this was truly "the beginning of an era" (*IS* 12/3).[74]

As noted earlier, the place of the Situationists in history is largely bound up with the way in which the events of May 1968 confirmed their theses. In the thick of these events, they sent a telegram to the In-stitute of Social History in Amsterdam that began, "We are conscious of the fact that we are beginning to produce our own history."[75] Later on, they were continually referring to that "joli mois de mai."[76] There are some observers, however, for whom the Situationists' role in 1968 was strictly fortuitous. Thus Mario Perniola would write several years later that "the key to understanding their relationship with May 1968 is an arbitrary three-tiered identification of Situationist subjectivity, the revolutionary project of instituting workers' councils, and the proletarian psyche: the fact is that here are three quite distinct things whose *coming together* was not dialectical, as the SI mistakenly believes, but merely *con-tingent*."[77] But Perniola is only partly correct: the SI never claimed to have foreseen the date of the explosion, merely its *content* (*IS* 12/54; *SIA*, 270). May 1968 was indeed proof that something very much like revo-lution could occur in modern societies, and in a form very closely resem-bling the SI's predictions. In a book published in 1967, Henri Lefebvre concluded a few remarks on the Situationists by observing that they "pro-

74. Indeed, some of their concerns were a very far cry from those of the students. They were keen, for example, to relate their actions to history, as when they proposed to ex-hume the remains of Richelieu—"that foul statesman and cardinal"—from the chapel of the Sorbonne and pack them off to the Elysée or the Vatican (see Viénet, *Enragés et situationnistes*, 77; Eng. trans., 47).

75. Viénet, *Enragés et situationnistes*, 274. This telegram was sent by the Sorbonne Occupation Committee, strongly influenced by the SI.

76. Clearly referring to his role in May 1968, Debord ended up "admitting to being the one who chose the time and direction of the attack" (*OCC*, 263; *In girum*, 60) and reflecting that "no one has twice roused Paris to revolt" (*Pan.*, 79; Eng., 71).

77. Mario Perniola, "I Situazionisti," *Agar-Agar* 4 (Rome, 1972): 87.

pose not a concrete utopia, but an abstract one. Do they really imagine that one fine day or some decisive evening people will look at each other and say, 'Enough! We are fed up with working and being bored. Let's put an end to this!' And that they will thereupon proceed into endless Festival and start creating situations? Maybe it happened once, at dawn on 18 March 1871, but that particular set of circumstances can never recur."[78] In 1967, the SI quoted this remark without comment in their journal (*IS* 11/52). In 1969, they quoted it once more with considerable—and quite understandable—satisfaction (*IS* 12/6; *SIA,* 227–28).

It is recognized today that 1968 was one of the crucial turning points of the century. But the simplifying label of "student revolt" has served to distort the real picture. It has to be remembered that 1968 witnessed the first, and until now the only, general wildcat strike in history, with over ten million workers downing tools and a large portion of them occupying their workplaces. Over the preceding months there had in fact been several wildcats in France, and some had been accompanied by outbursts of "permanent festival"; in other words, the striking workers of May and June 1968 were not simply aping the students' occupation of the Sorbonne.[79] Nor did any economic crisis underlie the revolt, as the SI correctly pointed out (*IS* 12/6; *SIA,* 228); and quite clearly specific demands for university reform or for higher wages were not the most fundamental motor in a situation that was completely unexpected and that bordered on civil war. For several weeks, though, every agency of authority abdicated its role, a feeling of "everything is possible" prevailed, the upside-down world was set back on its feet—in short, a historical event occurred, but it was one that affected individuals in their most intimate and everyday being. One, too, that showed beyond doubt that a very large number of people yearned inwardly for a completely different life and that this desire, once it found expression, could quickly bring a modern state to its knees: exactly what the SI had always said. Even though another May 1968 has not yet occurred, the fact remains that the conditions which occasioned the first have not disappeared, and should the day come when people's desire to control their own lives drives them once again into the streets, not a few of the SI's precepts will surely be recalled.

In the immediate wake of this moment of glory, the SI gained considerably in strength. A succession of new members was admitted, and

78. *Position: Contre les technocrates* (Paris: Gonthier, 1967), 195.
79. See Gombin, *Origines du gauchisme,* 158; Eng. trans., 120.

national sections were once more set up—French, Italian, Scandinavian, and American, each of which succeeded in publishing an issue of their own SI journal.[80] The Italian section further distinguished itself thanks to a series of well-aimed interventions in connection with the Piazza Fontana bombing and other Italian events of the time.[81] The SI's theses enjoyed vast renown at this time in all kinds of places; one journalist went so far as to dub Debord's *The Society of the Spectacle* "the *Capital* of the new generation."[82] The truth was, however, that the SI was entering a terminal crisis, seemingly due to the shortcomings of a good many of the newcomers; a series of expulsions and splits left only Debord and two others in the organization, and in spring 1972 the Situationist International was disbanded.[83]

Debord and the Italian Situationist Gianfranco Sanguinetti offer an explanation of these developments in *The Veritable Split in the International*. They observe that the period is on the road to a real revolution and that Situationist ideas are clearly present on a wide scale and in many different struggles. From this they conclude that the role of the SI as an organization is complete, but their attempt to see the demise of the SI in terms of the supersession of a separate avant-garde—for which a revolutionary period does not have the same need as a period when the revolution is still far off (*VS*, 73; Eng., 68–69)—is not very convincing. They themselves admit that the SI has entered a crisis, which they blame on the great numbers of people, chiefly students and intellectuals, who contemplate and endorse the radical attitudes of the Situationists without being capable of giving this endorsement the least practical expression. Their depiction of these "pro-Situs," and of the social stratum

80. See the American *Situationist International* 1 (June 1969), for instance. Reprinted, Portland, Oregon: Extreme Press, 1993.

81. The contents of the sole issue of the journal *Internazionale Situazionista* (July 1969), and the other writings of the Italian section, are at present available only in French translation: *Ecrits complets (1969–72) de la section italienne de l'Internationale Situationniste* (Paris: Contre-Moule, 1988). On 12 December 1969, a bomb exploded in a bank on the Piazza Fontana in Milan, killing sixteen people. "Left-wing extremists" were widely blamed at the time, although a long and tortuous judicial inquiry would eventually confirm the much earlier conclusions of the Italian Situationists, as set forth in their pamphlet *The Reichstag Is Burning*, namely that the bombing was a provocation plotted by the secret police, with help from right-wing extremists, in response to the rising revolutionary tide in the country. There were to be more such "State massacres" in Italy over the next few years (among them the train "Italicus," the Piazza della Loggia incident in Brescia, etc.).

82. *Le Nouvel Observateur*, 8 November 1971, cited in *VS*, 20n; Eng., 18n.

83. The less than scintillating final years of the SI are evoked in "Notes pour servir à l'histoire de l'I.S. de 1969 à 1971," *VS*, 85–101; Eng., 83–94. A number of internal SI documents dating from this period may be found in Dumontier, *Les Situationnistes et mai 68*.

of lower- and middle-echelon management to which they belong, is brilliant and withering, but the authors' overestimation of the phenomenon,
as likewise in a more general way their conflation of "the modern revolutionary project" with the SI, nonetheless bespeaks a certain (and not
entirely new) megalomania, a certain loss of contact with reality. Debord and Sanguinetti note that the independent petty bourgeoisie has
faded away with the rise of the managers, technicians, and bureaucrats
who are the main creators and consumers of the spectacle; such lower
and middle ranks of management nevertheless remain—objectively if not
subjectively—close to the proletariat (VS, 59; Eng., 55).

The real failure of the SI lay in the fact that its theory never spread
significantly beyond the much disparaged milieux of the students and
intellectuals. A good many workers' struggles were under way around
1970, and occasionally a few snatches of Situationist theory found their
way into them, but no proletariat existed that *as a class* stood opposed
to the *totality* of the society of the spectacle. Debord and Sanguinetti
cite "people of color, homosexuals, [and] women and children [who]
take it into their heads to want everything that was *forbidden* them" as
contributors to a spreading general insubordination (VS, 22; Eng., 19).
But it was not by chance that prior to 1968 the SI had never mentioned
any of these groups. The campaigns waged by such segments of society
are often very energetic and sometimes lead to the overthrow of certain
representations, to genuine action in the first person, and to the taking
into account of people's own everyday life both as the means and the
end of struggle; yet reference is barely ever made by these movements to
society as a whole, and they are made up of people who define themselves solely in terms of one aspect of their existence.

Formally, at any rate, the Situationists subscribed to the theory that
only the proletariat, by virtue of its position in the production process,
and of its historical tradition, had the capacity to bring down the system. Paradoxically, their broadening of the concept of the proletariat so
as to cover everyone who was dispossessed in one way or another ac-
curately prefigured the future revolts of various "minorities." All real
struggles, whether of blacks in Los Angeles, students in Paris, or workers in Poland, were characterized by the SI as "struggles against alienation," little heed being paid to the very different circumstances and the
very different demands in play in each particular case. This is not to
contest the legitimacy of seeking the essence of such struggles at a level
deeper than that of their explicit demands; the fact is, though, that the
SI's attempt to circumscribe their "in-itself" generally remained far too

abstract in character. The last of the Situationists poured scorn on the supposedly vague and abstract appeals addressed by Raoul Vaneigem— now dishonorably expelled—to "insurrectionaries of the will to live" (*VS,* 125; Eng., 113), yet they too were hard pressed to name the revolutionary subject. Indeed, Debord himself seemed to be placing his hopes in the automatisms of capitalist development, as when he and Sanguinetti argue that the contradiction between the economy and life has reached a qualitative threshold, while the opposition aroused by the economy must in turn bring about a return of the economic crisis in the traditional sense of the term (*VS,* 26–28; Eng., 24); all of which allegedly made the times more revolutionary than ever.

The most interesting aspect of *The Veritable Split in the International* is the attention it pays to an issue then in its infancy but with a great future ahead of it: the issue of pollution and ecological catastrophe, including the effects of the use of nuclear energy (*VS,* 31; Eng., 27). It was clear to Debord and Sanguinetti that capitalism had entered a phase of "galloping irrationalization" in this regard (*VS,* 37; Eng., 34). Industrial production was modeled on the agrarian system, striving to reap the absolute maximum possible in every season as though it too were permanently threatened by penury; concomitantly, it took on a pseudo-cyclical aspect, as programmed obsolescence became essential to the maintenance of output. The reality of industrial production, however, was not cyclical but cumulative, and this reality "returns in the form of pollution" (*VS,* 33; Eng., 30). In thrall to capital, science was just as useless as all the remedies proposed by governments. For the authors of *The Veritable Split,* looming ecological disaster was proof positive that the economy and the commodity were contaminating the whole of life and threatened the very survival of the species. They observed too that "capitalism has at last furnished the proof that it cannot develop the productive forces any further"—and this, not in the *quantitative* sense, as Marxist scholasticism had long predicted, but rather in the *qualitative* one (*VS,* 29; Eng., 26). Even such fundamental necessities as water and air were now part of the struggle (*VS,* 33; Eng., 30), rather like bread in the nineteenth century. The old slogan "Revolution or Death" had thus taken on a completely new significance (*VS,* 31; Eng., 30).

Today, with the benefit of twenty-five years of hindsight, we know that these circumstances have not generated any movement of radical opposition to a society where the gulf between technical and economic means has reached insane proportions; true, the environmental movement that does exist is vast, but it is utterly without any global perspective.

The Debord Myth

The events of May 1968 bestowed a measure of unanticipated notoriety on Guy Debord. Never having been fond of the limelight, least of all that of a society that he despised, and being of a naturally discreet disposition, he proceeded in the aftermath of 1968 to make himself more inaccessible than ever. He would have nothing to do with the many *groupuscules*, in several countries, all of whom claimed the mantle of the Situationists and spent most of their time in crude vendettas passed off as revolutionary activity. Nor did he heed the attempts to co-opt the luminaries of 1968 and turn them into literary editors, academics, politicians, or at the very least willing talkshow guests. His position was unwavering: "I would find it just as vulgar to be an authority in the resistance to society as to be an authority within society itself" (OCC, 269–70; *In girum*, 66). The very act of withdrawing, however, led to Debord's being described as "the most elusive of men with one of the most significant trajectories of the last twenty-five years,"[84] and he was accused by some of disappearing precisely as a way of burnishing the myth that surrounded him.

This alleged disappearance of Debord's was in actuality quite relative. During this time, he formed a friendship with Gérard Lebovici, a brilliant and unconventional cinema impresario who in 1970 had founded and financed the small publishing house Champ Libre. In 1971 Debord entrusted Lebovici with a new edition of *The Society of the Spectacle*, and from 1974 on, though in no official capacity, he began to play a decisive role in running Lebovici's unique company. Unique, because, ignoring considerations of profit entirely, Champ Libre published texts on the theory and practice of revolution that ranged from Hegel to Bakunin and from Saint-Just to the Spanish anarchists; the critique of Maoism and Stalinism rubbed shoulders on Champ Libre's list with such classics as Omar Khayyám and Baltasar Gracián, George Orwell and Karl Kraus, while forgotten writings of Clausewitz or the German Dadaists, of Georg Groddeck or Malevich, were given a new lease on life.[85] Naturally Debord's own works, and those of other Situationists, also appeared under

84. The first words of a biographical note on Debord in *Le Débat* 50 (May–August 1988): 239.
85. Simon Leys's *Les Habits neufs du président Mao* (Paris: Champ Libre, Bibliothèque Asiatique, 1971) was a genuine bombshell, for it was the first denunciation of the "Maolatry" then prevailing among French intellectuals. English translation by Carol Appleyard and Patrick Goode: *The Chairman's New Clothes: Mao and the Cultural Revolution* (London: Allison and Busby, 1977).

the Champ Libre imprint. Lebovici's most provocative act as a publisher, however, occurred in 1984, when he issued *L'Instinct de mort* [The Death Instinct], the memoirs of Jacques Mesrine, France's most infamous criminal and "master escape artist," considered public enemy number one until his barbaric elimination by the French police.

Lebovici and Debord deliberately maintained execrable relations with the press and the so-called intellectual world. Champ Libre acquired a terrible reputation in the eyes of many people, and, to quote Debord himself, "the publishing house was shrouded in a sinister atmosphere of continual conspiracy against the whole world."[86] Ample confirmation of this is supplied by the two volumes of its own *Correspondance* that Champ Libre published in 1978 and 1981, for the letters reproduced are full of exchanges of insults sometimes occasioned by the most trivial of considerations.

Lebovici had many enemies, made for the most part, no doubt, during his meteoric career in the film industry. In March 1984, he was found shot to death in a parking garage. The crime has never been solved, but the French press was long fascinated with the fate of this out-of-the-ordinary figure with his double profile as rich entrepreneur and patron of the ultra-left. All the newspapers found Debord's influence on Lebovici inexplicable; many spoke darkly of "manipulation," accused Debord of leading Lebovici "astray," or intimated that he somehow shared moral responsibility for the death. Some publications went much further, however, charging that Debord was associated with terrorist groups and that he had ordered the killing of his friend in accordance with the following "logic": "Lebovici was killed . . . for having refused, on one occasion, to do something that he had been expected to agree to do."[87] Confronted by these extraordinary insinuations, Debord took the uncharacteristic step of bringing suit; the courts found in his favor. The following year he published *Considérations sur l'assassinat de Gérard Lebovici*, a work in which he wrote above all of himself, enumerating the press's frequently bizarre claims about him (indeed, deriving a certain satisfaction from the Mephistophelian role he was often assigned) and deploying his well-known polemical talents.[88]

Accompanied by Alice Becker-Ho, whom he married in the early sev-

86. Debord, *Considérations*, 28.
87. Ibid., 54.
88. The offensive as well as fanciful statements made by the French press concerning Debord and Lebovici are collected in *Gérard Lebovici, tout sur le personnage* (Paris: Gérard Lebovici, 1984).

enties, Debord moved around a good deal, mainly between Paris, Auvergne, Arles, Italy, and Spain.[89] In 1988 he returned to social criticism with his *Comments on the Society of the Spectacle,* a book that aroused a good deal of interest, and not only in France. The following year the first volume of an autobiography appeared, significantly entitled *Panegyric.* In 1991 Debord parted company with Éditions Gérard Lebovici, later renamed Éditions Ivréa; beginning the next year, six of his books were republished by Gallimard, France's best-known publishers.[90] The French press was by this time mentioning Debord more than ever, and in *"Cette mauvaise réputation . . . ,"* published in late 1993—the only new text produced in the last five years of his life—he commented sarcastically on a large number of articles referring to him. Those who had been shocked by Debord's willingness to sign a contract with Gallimard were in for another surprise when a film made in collaboration with Brigitte Cornand for Canal Plus Television was aired on 9 January 1995, along with two earlier films of Debord's. This was *Guy Debord, son art et son temps,* in which Debord illustrates "his art" by means of a shorter version of the black, silent screen of his first film and "his time" by means of a selection of some of the most ominous television images of recent years, accompanied by occasional titles offering such comments as the following: "These, the most modern events in historical reality, have just perfectly demonstrated what Thomas Hobbes thought the life of man must have been like before the advent of civilization and of the State: 'solitary, poor, nasty, brutish, and short.'" Only hypocrites would pretend surprise at the bleakness of this picture of the state of the world; but of course there is no shortage of hypocrites.

On 30 November 1994, Guy Debord took his own life in his home at Champot (Haute-Loire) by shooting himself in the heart. He set forth the reasons for this act in a title that appeared at the end of the television broadcast: "Illness called alcoholic polyneuritis; first signs appeared in autumn 1990. At first almost imperceptible, but progressive. Became truly distressing only in late November 1994. As with all incurable diseases, there is much to be gained by neither seeking nor accepting medical care.

---

89. Alice Becker-Ho is the author of *Les Princes du jargon* (Paris: Gérard Lebovici, 1990), reprinted by Gallimard (Paris, 1993); and of *L'Essence du jargon* (Paris: Gallimard, 1994).

90. For Debord's account of his "contested divorce" from Éditions Gérard Lebovici, see *"Cette mauvaise réputation . . . "* (Paris: Gallimard, 1993), 86. As for the Gallimard arrangement, it was eventually broken off in 1997, after Gallimard had published a book slandering Debord, and future publication was entrusted to the publishers Arthème Fayard.

This is the opposite of an illness that you contract through an unfortunate lack of prudence. On the contrary, contracting it requires dogged determination over a whole lifetime."

As noted earlier, Debord allowed himself to be called a theoretician; he always described himself, however, as a filmmaker and presented this as his only real *métier* (see for example *IS* 12/96). True to the idea that the work of destruction of the old values could not continue indefinitely and that it was needful to proceed to a new and positive use of elements already existing in the world, he followed his first film, which was devoid of images, with others that contained them. It was very rare for him to do any shooting himself, and practically all the images he used were *détournéments* from various fiction films, historical documentaries, newsreels of political events, or advertisements.[91] These accompany a voiceover text, though as a rule without illustrating it directly. In the two short subjects *On the Passage of a Few Persons through a Rather Brief Period of Time* (1959) and *Critique of Separation* (1961), this text includes sometimes melancholy thoughts on the life of the Situationists and their historical role. Debord nevertheless once told the other Situationists that he had never made a Situationist film (*IS* 7/27), and indeed the SI made it clear from the beginning that none of its interventions should be viewed as anything more than *prefigurements* of future Situationist actions. Other film projects of Debord's dating from this period were never realized, but later his friendship with Lebovici gave him an opportunity to return to his first love, the cinema. In 1973 he "brought *The Society of the Spectacle* to the screen" as a film in which the reading of passages from the book was accompanied by a collage of images. Unlike Debord's early films, *The Society of the Spectacle* was shown in movie theaters, albeit on a very modest scale. To the press's reactions, which varied widely, Debord's riposte was another, medium-length film, *Refutation of All the Judgements, Laudatory as Well as Hostile, Passed up to Now on the Film "The Society of the Spectacle."* As an epigraph to this film, Debord quoted Chateaubriand: "There are times when contempt should be dispensed only in the most economical manner, by reason of the great number of persons in need thereof" (*OCC,* 161; *Films,*

---

91. Even the few frames that he did shoot, however, were sufficient to place Debord among the all-time great *cinéastes*—or at least that was the view expressed in *La Quinzaine Littéraire* for 1 July 1981, as quoted in *Ordures et décombres déballés à la sortie du film "In girum imus nocte et consumimur igni"* [Rubbish and Refuse Unpacked in Response to the Film *In girum imus nocte et consumimur igni*], ed. Anon. [Debord] (Paris: Champ Libre, 1982), 31.

119). Of those who had passed *laudatory* judgments, he observed that they had "loved too many other things to be able to love" his film (*OCC*, 246; *Films*, 120).

Debord's masterpiece in the cinema, announced as his last film, was *In girum imus nocte et consumimur igni*, which was made in 1978 and released in 1981. The title is a palindrome meaning "We go round and round in the night and are consumed by fire" (see *OCC*, 242; *In girum*, 43). To ensure its exhibition, along with that of all Debord's films, Lebovici bought a small Latin Quarter cinema, the Studio Cujas, and dedicated it exclusively to this purpose. In 1984, however, in protest against the press campaign that followed Lebovici's murder, Debord withdrew all his films from circulation, with the result that no one was able to see any of them until, in 1995, *The Society of the Spectacle* and *Refutations* were shown on television along with *Guy Debord, son art et son temps*.

Critical opinion on Debord's films is sharply divided. The myth surrounding their director, coupled with the impossibility of seeing them for over a decade, caused these films to become the object of considerable fascination in certain quarters. Some critics describe them as utterly original, evoking the debt owed Debord by other "avant-garde" directors such as Jean-Luc Godard.[92] Most observers, however, even once they could no longer ignore Debord's other activities, have persistently failed to evince much interest in his cinema. Debord himself attributed this lack of interest to a conspiracy of silence provoked by the fact that his cinema was even more transgressive than his theoretical works and constituted an intolerable "excess" in the eyes of the spectacle's minions (*OCC*, 168; *Films*, 123). "So great was their distaste that they stole far less often from me here than elsewhere" (*OCC*, 213; *In girum*, 19–20).

Debord's personality emerges particularly clearly from his films, especially *In girum*—although that personality can hardly be detached from any of the public actions of someone who, as he himself put it, never did

92. At the time of this writing the only really serious discussion of Debord's cinema is Thomas Y. Levin's long and well-disposed article "Dismantling the Spectacle: The Cinema of Guy Debord," in *Passage*, 72–122. Three articles devoted to Debord appear in *Cahiers du cinéma* 487 (January 1995). A telling instance of the "precursor of the video neo-avant-garde" approach to neutralizing Debord is the would-be retrospective devoted to him by the "Rassegna video d'autore" of the Taormina Arte festival in 1991; cf. the catalogue accompanying this event: *Dissensi tra film, video, televisione* (Palermo: Sellerio, 1991), 239–68. In this connection, Debord himself cited an article, in the periodical *Trafic* (winter 1991), in which Serge Daney poked fun at the public debate on his films at Taormina and pointed out that hardly any of the participants had ever seen them ("*Cette mauvaise réputation . . .*," 68).

anything except follow his own tastes and "seek to experience, in the
course of my life, a good number of poetic situations."[93] Someone well
acquainted with Debord has described him as "the freest man that I ever
met." Debord certainly interested his contemporaries not only by virtue
of his theoretical and practical contributions but also by reason of his
persona and by reason of the living example he set. His glory is that he
never sought to make a career for himself, or to make money, despite
the many offers he must have had in this regard; that he never played
any part in public affairs, nor received any diploma from the state, except for his *baccalauréat;* that he never mixed with the celebrities, nor
made use of the channels, of the society of the spectacle; and that he
nonetheless contrived to play an important part in the history of his time.
Debord exemplifies a quest for personal consistency, a consistency that
did not arise, as in others, from an ascetic ideal, but rather from a genuine disgust for the world surrounding him: "From the outset I saw fit
to devote myself to the overthrow of society," he asserts; this was in a
period when any such outcome was a distant prospect indeed, and "since
then I have not changed my attitude once, or even on several occasions,
as others have, with the changing of the times; rather, the times have
changed in accordance with my attitude" (*OCC,* 215–16; *In girum,* 22).
This was not meant to imply swearing allegiance once and for all to
some immutable truth but attending closely to the ever new conditions
under which a project that remained identical in its fundamental intent
had to be developed. The Situationists themselves often stressed that their
theory had evolved and overcome initial errors (*IS* 9/3; *SIA,* 135; *IS*
11/58; *VS,* 49–50; Eng., 45–46), yet they saw very little merit in anyone's arriving at the same conclusions as they, but years afterward.

The singularity of a Debord is perhaps greater in France than it might
be elsewhere. France's intellectuals, bound to the state as functionaries
since the time of Richelieu, have developed an endless capacity, especially in recent decades, for adapting to the fashions of the moment, for
collaborating with people they previously detested, or for making their
peace with the state the moment there was something in it for them.
The 1968 generation has illustrated this tendency to perfection—one has
only to think of how the grotesque Maoist Althusserians metamorphosed
in a few years into "new philosophers" or "postmodernists." This is the
context in which we should place the proud isolation defended in De-

---

93. *"Cette mauvaise réputation . . . ,"* 24.

bord's last books and summed up in his pronouncement, "I have lived everywhere, except among the intellectuals of these times."[94] The firmness of this posture meant that Debord found himself, not perhaps without a degree of pleasure, almost entirely on his own. He broke with almost everyone who ever collaborated with him, often on the worst of terms, and would note with some satisfaction that those expelled from the SI or distanced from him in some other way almost always ended up making one kind of accommodation or another with the system.

Debord claimed, and there is no reason to doubt him, that he never asked anything of anyone, that it was always others who approached him. The fascination that he holds for many people may be attributed to his *style*, in his life as in his writing. There is a remarkable combination in him between a formalist, austere, and "classical" tendency and a constant appeal to disorder, hedonism, and the most extreme revolutionary fervor. Debord's aristocratic spirit and predilection for the seventeenth century coexist in paradoxical harmony with the agenda of the proletarian revolution, approbation for certain types of youthful banditry, and the cartloads of insults tipped on his opponents. It would be trite, however, to characterize this mixture as "aestheticism." Debord has often been compared to André Breton on account of it, as also on account of the firmness he applied to running the SI and the rigor with which he defined orthodoxy within the ranks of these enemies of all orthodoxy.[95] Another modern figure to whom Debord might be likened is Karl Kraus, for the two have very many common traits: the extreme care taken with words; the finely hewn sentences, so well designed to condemn without appeal or discussion; the high-handed dismissal of all "public opinion," especially as represented by the press; the lone struggle against a world for whose approval or condemnation they cared not a jot; and the lack of interest in any kind of "career." Both had very high opinions of themselves, and both drew on great reservoirs of contempt.

---

94. Debord, *Considérations*, 77.

95. The first to compare Debord to Breton was in fact Asger Jorn. After his departure from the SI, Jorn recalled that in the wake of CoBrA's dissolution he had wanted to found a new group but one that would avoid the confusionism, and the Nordic accent, of CoBrA. This led him, he writes, "to seek the collaboration of a man who to my mind could be the ideal successor to André Breton as a fertile promoter of new ideas. I refer to Guy Debord—and nothing since that time has caused me to revise my opinion of him." Jorn also appreciated Debord's "politico-Latin training." See Asger Jorn, *Signes gravés sur les églises de l'Eure et du Calvados* (Copenhagen: Borgen, 1964), 290 and 294. Later, along with many other people, the French press decided that Debord and Breton were alike in that they were both "popes"; even Debord did not seem to find the comparison particularly shocking (see *Considérations*, 49).

Perhaps most significant of all, both related in the same way to their public and to their admirers. The more admirers of such figures are spurned, the more avidly they tend to attach themselves to these "masters," and in this sense Debord, like Kraus, exemplifies the paradox of extreme freedom appearing to others as extreme authority. Elias Canetti tells how, having been a fervent admirer of Kraus in his youth, he dared not for many years read a single line of any authors whom Kraus had disparaged.[96] Likewise there are not a few people, in France and elsewhere, who have made articles of faith out of any and all of Debord's opinions, whether of persons or of wines, as out of his way of writing, or out of what they supposed to be the way he led his life. And Kraus and Debord invariably found their contempt confirmed by "acquaintanceship with that *genuinely contemptible individual—the spectator*" (SS §195).[97]

To this sketch of the "character," we must add Debord's ability to stylize and dramatize events, lending them historical resonance by identifying the participants with those of moments in the past.[98] There is a whole culture of the "gesture" to be found here. Nothing was fortuitous in what Debord chose to present to the world, and the image of himself was worked up in the finest detail.[99]

Debord described his ambitions as "megalomaniacal" (*Pot.*, 277; *Oct.*, 89), and this beyond any results actually achieved; thus, again in his own words, there was to be "neither success nor failure for Guy Debord and his outrageous pretentions" (*OCC*, 281; *In girum*, 75–76). He had wanted a life of adventure, and, rather than exploring grottoes or dabbling in high finance, he chose an attack on existing society as the most seductive of enterprises. He proceeded to realize for himself something that according to his theory was now possible on a general scale, namely to live

96. See Elias Canetti, *Die Fackel im Ohr: Lebensgeschichte, 1921–31* (Munich: C. Hanser, 1993).

97. Champ Libre published Kraus's aphorisms in French for the first time (beginning in 1975). Debord's sole, somewhat stealthy mention of Kraus, however, was not exactly complimentary—see "*Cette mauvaise réputation . . . ,*" 120.

98. The title of *The Veritable Split in the International* is a *détournement* of the title of *The Alleged Splits in the International*, in which Marx and Engels explained the exclusion of the anarchists from the First International in 1872 (*PW III*, 272–314); in their correspondence, Debord and Sanguinetti signed as "Cavalcanti" and "Niccolò [Machiavelli]" respectively (see Éditions Champ Libre, *Correspondance*, vol. 2 [Paris: Champ Libre, 1981], 97–118).

99. Debord's claim that he had carried out a personal "revolution of everyday life" of his own was not devoid of foundation: two short novels by Michèle Bernstein, *Tous les chevaux du roi* [All the King's Horses] and *La Nuit* (Paris: Buchet/Chastel, 1960 and 1961, respectively), offer a lively account of the hedonistic and experimental life that she led with Debord, especially with respect to love relationships. It is true, of course, that much of this had to do with the climate of the times.

one's own life as a historical adventure. To a degree rarely achieved in this century, Debord succeeded in turning his life into a legend; by the time the SI was disbanded, that life had already long enjoyed mythical status.

"Is there any greater action in the world than leading a party?" asked Paul Gondi, Cardinal de Retz (1613–79), and his words might well be applied to Debord.[100] Debord was a great admirer of Retz; he quotes his *Mémoires* in several places and has him make ephemeral appearances in his last films and writings. He clearly identified, to the point of playfully adopting his name, with this distinctly unecclesiastical cardinal who was the moving spirit of the Fronde and who on several occasions roused the Parisian populace, amidst which he lived without being of it. As early as 1956, Debord noted that "the extraordinary ludic value of Gondi's life, as of that Fronde of which he was the chief architect, have yet to be viewed in a truly modern light" (*Pot.*, 242). What Debord admired in Retz was the fact that throughout his adventurous life and continual conspiracies he was motivated not by ambition but by the desire to rejoice in the drama of situations, to dabble with sets of historical contingencies. Retz was in the highest degree an embodiment of the baroque conception of the world as a great theater where one must play a part, strike the imagination, create dramatic effects, present what one has to say in an unprecedented way, and thus take center stage; the Situationists learned a great deal from Cardinal de Retz. Even though he lacked the protean quality that allowed Gondi to play the most varied roles, Debord too conceived of himself as a "leader of the game," a strategist carefully observing the dynamics of human groups and intervening only at the most propitious moment. And both men, following a relative failure on the stage of history, derived great pleasure from the narration of their past actions, sometimes perhaps even exaggerating the importance of their part in events.

The conception of history as a game—albeit at times a very serious game, an interplay of forces—led Debord to take a great interest in *strategy*, both in the strict military sense of the word and in the sense of a calculus of those forces, prospects, and human factors that may offer "game leaders" the opportunity to deploy their intelligence. In his film *In girum imus nocte et consumimur igni,* he depicted himself as the commander of an army of subversion (*OCC*, 261–63; *In girum*, 59–61), and

<hr>

100. Cardinal de Retz, *Oeuvres* (Paris: Gallimard, Bibliothèque de la Pléiade, 1984), 147.

the whole film is replete with military metaphors and images of battle. Some years earlier, Clausewitz had become one of the authors most often cited by the Situationists; Champ Libre undertook the publication of his complete works, along with that of other classics of strategy. Debord even devised a war game that was produced in various versions and published an account of a typical game in which he and Alice Becker-Ho were the two players.[101]

Debord concluded that the theory he had developed was in no sense a philosophical exercise, for "theories are made only to die in the war of time: they are stronger or weaker units to be thrown at the right moment into the combat" (OCC, 219; In girum, 24–25). All history is nothing but a perpetual conflict, a few rules of which we must learn as best we can. Such considerations carried Debord beyond mere military strategy to authors who had sought to define the rules of the game of history and society: Machiavelli, Baltasar Gracián, Castiglione. This interest of his could be interpreted as a desire to remain moored to a world still essentially *intelligible*, where the passions could run their own course because they enjoyed a margin of uncertainty in a universe that was in other respects by no means an indecipherable chaos but indeed to a high degree predictable. Such had been the world of Retz. In this perspective, politics was a great chess game, complete with its surprises and its rules of play. Debord's strategic conception was clearly of eighteenth-century inspiration, and it is not surprising that he had little to say about modern notions of strategy. This adherence to the classical model in which two armies, following lengthy preparatory maneuvers, confront one another in a set battle, constitutes at once a major strength and a major weakness of Debord's thought, for it tends to reduce society to two opposing monolithic blocks, neither of which has any serious internal contradictions, and one of which may be either the proletariat, or simply the Situationists, or even just Debord himself.

On many occasions Debord admitted to an affinity for the baroque. Perhaps this had to do with the fact that the baroque transcended the "Classical-Romantic dichotomy" which the Situationists deemed "already so unfortunate in Marx" (IS 7/52); or else with the observation that the feudal lords of the baroque period had enjoyed the "free play of [an] irreversible time" (SS §140), the "relatively playful conditions" ensured by a semi-independence from the state (SS §189). Progress might have

---

101. Alice Becker-Ho and Guy Debord, Le "Jeu de la guerre," relevé des positions successives de toutes les forces au cours d'une partie (Paris: Gérard Lebovici, 1987).

brought such a life within everyone's reach, turned everyone into a "master without slaves," but instead the baroque world had been replaced by the bourgeois world of calculation and commodities. In their campaign against functionalism and in favor of play, the young Letterists already set great store by the baroque for the importance it lent each work of art as a creator of atmosphere and a generator of a style of life (*Pot.*, 157: *Dérive*, 54; *IS* 1/10). The most profound reason for Debord's interest in the baroque, however, is that it was the highest expression of the art of time, of historical time; in his words, it was "the art of change": the baroque and its sequels, "from Romanticism to Cubism," exuded the negative work of time, dissolving all attempts by various classicisms to congeal the state of society at a particular moment into a permanent condition of human life (*SS* §189). "Theater and festival, or theatrical festival—these were the essential moments of the baroque" (ibid.), for they were moments that expressed *transition*. There was thus a sense in which the baroque prefigured that "supersession and realization" of art to which the Situationists aspired. The transcendence of art had to usher in a life enriched at every instant by an outpouring of creativity, by a lavish spirit quite unmindful of conservation—not by imprisonment in works of art with claims on eternity.

One of the spurs to the baroque sensibility was an acute awareness of human fragility with respect to time. Debord for his part gave the Situationist project a kind of existential underpinning: the acceptance of the passage of time as opposed to traditional art's reassuring fixation of time and embrace of the eternal. We have already seen that he conceived of history as the essence of man and condemned the negation of history by the false eternal present of the spectacle. In his *Rapport sur la construction de situations,* he writes: "The main affective drama in life, if one discounts the perpetual conflict between desire and a reality hostile to desire, must surely be the feeling of time slipping away. The Situationist attitude here, in contrast to aesthetic procedures that tended to still emotion, is to bank on that very slipping away of time" (*Rapp.*, 700). "Constructed situations" differed from traditional works of art by virtue of their rejection of any wish to create something lasting (*IS* 4/10; *Dérive*, 100). Thus the antagonism between life and survival also exists on the artistic plane as the antagonism between life and "survival through the work" (*IS* 7/6; *SIA*, 78).

"The sensation of time slipping by has always been a keen one for me, and I have been attracted by it as others are attracted by the void, or by water" (*OCC,* 277; *In girum,* 72). The deep theme of Debord's adventure is contained in the words "O, gentlemen, the time of life is short! . . . An if we live, we live to tread on kings."[102] Contrary to the lesson of exchange-value, which is the illusion that everything is always possible, because everything is equivalent, the qualitative, like passion, can arise only from a consciousness of the irreversibility and uniqueness of human actions. "But those who have chosen time as their weapon know that it is also their master; and that they cannot complain about this. It is also the master of those without weapons, and indeed in their case a harsher one" (OCC, 254; In girum, 53). Likewise in the spectacle the "social absence of death" is simply the reverse side of the absence of death: "the consciousness of the spectator can have no sense of an individual life moving toward self-realization, or toward death" (SS §160). An unmistakable sign of the "pro-Situationist's" ineptness is thus the refusal to recognize this dimension: "Time frightens him because it is made of qualitative leaps, of irreversible choices, of occasions which will never return" (VS, 47; Eng., 43). That is why such people, "who have not yet begun to live, but who are saving themselves for a better period, whence their immense fear of growing old, expect nothing less than a permanent paradise" (OCC, 254; In girum, 53). They are the very opposite of Debord's companions of 1952, who never "left these few streets and these few tables where the culminating point of time had been discovered," where "time burned with more heat than elsewhere, and would never suffice" (OCC, 235, 239; In girum, 38, 41), where one heard "the roar of the cataract of time" and declaimed, "Never again will we drink so young" (Pan., 39; Eng., 28).

Debord's writings, and especially the last ones, are notable too for the beauty of their many quotations. Pride of place is accorded those which deal with the vanity of human beings and the slipping away of time: Omar Khayyám and Shakespeare, Homer and Ecclesiastes. In 1980, Debord published a French translation of the fifteenth-century Spanish poem Coplas de Don Jorge Manrique por la muerte de su padre, whose author, in mourning for his father, reflects that "qualquiere tiempo passado/fué mejor" (any past time/were better).[103] This mood, coupled with Debord's extreme contempt for the petty lives of those who passively submitted to the spectacle, eventually turned him, like King Solomon, into a "contemner of the world" (Pan., 36; Eng., 25); they also turned him into a figure comparable to the great moralists of the French classi-

---

102. Henry IV, Part I (V, ii, 81, 85). These lines serve as an epigraph for chapter 5 of The Society of the Spectacle.

103. Jorge Manrique, Stances sur la mort de son père (Cognac: Le Temps Qu'Il Fait, 1996), 7, 49.

cal period. By this time, Debord no longer felt in the least as though he were in the vanguard of a powerful social movement, but his claim to being the only free individual in a society of slaves gave birth to many pages of a sober beauty very rarely encountered today.

Yet this shift of emphasis in Debord's thinking—which led him to the sad conclusion that François Villon was right when he said "Le monde n'est qu'abusion" (The world is nothing but deception; *Pan.*, 84; Eng., 77)—did not prevent him from remaining a highly vigilant witness to his time. Sojourns in Italy in the seventies gave him the chance closely to observe a situation which in many ways resembled the kind of social revolt that he had always called for and to study the countermeasures taken by the authorities. "Italy sums up the social contradictions of the entire world," he wrote, "striving in an all too familiar way to solidify in a single country the repressive Holy Alliance of class power in both its bourgeois and bureaucratic-totalitarian versions" (*Pref.*, 108–9; Eng., 19). Debord and his Italian friends were among the first to accuse the state of manipulating the terrorism of the period so as to check subversive tendencies rendered particularly threatening by the fact that the workers were escaping from the traditional control of the Communist Party.[104] In his *Preface to the Fourth Italian Edition of "The Society of the Spectacle"* (1979), Debord analyzed the part played by the abduction of Aldo Moro and the function of the Italian Communist Party in the resolution of the state crisis; his conclusions are generally accepted today, but at the time they were completely beyond the pale. "The Italian authorities' version," he wrote, "was not credible for an instant. Its intent was not to be believed but to be the only version on offer" (*Pref.*, 102; Eng., 12). Years later, Italian parliamentary commissions would themselves find that the Red Brigades had been manipulated in some way by a faction within the state apparatus.

The Spectacle Twenty Years On

What he observed in Italy clearly informs a great deal of the analysis Debord offers in his *Comments on the Society of the Spectacle* (1988). His main thesis is based on the perception that in many countries "diffuse"

104. Thus in 1975, using the pseudonym "Censor," Gianfranco Sanguinetti issued his *Rapporto veridico sulle ultime opportunità de salvare il capitalismo in Italia* [A Veracious Report on the Last Chance of Saving Capitalism in Italy], a pamphlet purporting to have been written by a member of the *haute bourgeoisie* who saw participation by the Communist Party in the Italian government as the only hope of defusing subversive action by the workers. The hoax was successful and created quite a stir in Italy. Debord quickly translated the text into French (1976; see Bibliography 1).

spectacular power and "concentrated" spectacular power have now been combined in an "integrated spectacle" of which the Italy and France of the seventies were the pioneers (*Comm.*, 19; Eng., 8). In the combined system, the essential domination of the diffuse spectacle over the concentrated version is nevertheless accompanied by the introduction of a generalized *secrecy* and *falsification,* traits hitherto specific to authoritarian regimes. Unlike its predecessors, the integrated spectacle lets no part of the real society escape its control: instead of hovering above reality, it has "integrated itself into reality." Reality thus no longer "confronts [it] as something alien," for the integrated spectacle has been able to reconstruct reality to suit itself (*Comm.*, 20; Eng., 9). The continuity of the spectacle is its main achievement, in that it has successfully "raised a whole generation moulded to its laws" (*Comm.*, 18; Eng., 7); anyone who grows up under its rule speaks its language, even if their subjective intentions are quite at odds with it (*Comm.*, 39; Eng., 31). Never before has a system of government attained such a state of perfection as the integrated spectacle, which is why "all those who aspire to govern want to govern this [society]" and use the same methods to do so (*Comm.*, 30; Eng., 21). Debord stresses the great distance separating us from the era of pre-spectacular democracy, which now seems almost idyllic by comparison. Among those in power as much as among their opponents are many who have been too slow to grasp the kind of change that has come about and who remain unaware of "what obstacles" governments have been freed from (*Comm.*, 89; Eng., 88).

Comments is a short, dense book from which the optimistic tone used by Debord as late as 1979 has disappeared. By 1988, Debord no longer sees any sign of an organized force capable of opposing the spectacle, and he declares right away that he does not mean to consider "what is desirable, or merely preferable"; his comments are to be confined to "recording what is" (*Comm.*, 16; Eng., 5)—even if one can never completely rule out a future reversal of history (*Comm.*, 76; Eng., 73). Not that the necessary conditions for revolution are absent—but "it is only governments that think so" (*Comm.*, 86; Eng., 84). Within the integrated spectacle, struggles are being waged everywhere, but they almost always have an incomprehensible aspect and their essence remains veiled in secrecy. In the main, they are conspiracies *in favor of* the established order (*Comm.*, 77; Eng., 74), conflicts between different factions of the power structure, or, even worse, a pre-emptive counterrevolution—as when a spectacle of terrorism is set up to make the state appear as the lesser of two evils (*Comm.*, 33; Eng., 24).

Debord stresses that the tendency to see plots or the machinations of police and secret services everywhere—in short, the "conspiracy theory of history"—was indeed until recently a reductionist belief (*Comm.*, 63; *Eng.*, 59); today, however, secret police forces play "the pivotal role" in spectacular societies (*Comm.*, 81; *Eng.*, 79): it is they, along with other agencies operating clandestinely, who continually disseminate contradictory "information" on all aspects of life, so making it impossible to form a clear picture of anything. In this context, the police work in tandem with the media: with the disappearance of any kind of community (*Comm.*, 29; *Eng.*, 19), the individual's contact with the world is entirely mediated through images selected by others, who can define their content at will (*Comm.*, 36; *Eng.*, 27–28). In contesting every genuine trace of the historical past, the spectacle's aim is to suppress the knowledge that it is itself a "usurper" only just risen to power (*Comm.*, 26; *Eng.*, 16.); it hopes in this way, by removing every point of comparison, to impose itself as the best, indeed the only possibility. The spectacle creates a perpetual present where the constant reiteration of the same pseudo-novelties erases all historical memory (*Comm.*, 23–24; *Eng.*, 13); consequently no event can be understood in terms either of its causes or of its effects, and all logic, not only dialectical logic but even simple formal logic, is obliterated (*Comm.*, 36–38; *Eng.*, 28–31). Under such conditions it becomes possible to tell any lie, no matter how inconsistent and fantastic. Any claim made in the mass media, once it has been repeated two or three times, becomes true (*Comm.*, 28; *Eng.*, 19); and, by the same token, "when the spectacle stops talking about something for three days, it is as if it did not exist" (*Comm.*, 29; *Eng.*, 20). The past itself may be remodeled with impunity, as may a person's public image (*Comm.*, 27–28; *Eng.*, 18). And if perchance some truth or other should percolate through, the charge of "disinformation" is always ready to hand (*Comm.*, 51–55; *Eng.*, 44–49). All the autonomous science, genuine learning, and taste for independent and rigorous thought that distinguished the high bourgeois era is fast disappearing. It has become well-nigh impossible to "read" all the items of information and all the lies on offer, each of them corresponding to some particular interest or other. The items collide, overlap, and operate in highly sophisticated ways: many are tricks, and many openly acknowledge their mendaciousness the better to distract our attention from something else (*Comm.*, 60–61; *Eng.*, 56). Referring to two major disasters of the eighties, Debord remarks that people with a large investment in "under-sea tunnels will be favorably disposed to the hazards of ferries," while the "outraged" competitors of the Swiss pharmaceutical firm that polluted the Rhine valley were hardly concerned with the fate of the river (*Comm.*, 84; Eng., 82). Most events reported, however, are as difficult to fathom as the assassination of Olaf Palme (*Comm.*, 66; Eng., 62) or the case of "the mad killers of Brabant" (*Comm.*, 60; Eng., 55), even though they surely contain a "message."

In these circumstances, it is obvious that no real "public opinion" can now take form (*Comm.*, 23; Eng., 13), that the very notion of scandal is anachronistic (*Comm.*, 31; Eng., 22), and that the people who make the decisions are the self-same people who tell us "what they think of them" (*Comm.*, 17; Eng., 6). How could "citizens" still be said to exist in such a context? "Those who are always watching to see what happens will never act: such must be the spectator's condition" (*Comm.*, 31; Eng., 22). To make matters even worse, an "all-powerful economy" that has "lost its reason" (*Comm.*, 46; Eng., 39) deprives the spectacle itself of any strategic vision (*Comm.*, 30; Eng., 20), prodding it more and more to act against the very survival of humanity, as witness, most egregiously, the issue of nuclear power (*Comm.*, 44–45; Eng., 37–38). A stage has now been reached at which the spectacle ceases to obey even the laws of economic rationality (*Comm.*, 61; Eng., 56).

In such a world there is nothing whatever "archaic" about the Mafia. Obscurantism, its incubator, is everywhere on the rise, albeit in new forms. Blackmail, intimidation, extortion, the law of *omertà*—these are precisely the methods whereby the groups in power settle their affairs with a complete disdain for bourgeois legality (*Comm.*, 67–71; Eng., 63–67). No more perfect "modern prince" for our times could therefore be found than General Noriega, a man who "sells everything and fakes everything" (*Comm.*, 62; Eng., 58).[105]

As already noted, Debord now discerns no real opposition to the system and distrusts anyone laying claim to such a role. If the spectacle falsifies everything, it must also falsify the critique of society, and indeed it has gone so far as to cultivate a domesticated or "farmed" variety of social criticism (*Comm.*, 77; Eng., 74–75), deliberately supplying those who are not liable to be satisfied by the standard explanations with supposedly restricted information, from which, nevertheless, the really essential material is missing. And that is not all, for the integrated spectacle's "highest ambition" is "to turn secret agents into revolutionaries,

---

105. These remarks were made more than a year before Noriega's downfall; in the end, perhaps, the general's provocations and play-acting simply went too far. This outcome would have appealed to the admirer of Retz in Debord.

and revolutionaries into secret agents" (*Comm.*, 21–22; Eng., 11). Thus "no one can be sure that they are not being tricked or manipulated" (*Comm.*, 85; Eng., 83). Such a system has every reason to defend itself, because it represents "a fragile perfection" (*Comm.*, 30; Eng., 21) and can no longer survive reform, even of its "most trifling detail" (*Comm.*, 82; Eng., 80). Henceforward the main enemy of the spectacle will be the spectacle itself: its warring factions broadcast a mass of false or unverifiable information that makes calculations extremely difficult, even for those at the commanding heights of society. The spectacle's main problem, in a word, is that its jettisoning of all logic, all sense of history, all contact with reality, eventually makes it incapable of managing society in a way that makes sense, even from its own point of view.

When Debord's *Comments* first appeared, some of its theses may well have seemed rather startling. One might have been excused for wondering whether Debord, who had probed so deeply into the roots and mechanisms of power in the modern world, had somehow been converted to a "primitive" view of domination that saw intrigue and espionage everywhere. There is no denying, however, that the years since the book's publication have confirmed its claims in myriad ways. In the wake of the collapse of the Eastern European regimes, the preponderant part played in those events by the secret services of the countries concerned became quite clear: they had not hesitated to organize protest demonstrations or to add fuel to the flames by spreading rumors about supposed assassinations, as in Prague in 1989. It now appears that in the former East Germany almost all the leaders of the opposition to the Stalinist regime worked for the secret police, or "Stasi." Perhaps it would be more accurate to say that a portion of the evidence upon which these charges are now being based was forged earlier by interested parties as ammunition for future use against their rivals: the Stasi archives have been opened, but a good many documents could well have been falsified by the Stasi itself, which may indeed still be operating under cover. Meanwhile, we can only speculate as to the possible role of the Stasi chief Markus Wolf in the run-up to the capitulation and recycling of the country's Stalinist bureaucrats.

In Rumania, distortion by the media was especially flagrant: the Western press cleverly used photographs of the victims of repression in Timosoara to support fatality figures that had in fact been multiplied tenfold, thus effectively fanning the flames of revolt.[106] The numbers of dead at

---

106. After writing these lines on a "fact" that had by then been widely reported, particularly in France, I was told by a participant in the Timosoara revolt that the scale of the

Tienanmen Square in 1989 seem likewise to have been much exaggerated. During the Gulf War, the long list of Saddam Hussein's crimes was eked out by the worldwide distribution of the picture of an innocent cormorant soaked in oil, the presumed victim of Iraq's destruction of wells; only after the war did someone point out that no such cormorant ever visited the Gulf region during the spring, at which point it was admitted that this was a file picture of a bird caught up in an ecological catastrophe in Brittany years earlier. More important, for all the media's chatter about the "global village," the fact is that we were never told how many Iraqis died in the Gulf War. Fifteen thousand? One hundred and fifty thousand? No one knows. All information released had to conform absolutely with the interests that controlled its sources. Sometimes there may be comfort to be drawn from the fact that the world may not be quite as terrible as it appears in the media; on the other hand, we have to reckon with everything that the media systematically conceals. Debord's *Comments* makes the perhaps extravagant claim that numerous people who would normally be considered beyond suspicion, particularly among artists, are in fact associated with the secret services of the state; and indeed we have now learned that many of the writers of the former East Germany were police informers. And the export of Pop Art to Europe in the early sixties was supposedly decided upon at the highest level of the United States government and organized by the CIA.[107]

Italians may well need less convincing than others when it comes to the scathing views set forth in *Comments:* they are, after all, only too well acquainted with the interpenetration of Mafia and politics, and more generally with the creation of new logics of influence-peddling based in the main on access to certain secrets (*Comm.*, 65; Eng., 61). Anyone in Italy who followed the official inquiries into an event such as the "tragedy of Ustica," when, on 27 June 1980, a plane with eighty-one people on board crashed into the sea, probably brought down by a missile "of unknown origin," or into the "state massacres" of the seventies, knows full well what it means to be inundated with countless contradictory versions of the truth, all presented by so-called experts, so that it becomes quite impossible to identify the real interests involved. What Debord describes is the combination of the oldest with the most modern methods of domination, and this is an area where Italy probably leads the world.

---

tragedy was in fact even greater and that the figure of four thousand dead was a serious underestimate. Whatever the truth of the matter, the point is that it is extremely difficult in our "global village" to get any clear picture of events at all.

107. Or so says Enrico Baj; see his *Cose dell'altro mondo* (Milan: Elèuthera, 1990), 72–73.

One might reasonably object, nevertheless, that there is nothing so very new about such phenomena. The cases of many powerful figures of the past cast not a little doubt on the claim that "for the first time in history it is possible to govern without the slightest understanding of art or of what is authentic and what is impossible" (*Comm.*, 57; Eng., 52).

There seems, however, to have been some hesitation on Debord's part about the question whether the spectacle is in crisis or not. The social agitation of the seventies, and perhaps also a wish to assign as much significance as possible to 1968 (and hence to himself), led him (in *Comments*) to assert that nothing is as it was. In 1979 he had written that the spectacle began by "believing itself loved," but "now it no longer promises anything. It no longer says: 'What appears is good, what is good appears.' It simply says 'It is so.'" And that was why "its inhabitants have split into two parties, one of which wants this society to disappear" (*Pref.*, 110, 112; Eng., 21, 23). A few years earlier still, he had observed that "the spectacle does not debase men to the point of making them love it" (*OCC*, 165; *Films*, 121). *Comments* asserts that modern society is now content merely to intimidate, being well aware that "its innocent air has gone forever"; "no one really believes the spectacle," which indeed inspires "general contempt" (*Comm.*, 84, 65, 63; Eng., 82, 60, 59). Today "servitude" offers no compensatory advantage and "truly wants to be loved for itself" (*Pan.*, 84; Eng., 77). In short, the spectacle no longer has the approbation of its subjects, and this amounts to a considerable defeat. Debord's chief claim to glory, in his own view, is that he "helped bankrupt this world."[108] In his presentation of the reprint edition of *Potlatch*, he asserts that the ideas expressed therein "eventually brought ruination" to the "banalities" of that period (*Pot.*, 8–9).

All of this sits uneasily with the analysis, also proposed in *Comments*, according to which the spectacle is more highly perfected than ever and that it "has succeeded in raising a whole generation moulded to its laws" (*Comm.*, 18; Eng., 7). The fact is that the last of Debord's works are by no means concerned with the struggle between masses in revolt and the spectacle but rather with the imbecility of a world where everyone has succumbed to the spectacle's tyranny.

The truth may well lie somewhere between these two extreme positions, to which Debord was led by two contending needs: the need to magnify the historical changes provoked by the SI and the need to point up his own uniqueness against the backdrop of a sombre world. From a

108. Debord, *Considérations*, 92.

less psychological point of view, it is certainly arguable that the spectacle now generates far less enthusiasm than it once did, that people who
truly believe in it are few and far between, but that there are many who
know how to turn participation in it to their own account. On the other
hand, to say, as Debord does, that "the reigning imposture may have been
able to get anyone and everyone's approval, but at least it will have had
to do without mine," has something overweening about it and under-
estimates the antagonists that spectacular capitalism continues to arouse
more or less everywhere.[109] We shall return to this issue in Part 3.

109. Ibid., 91.

Part 3 | Theory Past and Present

The Situationist Critique in Historical Context

It is worth considering the place of the Situationist critique within modern French thought, both Marxist and non-Marxist, for this will make it easier to see to what extent that critique ran counter to the mainstream in the sixties but also how close it was, objectively, to some other currents.

French Marxism has always presented several peculiarities. In the first place, it has to be remembered that socialist thought in France was traditionally less Marxist than elsewhere, much to the benefit of such authors as Proudhon and Fourier. When it did claim allegiance to Marx, French socialism was hopelessly split into two strands that never really came together: on the one hand there was a "Marxism for the people," reduced to the bare bones and highly pedagogical, which the French Communist Party offered as a catechism to its faithful; on the other hand, reemerging with each generation, was the "intellectual" version, refined to the point of "baroque sophistication" and invariably tending to combine Marx with any number of other authors and to read him through lenses borrowed from elsewhere.[1] "Marx was in turn Hegelian-ized, Kierkegaard-ized, abundantly Heidegger-ized—in short, 'revised' in one way or another before having been properly assimilated."[2] The unsatisfactory results of such enterprises, along with the fact that their proponents were for the most part thinkers, whether within the universities or elsewhere, who were paid by the state, generally meant that "critical Marxism" was rapidly transformed into a critique of Marx himself and ultimately into a condemnation of him. A kind of champion and pioneer here was the journal *Arguments*—a favorite target of the Situationists—which followed this trajectory perfectly during the few years of its

1. Daniel Lindenberg, *Le Marxisme introuvable* (Paris: Calmann-Lévy, 1975), 243. My discussion here is based in some respects on Lindenberg's account.
2. Ibid., 9.

existence (1957–63).[3] The *Arguments* group nevertheless contributed a good deal by way of translations into French—many of which the Situationists made great use of—including the first publication in French of works by the young Lukács, Korsch, Marcuse, Reich, and Adorno. Before long the theorists of *Socialisme ou Barbarie* would follow in the footsteps of those of *Arguments*, and after 1968, as everyone knows, apostate "Marxists" were two a penny.[4]

French Marxism has always stressed particular aspects of Marx's work and downplayed others. It has often preferred the young Marx, the critic of the "alienation of the human essence," to the Marx of the critique of political economy; at other times, however, the "mature Marx" has been contrasted in the most absolute way to the young Marx. In either case, the question of alienation was detached, if not flatly opposed, to the question of political economy. In the main, French Marxist intellectuals have chosen to confine themselves to the social sphere and to the "superstructure." Their analyses have almost always had an abstract and philosophical character, with ethical and aesthetic overtones, and this holds good for authors as diverse as Sartre, Lefebvre, and Althusser. A basic misunderstanding occurred at the start and indeed survives in many milieus today: the rejection of economic determinism, which was identified with Stalinism, led to a confusion between simply *observing* the deterministic character of capitalism and *approving* of it.[5] The fact is, however, that the fetishistic nature of a commodity-driven society cannot be wished away by the mere assertion that "in reality" the subject, even a subject created by means of capitalist socialization, is somehow independent or that the tendency of "economic laws" to become autonomous is mere illusion. Even Debord fell prey to the idea that the automatism of value could be explained in terms of conscious acts on the part of presupposed subjects. He held that history is produced exclusively by human actions; thus an SI text of 1970 speaks of "history, that is to say those who make it," while elsewhere Debord describes the revolution as "a system of human relations" (*VS*, 161, 72; Eng., 138, 68).

---

3. The complete run of the journal has been reprinted in two volumes (Toulouse: Privat, 1983).

4. For a withering critique of some of these authors (Glucksmann, Castoriadis, etc.) from a perspective very close to that of the Situationists, see Jaime Semprun, *Précis de récupération* (Paris: Champ Libre, 1976).

5. Richard Gombin sees the rejection of economic determinism as the defining trait of "leftism," thus excluding even "extreme communists" from the category (*Les Origines du gauchisme* [Paris: Le Seuil, 1971], 70; Eng. trans. by Michael K. Perl: *The Origins of Modern Leftism* [Harmondsworth, Middlesex: Penguin Books, 1975], 56).

This kind of "subjectivism" betrays the fact that Situationist theory has roots in existentialism. Whereas Debord's thought differs radically from the predominant thought of the sixties—everything claiming to be "modern" around 1968 was strictly anti-Hegelian, even when it also claimed to be Marxist—it certainly belongs in many respects to the philosophical generation that asserted itself in the fifties.[6] Thus the humanist and historicist Marxism of a Sartre presents not a few parallels with Situationist ideas, even though the Situationists expressed the greatest contempt for Sartre, denouncing him variously for Stalinism, eclecticism, or just plain "imbecility" (*IS* 10/75–76; *SIA,* 179–81). Like Lefebvre before them, the Situationists criticized existentialism for taking lived experience as it presents itself today and identifying this with the entire possible range of reality. Still, there is no denying that Sartre's work deals, albeit from a different standpoint, with such conceptions as "situation," "project," lived experience, and praxis. And Sartre's confident view of the individual shaping his own fate within history, and the distinction he draws between "things" and "men," or in other words the central role of a strong "subject," clearly have echoes in Debord. Even if one cannot speak here of "influence" in the strict sense of the word, it is hard to imagine that Debord was not inevitably affected by the particular cultural climate that prevailed in his youth. There is a sense in which Isou's Letterism constituted an extreme wing of the existentialist movement. And *Socialisme ou Barbarie* was clearly involved in some ways with phenomenology.[7]

In France, an effective understanding of Marx was hindered by a long-standing resistance to Hegel. Up until about 1930, Hegel had no entrée into the French intellectual world, and when he did finally make his way in, he did so as an "existentialist"; he was then interpreted for a long time in the light of Alexandre Kojève's important but highly idiosyncratic reading. Generally speaking, French Hegelians were not Marxists, and often French Marxists were not Hegelians, or even, like Althusser, explicitly anti-Hegelian. The revival of Marx in the sixties, or at least of a particular way of understanding him, was in reality—like the renewed interest in Freud or Nietzsche—a *reaction* against the preeminence that

---

6. See Vincent Descombes, *Le Même et l'autre: Quarante-cinq ans de philosophie française (1933–1978)* (Paris: Minuit, 1979), 24. Despite its many shortcomings, this book serves, read *ex negativo,* as a useful account of Situationist theory (which Descombes never mentions) and as a guide to what distinguishes that theory from its contemporaries.

7. Claude Lefort was a student and friend of Maurice Merleau-Ponty's and edited his posthumous writings.

Hegel, along with Husserl and Heidegger, had enjoyed for the previous three decades.[8]

Debord belongs to the small company of French Hegelian Marxists, and he always proudly acknowledged this association. The main point here is certainly not his occasional quoting of Hegel, which at times recalls a similar habit among the Surrealists, refreshing if somewhat superficial. Sartre certainly, and Debord by a perhaps more indirect route, came under the influence of Kojève's interpretation, as presented in his famous courses of the thirties.[9] Kojève accentuated struggle and the tragic dimension in Hegel rather than the theme of final reconciliation. His reading centered on man and his history, explicitly disregarding a nature that knew nothing of difference or of the negative. The motor of the human, for Kojève, was desire, expressing itself as the consciousness of a lack, of a negative principle. By denying things as they are given, man creates, and creates truth—itself a product of historical action. The negative, and nothingness, which had been contested by neo-Kantian and Bergsonian philosophies, were reaffirmed by Kojève, and in his wake by Sartre, who viewed the possibility of negating the existing world as the ground of human freedom.

The precise attitude to the negative adopted by Debord, by the Letterists and Situationists, is not easy to pin down. In the fifties, when art had grown particularly repetitive, they scorned the void, the nothingness, of bourgeois culture of which existentialism was for them a mere variant; they poked fun at "Merleau-Ponty's dialectical nothingness"—a "void that does not even bother to conceal itself" (Pot., 220). If the Letterists were Dadaists, they were exponents of "positive Dadaism" only (Pot., 43). On the other hand, great importance was attributed to negation, to the necessity of destroying the existing order before creating a new one. One of the SI's achievements, in its own eyes, was to have made its "unknown theory" known to "the subjectively negative part of the [revolutionary] process, to its 'bad side'"—a "bad side" to which the SI itself belonged (VS, 14–15; Eng., 12–13). "The negative vanishes along with the positive that it negates" (OCC, 145; Films, 114). It should be remembered that in this theoretical context destruction and negation are always taken in a Hegelian sense, that is, as "the negation of the negation" and as a transition to the next stage.

8. See Descombes, Le Même et l'autre, 13.

9. Debord also had a direct acquaintanceship with the teaching of the other great French interpreter of Hegel, Jean Hyppolite, whose courses at the Collège de France he sometimes attended around 1967.

Such an approach is of course diametrically opposed to any proc-
lamation of the "death of man," of "history without a subject," or to
any identification of the motor of history with "structures." Debord sees
structuralism as the chief apologetic ideology of the spectacle, denying
history and seeking to freeze presently existing social conditions as immutable structures (SS §196); he mocks structuralist thinking as "an academic approach fit for . . . middle-range managers" (SS §201) and as "a
thought underwritten by the State" (SS §202). In a more general way,
structuralism—which itself perceived May 1968 as the refutation of its
own theses, as witness Claude Lévi-Strauss exclaiming that in the aftermath of those days objectivity was abandoned and structuralism was
"no longer in fashion"[10]—has sought like other theories of the sixties
and seventies to show that the very idea of revolution is an implausible,
illogical, and ridiculous notion. This might well be viewed as a parallel,
on the plane of ideas, to the actual destruction of all the social bases of a
possible revolution, "from trade unions to newspapers, and from cities to
books" (Comm., 82; Eng., 80). Nor does this in any way run counter
to the fact that structuralism has aspired at times to a "critical" role, or
to the discovery by the editors of the journal Tel Quel of an "isomor-
phism" between aesthetic and political avant-gardes, in that works such
as those of Joyce and Mallarmé indeed demolish "bourgeois codes" and
are thus superior to the products of "socialist realism" (which products,
one cannot help but recall, these same discoverers had been praising to
the skies but a few years earlier).[11]

For a while, from about 1965 to about 1975, the abandonment of
Marxist theory depended to a great extent on the notions of "desire"
and of "the imaginary"; in this connection, it suffices to evoke the names
of Castoriadis ("who believes no doubt, here as in other areas, that talking about something is the same thing as having it" [IS 10/79]), Deleuze, and Lyotard. It is true that these concepts had played a big part
in all attempts to liberate individual lived experience, especially those of
Surrealism. The Situationists themselves belong to this tradition, but the
great originality—and in a sense too the limitations—of their ideas in
this area is their conception of desire as a force that is not *unconscious*
and bound to *needs* but instead *conscious* and chosen by the individual.
Debord did not share the Surrealists' faith in "the infinite richness of the

10. Quoted in the New York Times, 31 December 1969, as cited by Mark Poster, Existential Marxism in Postwar France: From Sartre to Althusser (Princeton: Princeton University Press, 1975), 386.
11. See Descombes, Le Même et l'autre, 150.

unconscious imagination. . . . We now finally know that the unconscious imagination is poor, that automatic writing is monotonous" (*Rapp.*, 691; *SIA*, 19).[12] In contrast to need, desire is a pleasure and should be increased as much as possible. At the outset, the SI announced that "the truly experimental direction of Situationist activity consists in the setting up, on the basis of more or less clearly recognized desires, of a temporary field of activity favorable to those desires. This alone can lead to the clarification of the original desires and to the confused emergence of new ones" (*IS* 1/11; *SIA*, 43); the point to note here is that recognizing, defining, and developing one's own desires are conscious activities. Need, on the other hand, though clearly it cannot be suppressed, is often antagonistic to desire and lends itself easily to exploitation: "Habit is that natural process whereby desire—fulfilled, realized desire—declines to the level of need. . . . But our present economy is geared directly to the manufacture of habits, and manipulates people with no desires" (*IS* 7/17; *SIA*, 87). Capitalism is continually creating artificial needs, which have never existed as desires and which block the fulfillment of genuine desires (*Prelims.*, 344; *SIA*, 307). For Debord, desires are not a *part* of life that one leaves behind, once they have been satisfied, in order to get back to "serious matters." On the contrary, all human activities could well take the form of the fulfillment of desires and passions; this cannot occur, however, without mastery over one's own milieu and over all its material and intellectual means, and in the long term such mastery implies the conversion of all productive activity into *play*.[13]

The Situationists' refusal of the fashionable identification of desire with erotic or sexual desire, which was already a restriction, is also worthy of note. In an address of 1958, Debord rebuked Surrealism for its "participation in that bourgeois propaganda which presents love as the only possible kind of adventure possible under modern conditions of existence" (*IS* 2/33). And in 1961 he pointed out "how much the image of love elaborated and propagated in this society has in common with drugs. The passion involved is first of all presented as a denial of all other passions; then it is frustrated, and finally reappears only in the compensations of the reigning spectacle" (*IS* 6/24; *SIA*, 72).

The Situationists thus stood opposed to those theorizations of the dissolution of the subject by impersonal drives that have so frequently

12. The CoBrA group had already rejected the Surrealist cult of the irrational.

13. It may come as a surprise to many people that this vision is very close to that of Marx, so often accused of "fetishizing labor": Marx invokes the composing of music as an example of an activity combining a playful aspect with a serious application (*Grundrisse*, 611).

been offered over the last few decades. At the same time, however, their indifference to the unconscious sphere prevented them from registering its full weight and from appreciating its force as a causative factor in the persistence of the present social order. Still, they viewed the contribution of early psychoanalysis as positive, calling it "one of the most redoubtable eruptions yet to have begun making the moral order tremble"—even if Freud's unjustified conflation of the capitalist order with a supratemporal "civilization" was already an open door to every kind of future co-optation (*IS* 10/63).

We have seen that Debord conceived of both individual and collective liberation as a *coming to consciousness* and a recognition that what appear to be autonomous forces are in reality the work of man; in his view, the revolutionary project is "the consciousness of desire and the desire for consciousness" (*SS* §53). The unconscious, as it manifests itself today, is by no means a pure spring whose demands, were they satisfied, would lead straight to joy, or to revolution. Like the imaginary,[14] the unconscious is a product of history, and its irrationality is not a primal agency in opposition to a too "rational" world but rather a receptacle for all the oppressions of the past; the original impulse of psychoanalysis was not to justify either the unconscious or the world but to criticize both of them (*IS* 10/79). As early as the days of the Letterists in fact, Debord wanted to invent *new* passions, not live passions that already existed (*Rapp.*, 701).

If these positions put Debord very far away from Marcuse, as likewise from many other ultimately Rousseauist approaches, they bring him, by contrast, very close to Marx. The Situationists declared themselves in agreement with the Marxian precept that "the whole of history is nothing but the gradual transformation of human nature" (*IS* 10/79). There was no such thing, in their view, as some original human nature, complete with its desires and its imaginary register, that a bad society had later perverted. This is one of the places where Debord's rejection of any notion of an ontological subject is unequivocal.

True, the Situationists might seem at first glance to have a certain affinity with the kind of "Freudo-Marxism" that typically evokes Marcuse and Reich. There are indeed some resemblances between Marcuse's analyses and Debord's, but there is certainly no parallelism between the two as regards their respective influences on the events of May 1968. "Freudo-Marxism" was not at the root of 1968 in France; rather, it was

14. The Situationists rejected one of the most popular slogans of May 1968, "Imagination to Power," as "impoverished" and "abstract" (*IS* 12/4; *SIA*, 226).

incorporated into the movement in the immediate wake of May.[15] Thus, whereas the earlier books of Marcuse had not met with much success in France—*Eros and Civilization,* for instance, which appeared in French translation in 1963, is said to have sold only forty-odd copies in the next five years—*One-Dimensional Man* was published in May 1968 and was soon selling at the rate of about a thousand copies a day.[16] It is also important to recall that Marcuse was read at the time in a rather confused way: as bizarre as it may seem now, many students of that period evinced great enthusiasm for the idea of the sexual revolution while simultaneously becoming enraptured by Maoism and swelling with admiration for a far-off "cultural revolution" in China which until then only the Situationists had exposed as nothing more than a "power struggle" (*IS* 11/5; *SIA,* 187).[17]

The favorite polemical targets of such authors as Foucault, Deleuze, Derrida, Althusser, Baudrillard, and Lyotard are the concepts of the *dialectic* and of *identity.* The first is deemed incapable of transcending the "logic of identity" or of accounting for *difference.*[18] These authors reject the idea of a subject endowed with an identity sufficiently strong to remain unmodified, in its nucleus, amidst changes. It is easy to see that the abandonment of such a subject must evacuate all meaning from the idea of an alienation that the subject is potentially capable of resisting. The concept of alienation had aroused an intense philosophical debate around 1955, just as Debord was clarifying his own ideas.[19] In the sixties, and especially after 1968, this concept was jettisoned. If the subject of history is structures, or language, or libidinal drives, then there can be no "essence" of man susceptible of misdirection by a maladjusted society. Similarly, by refusing to see the work of art as an expression of lived experience, "semiotics" took up a position diametrically opposed to the way in which the Situationists viewed the works of the past.

It would doubtless be an exaggeration to treat the philosophies that became fashionable after 1968 as a direct response to Situationist ideas,

15. See Gombin, *Les Origines du gauchisme,* 167; Eng. trans., 127.

16. Sales figures for *Eros and Civilization* are from Daniel Cohn-Bendit, as cited in R. J. Sanders, *Bewegung tegen de schijn* (Amsterdam: Huis aan de Drie Grachten, 1989), 271. Those for *One-Dimensional Man* are from "Matériaux pour servir à l'histoire intellectuelle de la France, 1953–1987," *Le Débat* 50 (May–August 1988): 59.

17. Lindenberg, *Le Marxisme introuvable,* 30.

18. The idea of a non-identical dialectic, like the one that Theodor Adorno sought to develop, seems never even to have crossed the minds of these thinkers. On the question of difference, see Descombes, *Le Même et l'autre,* 93.

19. "Matériaux pour servir à l'histoire intellectuelle de la France," 176.

even though their proponents were often well acquainted with those ideas. These new theorists clearly announced their hostility to the "Cartesian" subject and hence to a whole long philosophical tradition; they also very often went so far as to state that their theories constituted a particularly radical critique of existing reality. As often as not, however, the claim that they were searching in this way for the deepest and most thoroughly hidden roots of capitalism served merely to conceal a subtle sabotaging of radical theory. If the causes of the ill are not concrete historical phenomena, such as the commodity economy or the modern state, but instead phenomena of a very general kind, as for instance the fact of thinking in terms of "identity," then it is nonsensical to propose the supersession of these problems. The "semioticians" indeed took the view that the concept of revolution operated on the same mental terrain as the system in place, to which they preferred to oppose the infinite horizons of "difference" or of "drives." The very idea of revolution was denounced as a myth or a "grand narrative," as a figure of human existence that has always existed and that is consequently far from having a concrete historical existence in the present.

A more direct reference to Situationist thinking is to be found in the theory of the *simulacrum,* which explicitly denies the possibility of distinguishing true from false and hence also the existence of any *authentic* reality that could be falsified. This theme has been developed in particular by Jean Baudrillard, who was obviously much influenced by Debord and who was once a research assistant of Lefebvre's. Baudrillard accepts the definition of existing society as a spectacle, but he detaches this concept from its material basis and views the spectacle as a "self-referential" system in which signs are no longer travesties of reality but reality itself. He is thus happily relieved of the need to concern himself with a cumbersome "truth" which now does not need unmasking for the very good reason that it is quite simply nonexistent. In Baudrillard's view the exchange of signs now occupies the whole of social space. Resistance to this state of affairs is logically impossible, for it would perforce need to rely on such concepts as content, meaning, or subject, all of which, according to Baudrillard, have themselves become signs only. It is curious to see how Baudrillard takes Debord's conceptions and, while seeming to radicalize them, actually inverts them. His supposedly critical theory really does nothing more than dream of a perfect spectacle, one delivered from any material foundation—in other words, a system of consumption unbeholden to production and thus unconcerned by its contradictions. Once placed in this context, the term "society of the spectacle" can easily be integrated into the jargon of journalism, and indeed one now meets it so used every day—a development that Debord had himself foreseen (SS §203).[20]

It would be a serious error to try to associate Debord with more or less "postmodern" theories concerned with communication, images, and simulation. When adepts of such theories hail Debord for his alleged "prophetic" gifts, they are clearly laboring under a misapprehension. To reduce the spectacle to the simple fact that it is impossible to verify everything with one's own eyes, and that one is therefore dependent on often very untrustworthy means of communication, is to avoid the real question. If not as old as the world itself, such an observation goes back at least as far as Francesco Guicciardini, writing in the sixteenth century: "No wonder that we are ignorant of what has happened in past ages, or of what is happening now in distant countries and remote cities. For if you note it well, you will perceive that we have no true knowledge even of the present, and of what goes on from day to day in our own town. Nay, often between the palace and the market-place there lies so dense a mist or is built a wall so thick that no eye can penetrate it; so that the people know as much of what their rulers are doing, or their reasons for doing it, as they know of what is being done in China. And for this reason the world is readily filled with empty and idle beliefs."[21] The issue, however, is not just the lack of fidelity of the image relative to what it represents but also the state of the actual reality to be represented. In this connection, it is worth recalling the distinction drawn in Part 1 of this book between a superficial conception of commodity fetishism, which sees it as merely a false representation of reality, and another view, which recognizes it as a distortion brought about by man in the actual production of his world. The critique of the "spectacle" should help us understand not only how television speaks of Bosnia but also the much more important question of why such a war occurs.

Those who are determined to attribute to Debord a metaphysical hostility toward the visual and the image would do well to consider, not only his films, but also what he says with such disarming simplicity in his foreword to the second volume of *Panégyrique*, which is composed

20. For an even cruder use of Debord, see for example Claudio Vicentini, ed., *Il Teatro nella società dello spettacolo* (Bologna: Il Mulino, 1983), where the editor acknowledges that no one would want to deny the fact of spectacularization but wonders why it is considered such a bad thing.
21. *Ricordi politici e civili*, redaction C, §141; English translation by Ninian Hill Thomson: *Counsels and Reflections of Francesco Guicciardini* (London: Kegan Paul, Trench, Trübner, 1890), 63.

mainly of photographs: "The reigning deceptions of the time are on the point of causing us to forget that truth may also be displayed by means of images. An image that has not been deliberately separated from its meaning can add great precision and certainty to knowledge. Nobody had ever cast doubt on this until these last few years."[22]

What Debord criticizes is not the image per se but the image-form as an extension of the value-form. Like the value-form, the image-form precedes all content and ensures that struggles between the various social agents are nothing but struggles over distribution. Thus both bourgeois and workers—to confine ourselves to the classical model—express their seemingly irreconcilable interests in a shared form, the money-form, which is absolutely not neutral or "natural," as is tacitly suggested, but which on the contrary constitutes the real problem. Similarly, in the spectacle, every content, whatever its nature, even one that claims to be in opposition, perforce manifests itself in the never innocent form of the spectacular image.

The Aporias of the Subject and the Prospects for Action

Here, as in other places, Debord transcends the conception of a subject ontologically antagonistic to capitalism while at the same time in a sense cleaving to it. The implicit abandonment of that conception in the analysis of the image-form, as just outlined, coexists in Debord with a discourse concerned with "communication" that has much in common with another favorite theme of the new Left, that of *manipulation*. On the basis of this concept, the advent of the commodity-based society, like that of oppressive societies of the past, is conceived of as an external aggression from an unspecified source against an already constituted subject that is "different" from the social order imposed by the "ruling classes." Such systems, which are contrary to the interests of the great majority, have inexplicably maintained their hegemony for millennia by means of a subtle "manipulation" supplementing a violence that is never of itself sufficient. The importance attributed by the Situationists to the betrayal by representatives of those whom they represent, and their subsequent well-nigh obsessional preoccupation with issues of organization, are clear signs of a fundamental delusion that affects the whole of the Left: the notion that the masses, proletarians, individuals, or subjects are manipulated, seduced, corrupted, fooled—that they can neither express

22. *Panégyrique*, vol. 2 (Paris: Arthème Fayard, 1997), "Avis."

themselves nor act autonomously. If only they were left to their own de-
vices, capitalist society would supposedly vanish in an instant like a bad
dream. No explanation is offered, however, as to where such a ready-
made subjectivity might have taken shape. We really have no good reason to believe that it ever existed in the past—save perhaps in some kind
of fragmentary form—only to be demolished by the corrosive action of
the commodity. The postulation of such an a priori status for the subject is a mainstay of the modernist Left, yet it absolves capitalism, without even realizing it, of its most grievous fault, namely that it prevents
the formation of that very conscious subjectivity many of whose necessary preconditions it has itself created. A mistaken response to this
problem is that offered by structuralism, for which the subject is not yet-
to-be-realized for the simple reason that the subject *cannot* exist; the
present society is thus implicitly accorded the status of an eternal human condition.

Ever since the action of the historical proletariat reached its climax
and the class was successfully integrated into capitalist society—thus
transforming a semifeudal society into a truly capitalist one—the Left
has been placing various pretenders upon the vacant throne of "the good
cause": Third World peoples, women, students, immigrants, the "excluded," data-entry keyboarders—even such disembodied phenomena as
sexuality, creativity, everyday life, and so on.[23] The militant spirit with
which some of these categories at times defend their interests tends to
obscure the fact that none of them, at any rate in their current form, is
external to the value-form and the money system.

The Situationists even believed that they had discovered the vastest
and most irreducible subject possible: "life." Unfortunately, this approach
does not solve the problem of the subject, as is demonstrated by the rigid
dichotomous vision to which it leads. The relationship of society to the
spectacle comes to be pictured as one between life and non-life. To the
commodity, the economy, and the spectacle, defined as "a negation of
life that *has become visible*," as "non-life," and as "the life, moving of
itself, of that which is dead"[24] (SS §10, §123, §215), is opposed life as
flux. Any attempt to interrupt the flow of time is construed as reification. It would certainly be a mistake to tax the Situationists with "vitalism" in any traditional sense, in the sense that Bergson or Simmel

23. Identifying the "revolutionary subject" with a proletariat redefined in an excessively broad way was nevertheless generally much more realistic than identifying it with a
circumscribed sociological population segment, as Marcuse did apropos of students.

24. As Debord informs us, this is the definition of money given by Hegel in the *Je-
nenser Realphilosophie*.

was a vitalist.[25] They in no way meant to criticize social institutions or art as extraneous to life as it actually exists today. When some critics described them, precisely, as "vitalists," they protested that they had formulated a "most radical critique of the poverty of all the life that is permitted" (*IS* 5/4). Undoubtedly they wished to contrast life and its reifications, but they wished to do so in the name of *another* life. Yet just as Bergsonism left a deep mark on French existentialism, no matter how much existentialism might deny it, it likewise exercised a not insignificant influence on Debord, chiefly in respect of the definition of temporal flux as a truly human dimension.[26]

One wonders, too, how far Debord's theories are open to a criticism often leveled at Lukács's *History and Class Consciousness,* which many have accused of transforming the concrete and historical problematic of fetishism into a set of generic and anthropological concerns. It is true that in Lukács's account reification arises from a failure of facts to dissolve into processes and ultimately indeed from the very existence of facts, the very existence of a material world. And if the material world cannot be abolished, we are obliged to infer that disalienation for Lukács must take place, as it did for Hegel, in the sphere of consciousness, and that it is on this plane that the "total man" is to be infused with life. Adorno also takes *History and Class Consciousness* to task for focusing its criticism on a form of consciousness, namely reification, when what need criticizing are the actual conditions under which men live and not the way in which those conditions present themselves to the mind.[27] Attempts have even been made to insert Lukács's book into a late-nineteenth-century tradition of "vitalism" in the broadest sense. The basic thesis of this current of thinking is said to be the necessity of things dissolving into a continuous movement, singular moments of which are erroneously fixed by the intellect. Alienation is identified in this context as the division between subject and object and described in terms of the existence of a world irreducible to the subject; the remedy proposed is the reduction, at the level of thought, of things to movement.

Is something of this to be found in Debord? He writes that it is of the essence of the spectacle that "it arrogates to itself everything that in human existence exists in a fluid state so as to possess it in a congealed

25. It would be equally mistaken to call Lukács a vitalist: he specifically rejected "irrationalist philosophies from Hamann to Bergson" (*HCC*, 110).

26. To have been influenced by Bergson, Debord would by no means have had to study him in any detail: the whole of French cultural life was long impregnated with Bergsonism.

27. See Theodor W. Adorno, *Negative Dialectics* (1966), trans. E. B. Ashton (New York: Seabury Press, 1979), 190.

form" (*SS* §35), so implying that fluidity corresponds to the human dimension. Similarly in Lukács we encounter the conviction that the very emergence of something qua "thing" is already a reification: "the recognition that social facts are not objects but relations between men leads eventually to the point where facts are wholly dissolved into processes" (*HCC*, 180). Debord tells us that in the spectacle "concrete things are automatically masters of social life" (*SS* §216) and that things have everything that living people lack: "it is *things* that rule, that are young—things themselves that vie with each other and usurp one another's places" (*SS* §62). In 1958, Debord announced that "it is a matter of producing ourselves, and not things that enslave us" (*IS* 1/21; *Oct.*, 90). Later he condemned the history produced by bourgeois society as merely "the history of the abstract movement of things" (*SS* §142). It must of course be stressed that Debord is referring to the commodity, not to the thing as such, and that he explicitly describes "coagulation" as a consequence, not a cause, of the spectacle (*SS* §35). The question is not just a terminological one, however, and Debord does indeed seem to concur in Lukács's desire to reduce everything to process. He thus characterizes the proletariat as "that class which is totally opposed to all reified externalizations" (*SS* §114). The most important point here is to make it as clear as can be that, in a society ruled by value, things are *in effect* "masters of social life"—but only because the autonomous social relations that govern social life have become objectified in them.

Debord dissents, however (and in this respect he is close to Marx, as also to André Breton), when it comes to another central tenet of vitalism and of *History and Class Consciousness*—a tenet embraced too by Max Horkheimer and Adorno in their *Dialectic of Enlightenment,* and by Herbert Marcuse: the charge that science, technology, and their quantitative methods are intrinsically reifying forces. We saw earlier that the Situationist project, at least at the start, was to equip a technological society with the means to "imagine what can be done with" its technology (*IS* 7/17; *SIA,* 87). When, later on, Debord turned his attention to the disasters produced by science, he did not lay the blame at the feet of science per se, but instead, evoking "the opposition to slavery that formed a significant part of its own history," he denounced the subordination of science to a "spectacular domination" that had "cut down the vast tree of scientific knowledge merely in order to make itself a truncheon" (*Comm.*, 46–47; *Eng.*, 39–40).

The Situationist dichotomy between life and non-life echoes a strong and simple opposition between "true" and "false." "True" social life is said to be "falsified" by the spectacle. "Truth" is conceived of by Debord in a static mode: it is no coincidence that he speaks on several occasions of something finally "discovered" or "revealed" in this connection. The words *mensonge* (lie, falsehood) and *mensonger* (deceitful) occur very frequently in *The Society of the Spectacle*, while the stress laid on "communication" likewise implies the notion of a truth veiled in falsehood but simply awaiting the moment when the veil will be torn aside and light shed.[28] A truth so pictured ought logically to belong to that subject, inalienable in its essence, which we spoke of above. The spectacle is described as "repressing all directly lived truth beneath the *real presence* of . . . falsehood" (*SS* §219), and the task of the revolutionary proletariat is the "'historic mission to establish truth in the world'" (*SS* §221). So inimical is the spectacle to truth that Debord likens it to a reign of madness, citing the comparison drawn by the psychiatrist Joseph Gabel between ideology and mental illness (*SS* §§217–19); similarly, the spectacle contradicts the very simplest of verities: "Saying that two and two make four is on the point of becoming a revolutionary act."[29] In his *Comments on the Society of the Spectacle*, Debord alludes frequently to the "completely illogical" character of the spectacle (*Comm.*, 36; Eng., 28). The notion of "secrecy," which is pivotal to this book, itself implies a truth existing beyond the reach of any manipulation—a concept of which the Hegel of the preface to *The Phenomenology of Mind* would doubtless have been somewhat skeptical. One sometimes gets the impression when reading Debord that he conceives of truth as a "reflection," after the fashion of Leninism and positivism; but when he observes that all logic disappears with the disappearance of dialogue, which is its social basis, he seems to return to a more mediated view (*Comm.*, 37; Eng., 29).

Nor does Debord ever make it clear whether the spectacle is merely a *false representation of reality* or whether it is in fact a *falsification of reality itself;* it is nevertheless possible to discern in his writings a growing preference for the second alternative. According to the *Comments,* the spectacle now has the means to falsify production as well as perception (*Comm.*, 20; Eng., 10). Just so long as one does not take it to mean the "manipulation" of a reality given once and for all, however, the concept of falsification as used by Debord is a very serviceable one. On the other hand, the notion that reality can be falsified creates conceptual

---

28. On *mensonge* and *mensonger,* see *SS* §§ 2, 102, 105, 106, 107, 108, 110, 111, 206.

29. *Considérations sur l'assassinat de Gérard Lebovici* (Paris: Gallimard, 1993), 55.

problems: by reference to what, or to what "authentic" other reality, could it be falsified? Here Debord's theory appears suddenly to embody what might be called a "Platonic" inheritance: phenomena with a concrete existence are apparently comparable with their models; bread and wine, for instance, products with whose adulteration Debord was much concerned, are judged by comparison with "real" bread or "genuine" wine. The term of comparison is not, of course, some "archetype" of wine floating in a Platonic heaven of ideas, but wine as it existed before the industrialization of agriculture. This clearly does not constitute any philosophical gauge of "authenticity," but it unquestionably constitutes a *palpable* reality. Debord likewise sets great store by exactitude in the definition of words, making language and language's older forms responsible for preserving the truth; and, following in the footsteps of George Orwell, Debord lambasts the new-speak that the spectacle has created for its own purposes.

The only possible solution here, one supplied in fact by Debord himself, is to be clear that the "authentic" is not being proposed as an absolute or as a static essence.[30] On the contrary, the subject and the subject's needs undergo a slow development (*SS* §68). Human history is the history of the subject's self-production through an interaction between the "self" and the subject's creations, which are always a reflection of that "self." A detached economy, and more generally every social agency, institution, and activity, by separating themselves off to the point where they emerge as autonomous powers, have had the effect of arresting this "organic development of social needs" and unleashing a "limitless artificiality" (*SS* §68).

Whereas it is impossible to decide what an "ontologically" true or authentic society might be like, it is perfectly feasible to assess the "ontological" falsity or inauthenticity of the society of the commodity. Value, as Marx shows in the opening pages of *Capital*, forcibly imposes equivalence upon things that are not equivalent. All the contradictions of the commodity, even its eventual crisis, are already contained in the "simple commodity-form," namely, "20 yards of linen = 1 coat."[31] But here

30. Initially the Situationists thought of *détournement* as a negation of the bourgeois cult of "authenticity." Michèle Bernstein labeled as "reactionary" such issues as "the real Henri II sideboard versus the fake Henri II sideboard, the fake canvas that is not signed," and so on (*IS* 2/27), but it is worth bearing in mind that these words date from 1958, when the general falsification of today was in its infancy.

31. "The simple, isolated, or accidental form of value. . . . (20 yards of linen = 1 coat, or: 20 yards of linen are worth 1 coat). . . . The whole mystery of the form of value lies hidden in this simple form. Our real difficulty, therefore, is to analyze it" (*Capital I,* 139). It is

we may go even further than Marx and, since the quantity has no significance, reduce the equation to "linen = coat." Linen is thus the same thing as a coat, or tea, or iron. In other words, "white = black." Obviously a society founded on such a principle is bound to come to a bad end.[32] It is thus quite possible to criticize capitalism, and especially the needs that are imposed on us, without immediately having to define what is "natural" or "just." At the same time, this objective demonstration of the falsity of capitalism gives the lie to postmodernist relativism, for which every social form is equally arbitrary and therefore in the last reckoning also equally justified.

Is it after all so desirable that everything in the world be a mirror of the subject? There are many authors whose critiques of alienation bring them to the point of wanting a world in which nothing at all remains alien to the subject. This is a position, however, which cannot be reconciled with the dialectical view that subject and object are not an ultimate duality and do not refer either to an ultimate unity; rather, they constitute one another in a reciprocal manner. Here we might well recall Adorno's critique according to which a fetishized concept of "totality" tends to institute a tyranny of the subject everywhere.[33] Adorno draws a distinction between the concept of reification, which he sees as justly critical of the fetishism of the commodity and of the unhealthy subordination of human beings to things, and the concept of "alienation," with which he associates the mentality of someone who "looks upon thingness as radical evil, [who] would like to dynamize all entity into pure actuality [and who] tends to be hostile to otherness." Such an absolute dynamism, however, "would be that absolute action whose violent satisfaction lies in itself, the action in which nonidentity is abused as a mere occasion."[34] For those over-preoccupied with reification, "inspired by the wishful image of unbroken subjective immediacy," Adorno recalls that "the total liquefaction of everything thinglike regressed to the subjectivism of the pure act. It hypostatized the indirect as direct. Pure immediacy and fetishism

---

indeed to the analysis of this form that Marx devoted most space; he deals much more quickly with the total form of value, the general form of value and the money-form, which are really just conclusions drawn from that main premise.

32. When the "cell-form" of bourgeois society is characterized in this way, it also becomes abundantly clear that the Hegelian negation of the principle of non-contradictoriness, with its celebrated opening equation, "being = nothingness," corresponds exactly to the reality of the world of commodities.

33. *Negative Dialectics*, 146–48.

34. Ibid., 191.

are equally untrue."[35] And he reminds "existentialists" that objectivity—here, the objectivity of metaphysical categories—and the non-identical, while they may indeed be the expression of a "sclerosed" society, can also indicate the real existence of the object world, failing whose acceptance and pacification the subject can never be anything but a tyrant.

The whole of Debord's theory, especially in its condemnation of "contemplation" and "non-participation," is characterized by a vigorous activism that sees any occasion when the subject is not shaping his world as an abdication. In the power of workers' councils, he writes, "the proletarian movement becomes its own product; this product is the producer himself, and in his own eyes the producer has himself as his goal" (*SS* §117); likewise the power of councils "aspires to be recognized—and *to recognize itself*—in a world of its own design" (*SS* §179). What is involved here, without any doubt, is the unity of subject and object. Obviously, however, Debord does not apprehend this unity in the form of a total identity but rather in that of a world where objectifications standing absolutely opposed to the individual have been obviated. The very notion of the *dérive*—as also in a more general way that of *aventure*—presupposes a world that is unknown and "other" relative to the subject. An SI text of 1970 quotes Hegel's *Science of Logic* to the effect that "contradiction is the source of all movement, all life," whereas identity is a dead thing (*VS*, 153; Eng., 132).[36] The end of reification as it exists is not taken by Debord to entail a state of motionless repose, without conflict or otherness; on the contrary, a liberated humanity will "at last be able to surrender itself joyously to the true divisions and never-ending confrontations of historical life" (*Pref.*, 112; Eng., 22).[37] Nor is he opposed to the idea of losing oneself in the outside world, but he wants a world that gives one the desire to get lost in it (*SS* §161). Once again we are reminded of the Marx of the *Economic and Philosophical Manuscripts of 1844:* "it is only when man's object becomes a *human* object or objective man that man does not lose himself in that object. This is only possible when it becomes a *social* object for him and when he him-

---

35. Ibid., 374.

36. The text in question is "Communiqué of the SI concerning Vaneigem," which severely criticizes Raoul Vaneigem just after his resignation from the group. In Vaneigem's *Revolution of Everyday Life* it is indeed possible to discern the desire for a total correspondence between self and world, and at times this wish does not seem to be far from mysticism, a tendency that made its appearance on various occasions in the ranks of the Letterists and Situationists.

37. Whereas others talked of "the end of history," the Situationists wanted at last to enter true history and to leave *prehistory* behind (*IS* 4/36; *VS*, 35: Eng., 32).

self becomes a social being for himself."[38] Unitary urbanism was conceived of as the construction of a genuinely human milieu where people would deliberately wander off the beaten path and go *à la dérive*.

In many ways the Situationist theory partakes of an *optimism* that was peculiar to the fifties and sixties. When the Letterists first began developing their ideas, the Second World War and Nazism were but a few years in the past. The thinking of many people was deeply marked by the horrors that had occurred and by the determination to make sure that such things would never happen again. By contrast, the Letterists, and later the Situationists, rarely alluded to these matters. The possibility of the world's falling back into barbarism preoccupied them far less than it did others, and they were much more concerned about new technological means not being used in the service of freedom; in short, they were more afraid of the preservation of the status quo than of historical regression.[39]

By the nineteen-fifties the domination of nature had reached the point where its impact could easily be felt even on the plane of everyday life, though as yet no questions, whether ecological or of any other kind, were raised about "the price of progress." We know, of course, how sanguine that period was about the prospect of technology ushering in a reign of human happiness. Initially the Situationists hailed the automation of production as a harbinger of the liberation of humanity from thousands of years of bondage to toil; the whole Situationist program of a "civilization of play" was founded on this presumption. Debord several times cited Marx's observation that humanity never sets itself problems that it cannot solve (see for example *Pot.*, 187). The prime task was the creation of a social order that would use its technical means in the interest of the society as a whole and not in the interest of a single class and its desire to rule. Clearly this view continued to endorse the classic schema of the development of the forces of production leading to the overthrow of the relations of production. One is often struck, when reading the early issues of *Internationale Situationniste*, by the expressed certitude that society is evolving in the right direction even if its superstructures are for the moment not falling into line. At this time the Situationists had a good deal of confidence in the world's ability to rid itself of the spectacle.

38. *EW,* 352.
39. Adorno, for instance, felt driven to accept modern society as a lesser evil, fearing that any attempt to change it might lead to something worse.

On another plane society seemed to have succeeded in controlling its own mechanisms. The sustained growth rates, full employment, high wages, and lack of serious economic crises that were characteristic of the fifties and sixties were looked upon by many as durable achievements. Leftists especially felt that capitalism would never again do anything to interfere with this tendency, which, thanks to the famous "integration of the proletariat," guaranteed the system's stability.[40] The capitalist system of production was no longer perceived as inherently contradictory and bound in the long term to go into crisis; rather, it was seen as the outcome of a preinstituted will capable of directing the course of its development. The condemnation of the economy as a separate sphere, a cardinal point for Debord, is not, however, at odds with hopes placed in automation, which could help transform material production into a pure means, intended to satisfy human desires rather than enlist them in the development of an autonomous economy.

The nineteen-seventies were to demonstrate that "affluence" was revocable. So long as essential needs seem to have been definitively addressed, the question whether something better might not exist arises much more readily; or, to put it in Situationist terms, when *survival* is guaranteed, *life* becomes a demand. It was thus perfectly functional from the capitalist point of view when, in the seventies, the traditional crisis returned, complete with anxiety about employment and falling real wages. When you are surrounded by millions of unemployed workers, or in other words by unlimited potential scab labor, the assembly line once again comes to resemble a life line. This was a period, too, when a rising awareness of the threat of ecological catastrophe and a revival of the "cold war" were also putting the problem of mere survival back on the front burner.

Like any viable concept, the notion of the spectacle is in some degree bound to its time, that of the "cybernetic" welfare state and the high tide of Fordism, when capitalism claimed to have resolved its traditional contradictions, including its need to bar the majority of the population from the enjoyment of abundance.[41] It must nevertheless be acknowledged that

40. See for example the continuation of Cornelius Castoriadis, "Le Mouvement révolutionnaire sous le capitalisme moderne," *Socialisme ou Barbarie*, nos. 32 and 33 (April and December 1961); reprinted in Castoriadis, *Capitalisme moderne et révolution*, vol. 2 (Paris: Union Générale d'Éditions, Collection 10/18, 1979). English translation: "Modern Capitalism and Revolution," in *Political and Social Writings*, ed. and trans. David Ames Curtis, vol. 2 (Minneapolis: University of Minnesota Press, 1988), 258–315.

41. For a criticism of the concept of "the spectacle," see David Jacobs and Christo-

even at that time the critique developed by Debord and the Situationists, for all that it was the most advanced, succeeded no better than its rivals in identifying possible remedies. It is certainly not enough to point, as many do, to alienation and its discontents as a sufficient motor for a new revolutionary movement. The years after 1968 showed just how impossible it is to change society through individual action, with no program and no organization, by virtue of a slow infiltration of new mores or changes in the cultural climate, for each such innovation gets incorporated into an essentially unchanging whole. Debord had sought to designate a force having a real prospect of intervening, but the hopes he placed in the proletariat turned out in the long run to be illusory. In addition the Situationists overestimated the power of theory. When history is seen as a *prise de conscience,* of course, the role assigned to theory will inevitably be a very significant one, and in Debord's view the agitation of 1968 and its aftermath arose essentially from the spread of Situationist theory: "so great is the power of words uttered at their moment" (*OCC,* 258; *In girum,* 56).[42]

The difficulty of gauging the real possibilities of the Situationist critique and its practical application was exacerbated too by the lack of any answer to the question whether the critique of the spectacle is itself part of the spectacle or just how it might be possible to position oneself *outside* the spectacle. At the beginning of the nineteen-seventies, following the "success" of the Situationists, the objection was frequently raised that the dissemination of Debord's ideas, written work, and films meant that he was himself participating in the spectacle. Debord for his part put these objections down to an envy fueled by the fact that it had now become impossible to ignore his theories. It is hard, all the same, to explain how the world could be said, on the one hand, to be full (around 1970, at any rate) of resistance to the spectacle, while at the same time virtually nothing seemed to escape the Situationists' verdict of "spectacular opposition."

---

pher Winks, *At Dusk: The Situationist Movement in Historical Perspective* (Berkeley: Perspectives, 1975), 42–43.

42. "So great" indeed that Debord was convinced that if his friend Gianfranco Sanguinetti had only gone public, at the moment of Aldo Moro's kidnapping in 1978, with his conviction that this act was orchestrated by the Italian secret police, it might well have caused the whole charade to collapse. Sanguinetti subsequently published *Del Terrorismo e dello Stato: La Teoria e la pratica del terrorismo per la prima volta divulgate* (Milan: n.p., 1979), of which a French translation with a new preface by the author, *Du Terrorisme et de l'Etat* (Paris: n.p., 1980), has been translated into English by Lucy Forsyth and Michel Prigent as *On Terrorism and the State* (London: Chronos, 1982). See also Éditions Champ Libre, *Correspondance,* vol. 2 (Paris: Champ Libre, 1981), especially pp. 118–24.

This paradox may be explained in part by the extreme flexibility of the concept of "spectacle," which Debord at times takes in the restrictive sense of the culture industry, the mass media, and the reign of images. It is this sense that the Situationists have in mind when they evoke "the *indifference* that is displayed by proletarians, qua class, in face of all forms of the culture of the spectacle" (*IS* 4/4). The spectacle so conceived is "further removed than ever from social reality" (*IS* 8/15). In a more figurative sense, however, the notion of the spectacle refers first of all to Western capitalism, then by extension to all existing society, and finally even covers societies of the past, inasmuch as "power as a separate realm has always had a spectacular aspect" (*SS* §25).[43]

Furthermore, although the Situationists acknowledged that the society's rulers were not a monolithic group (*IS* 8/13; *SIA*, 198), Debord never went very deeply into the spectacle's internal articulations and contradictions (those contradictions which would once have been described as "secondary"). The Leninist strategy of exploiting antagonisms within the opposing camp in order to weaken it unquestionably gave rise to the dubious practice of forming tactical alliances; the fact remains, however, that the Situationist idea of a frontal assault by the weakest of the forces in play is at odds with every known rule of strategy, and almost certainly destroys any conceivable prospect of victory.

There are some who feel that in the *Comments on the Society of the Spectacle* a dark pessimism replaces Debord's earlier optimism, a pessimism according to which all opposition to the spectacle is now seen as set up by the spectacle itself, while not a single trace of a revolutionary force remains in the world. A careful reading, however, suggests that Debord does not at all mean to announce the spectacle's final victory.[44] He speaks a great deal of secret-police activity, for example, but nowhere does he intimate that such covert agencies are about to take over the world. On the contrary, he notes that the society of the spectacle has lost any ability to manage itself in a strategic manner and can only stand and defend its own "fragile perfection." In other words, once the commodity-form, thanks to the "integrated spectacle," has completed its investment of society, the very possibility of managing the mad laws of the econ-

43. Note that Debord is in danger here of slipping into a "dehistoricized" view of alienation, something that tends to happen when, like Lukács in *History and Class Consciousness,* one lays too much emphasis on the reifying effect of the division of labor, which of course considerably antedated the advent of capitalism.

44. This is stated explicitly in "*Cette mauvaise réputation . . .* " (Paris: Gallimard, 1993), 31.

omy is reduced to the vain gesticulations of legions of conspirators. De-bord's oft-contested claim that there is no more opposition because every-one is now part of the system actually refers to the fact that immanent oppositions to the system, such as the traditional workers' movement and the "liberation movements" of the Third World, have now definitively run their course. Only in fancy could they ever have been assigned a transcendent role, for in reality what these oppositions challenged were imperfect phases of capitalism in which large sectors of the population were excluded from the access channels of capitalist socialization. When the commodity system as such goes into crisis, however, the role of such immanent oppositions is at an end. The trouble with Debord's account is that his picture of such a crisis is formed on the inadequate basis of a critique of "manipulation"—which for him seems to mean the end of all opposition rather than the beginning of a new, real one. He has not the slightest doubt about the reality of the crisis of capitalism, however, and he identifies the cause thereof less in the dissatisfaction that the sys-tem creates than in the system's own dynamics. In his last book, "*Cette mauvaise réputation . . . ,*" he speaks of "the obvious dissolution of the entire system" and asserts that "nothing works any more, and nothing is believed any more."[45]

We are indeed witness to a crisis of the value-form itself—not merely of its secondary characteristics. The ecological emergency is but one fea-ture of this more elemental crisis. Others are the impossibility, in this era of globalization, for "politics" or for national states to continue op-erating as regulatory agencies, and the crisis of the subject as consti-tuted by value, especially visible in the crisis of the relationship between the sexes. The most tangible effects, however, are those produced by the eclipse of labor as the foundation of society. Only a small portion of the labor formerly needed is now required to keep production going; all the same, to operate under sufficiently profitable conditions very large investments of fixed capital are essential, and this is feasible only in the most advanced countries and in high-technology sectors. And since the de facto globalization not just of trade but also of production obliges the entire world to align itself on the productivity levels of the most highly developed centers, a large part of the planet is bound to lose on this play-ing field. The productive plant of disadvantaged countries, even though it may be capable of producing consumer goods, will no longer be able to employ living labor in such a way as to produce exchange-value in

45. Ibid., 47, 107.

the world market and will consequently be dismantled. Such countries and sectors as are thus excluded from worldwide conduits of value will nevertheless continue to exert an ominous pressure on the very few winners, generating endless wars, mafias, and murky trafficking in whatever marketable materials are still in their possession.

Debord was one of very few people to have understood that the collapse of the Eastern-bloc countries did not signify the triumph of the Western social model but on the contrary heralded another stage in the global breakdown of commodity-driven society. Regimes with planned economies had been merely a variant of that society designed for backward countries, and their raison d'être disappeared once basic industries had been set up.[46] But Debord was less on target when he wrote in 1992, in his preface to the third edition of *La Société du spectacle*, that the main problem for capitalism was, and would continue to be, "how can the poor be made to work?" (*SS*, xii; Eng., 10). As a matter of fact, the main problem for capitalism today is to decide what to do with the vast majority of humanity, for whom, qua living labor, it has no use in view of the degree to which production has been successfully automated.[47]

Two Sources and Two Aspects of Debord's Theory

What is truly new in Debord's theory derives ultimately from his assignment of a fundamental role in modern society to exchange and the principle of equivalence. This was already one of the cardinal concerns of the young Letterists, as witness the title of their paper, *Potlatch*. No explanation of this title was offered when the Letterists first began sending out their free newsletter in 1954, but in 1959, presenting the first and last issue of a projected "new series" (*Potlatch* was by now an internal publication of the Situationist International), Debord refers explicitly to the Indian custom of potlatch and announces that "the non-saleable goods that a free bulletin such as this is able to distribute are novel desires and problems; and only the further elaboration of these by others can constitute the corresponding return gift" (*Pot.*, 283). The reader may recall

---

46. Ibid., 30. The best account of this process is Robert Kurz, *Der Kollaps der Modernisierung* (Frankfurt: Eichborn, 1991).

47. This change of period is no better grasped by those who persist in using such categories as "imperialism" when it is perfectly plain that capital has no interest in going out to conquer spaces from which there is nothing more to be extracted and which would only become dead weight. The countries of the East and South have lately fallen to their knees begging to be exploited in exchange for mere survival, but the so-called imperialist centers have as little inclination to oblige them as they have to intervene in the world's trouble spots.

that potlatch was practiced by certain Native American tribes in Canada who survived into the twentieth century and that similar customs have been followed by cultures elsewhere. The idea is that the prestige of an individual or group may be asserted by means of a gift offered to a rival. The latter must reciprocate, if he wishes to avoid acknowledging the supremacy of the giver, with a more valuable offering, and so on back and forth, sometimes to the point where one party or the other ostentatiously destroys their entire fortune. Potlatching is thus based less on equivalence than on the deliberate waste of resources, which are surrendered without any certainty of ever receiving—indeed even with the secret desire *not* to receive—an equivalent value in return. Marcel Mauss introduced the notion of potlatch into anthropology in his celebrated work on the gift (1924), but it was above all thanks to Georges Bataille's *The Accursed Share* (1949) that it became part of the common currency of French thought and took on the role of a sort of alternative to the idea of an economy founded on exchange.[48]

To work out a critical theory based on the category of exchange, as Debord did, and as the Frankfurt School did in a different way, represented a significant advance relative to the Marxism of the old working-class movement, for which the only form of exchange that counted was the "unequal" one constituted by the trade in labor-power. In the eyes of "Marxists" of this persuasion, giving pride of place to exchange amounts to attending first and foremost to the social sphere, and to intersubjective relationships, to the detriment of any consideration for the relationship between man and nature, that is to say, for the objectivity that only the analysis of production can vouchsafe. When, in 1967, Lukács drew up the list of errors he felt he had committed in *History and Class Consciousness*, he made a number of observations which he would surely have considered equally applicable to that book's latter-day scion, *The Society of the Spectacle*. Thus, according to its author, *History and Class Consciousness* falls in with "the tendency to view Marxism exclusively as a

48. Marcel Mauss, *The Gift: Forms and Functions of Exchange in Archaic Societies*, trans. I. Cunnison (New York: Norton, 1967). And see Georges Bataille, *La Part maudite* (Paris: Minuit, 1967), 120–39; Eng. trans. by Robert Hurley: *The Accursed Share: An Essay on General Economy*, vol. 1, *Consumption* (New York: Zone, 1988), 63–77. Bataille had first discussed potlatch, in the wake of Mauss, in "La Notion de dépense," *La Critique Sociale* 7 (January 1933): 7–21; English translation by Allan Stoekl and others in Bataille, *Visions of Excess: Selected Writings 1927–1939* (Minneapolis: University of Minnesota Press, 1985), 116–29. The young Letterists may also have come across the notion in *Socialisme ou Barbarie*, in whose pages Claude Lefort summarized Mauss's *Essai sur le don* when this was reissued in 1950. In *Homo ludens* (1938)—a book that Debord quite liked—Johan Huizinga too had discussed potlatch.

theory of society, as social philosophy, and hence to ignore or repudiate it as a theory of nature. . . . I argue in a number of places that nature is a societal category [and] that only a knowledge of society and the men who live in it is of relevance to philosophy." And indeed Lukács discerns an echo of this tendency in "French existentialism and its intellectual ambience" (HCC, xvi). By the same token, the Hungarian philosopher rebukes his book, and the "tendency" to which it gave rise, for not having analyzed labor, but only "complex structures" (HCC, xx). Lukács asserts that this approach was nevertheless contrary to his subjective intentions and that he had not meant to abandon the economic underpinnings of history: "It is true that the attempt is made to explain all ideological phenomena by reference to their basis in economics but, despite this, the purview of economics is narrowed down because its basic Marxist category, labor as the mediator of the metabolic interaction between society and nature, is missing" (HCC, xvii). This inability correctly to gauge the weight of material objectivity is then linked by Lukács to his mistaken conflation of objectification and alienation.

Seen in this light, the concept of the spectacle would seem to make an absolute of what might be called the superstructure, the realm of circulation, of consumption—in short, the social. But Debord rejected the criticism leveled at him by Claude Lefort, who "falsely charges Debord with having said that 'the production of a phantasmagoria governs that of commodities,' whereas in fact *the very contrary* is clearly stated in *The Society of the Spectacle*, notably in the second chapter, where the spectacle is defined as simply one *moment* in the development of commodity production" (IS 12/48; SIA, 266).[49] Still, very great importance is obviously given in Debord's analysis to culture, that is, to the superstructure. In the early years, the Situationists justified their attempts to achieve a sort of "hegemony" in the cultural sphere on the grounds that culture was "the center of meaning of a society without meaning" (IS 5/5; SIA, 61). To use a more sociological language, one might say that they had identified culture as a locus of "consensus creation." In their definition, it covered a vast area, taking in everything that was not simple reproduction (Prelims., 342; SIA, 305). Later on, the Situationists turned their attention to the critique of ideology, and when Debord defines the spectacle as "ideology in material form," it is clear that he conceives of it as much more than a "superstructure."

In its analytical role, the concept of the spectacle explains how the

---

49. See Claude Lefort, "Le Parti situationniste" (review of Debord's *La Société du spectacle*), *La Quinzaine Littéraire*, 1 February 1968.

process of abstraction transforms both thought and production. It thus tends clearly in the direction of a supersession of such dualisms as those between "base" and "superstructure," "appearance" and "essence," "being" and "consciousness," which were made so much of by a sociologizing "Marxism" that failed to see that value is a "total social fact"—as Marcel Mauss would say—itself responsible for instituting division in different spheres. This brand of Marxism proceeded to pass off as "dialectics" its lucubrations on the "reciprocal relations" between the very realms that it had already made into watertight compartments. That the Situationists failed to respect the base–superstructure distinction was thus no shortcoming on their part but indeed an important theoretical advance for which support in Hegel and Marx could quite legitimately be claimed. Likewise their refusal to make labor the basis of their theory was by no means a fault. Conceptions of labor like that of the Lukács of 1967, mentioned earlier, turn a characteristic of capitalism into an eternal ontological necessity. To describe labor as "an organic exchange with nature" is to state a truth, but one with no more conceptual utility than the assertion that human beings must breathe in order to live. But if it is understood as a specific modality for organizing this exchange, then labor may be seen on the contrary as a historical datum potentially transcended by the evolution of capitalism itself. The bartering of measures of work objectified as commodities would be superfluous in the context of a directly socialized mode of production. The present mode of production is already socialized in the material sense, even if it is still unable to free itself from a system in which individuals partake of the collective product solely by virtue of what each contributes by way of labor. The Situationists' critique of work does not make them into old-fashioned bohemians, therefore, but rather into genuine anticipators, from a Marxist point of view, of a thoroughly modern phenomenon.

Debord's ideas have benefited in this regard from the fact that they began as reflections on art. The resulting emphasis is characteristically French, expressing a tendency to stress the "social" aspect as opposed to the "harsh realities" of economics.[50] Yet there is also a hidden animosity here—and a fully justified one, albeit somewhat distorted—toward a "Marxism" reduced to a mere guarantee of economic modernization. The particular way in which Debord and the Situationists came to be among the first to perceive, at least in part, the new conditions created

---

50. Thus authors including both Lefebvre and Sartre prefer the purely intersubjective concept of "action" to that of "labor," which implies a relationship between man and nature.

by the end of the Fordist period is a function of the *break* they represent relative to practically all previous social criticism. If they were able to break new ground in this area, at the same time exhuming a number of buried aspects of Marxian theory, this was precisely because they had *not* emerged from Marxism's internal debates. The Situationists understood that Marx's theories too needed to be subjected to *détournement*—to be turned around and inserted into a new context and in this way revalidated. And if they were ready to perform such a *détournement*, that readiness was founded on their experience of the decay of the arts. The situation brought about by the end (real or presumed) of poetry, like the desire to construct a passionate everyday life, was at the center of Debord's preoccupations long before he began thinking about Marxist theory. The artistic origins of the SI would turn out to be a serious obstacle later, when the need arose for a sect (itself conceived of as the supreme work of an art-without-works) to be transformed into a mass movement; yet it was precisely those origins which enabled the SI to find its "North-West Passage"—at any rate in the realm of Marxist theory.

As has already been stressed more than once, the various strands of Marxism all developed *within* the confines of a system of socialization defined by value and never went beyond calling for a "juster" organization of that system. Liberation from abstract labor, money, the state, and production as an end in itself was at best deferred to a far distant future, for consideration only after the social forms created by the commodity had been effectively extended to the whole of society. Even heretical Marxisms demanded nothing more in essence than a more radical or more democratic management of the existing arrangements. It is fair to say, therefore, that apart from the French utopian socialist tradition, as exemplified by Fourier, only the artistic avant-gardes in general, and on a more conscious level Surrealism, had ever voiced the demand for a liberation that was genuinely concrete and that, even if conceived in a somewhat ingenuous way, really looked beyond the horizon of industrial society. Only here, in other words, could one find the rudiments of a kind of thinking that transcended the categories manufactured by the commodity-form. And this was the tradition that carried Debord to a threshold that had remained beyond the reach of such theoretical undertakings as *Arguments* or *Socialisme ou Barbarie*, whose attempts to rejuvenate Marxism did not start from Marx himself and thus failed to grasp that the economism they objected to could most effectively be contested by recourse to "the *critique* of political economy." These groups

strove to make up for the shortcomings of Marxism as a whole by inter-
jecting foreign elements. Despite the great merit of its critical analysis of
the Soviet Union, *Socialisme ou Barbarie* clung to an entirely trivial, so-
ciologically inclined Marxism, far removed from a critique of the value-
form or of commodity fetishism, while at the same time incorporating
material in the most uncritical manner from other disciplines such as anthropology and psychology. This purely mechanical assimilation of elements that in themselves had not been subjected to critical scrutiny was
naturally unsatisfactory; it is hardly surprising that after a few years the
likes of Edgar Morin and Cornelius Castoriadis should have completely
turned their backs on any serious critical approach to society.

Debord was thus one of the few people in a position to carry a social
critique beyond the various forms of the Marxism of the working-class
movement, which in 1968 experienced one more deceptive Indian summer, just before the process of modernization ended and turned into a
catastrophe. It was not then easy to understand that almost all varieties
of opposition to capitalism had taken aim only at what was extraneous
to the pure value-form and that consequently it made no sense to continue along the same path. This reversal of perspective was apprehended
first in the realm of the arts.[51]

Avant-garde and formalist art between 1850 and 1930 meant destroying traditional forms far more than creating new ones. This process of
destruction had an eminently *critical* function linked to the historical period during which the social system founded on exchange-value became
dominant. The relationship between modern art and the development
of the logic of exchange-value was ambiguous in a number of ways. On
the one hand, modern art registered the dissolution of the ways of life
and modes of communication of traditional communities in a negative
fashion. Shocking by means of "incomprehensibility" was intended to
point up this disappearance. Well before the advent of the avant-garde
in any strict sense, nostalgia for a lost "authenticity" of lived experience
had become one of the central themes of art, as witness the work of
Flaubert. At the same time, however, art perceived that same dissolution
as liberating potential, as opening up new horizons to life and experience.
It thus gave an enthusiastic welcome to a process that amounted de facto
to the decay of pre-bourgeois social formations and the emancipation

51. See my article "Sic transit gloria artis: Theorien über das Ende der Kunst bei
Theodor W. Adorno und Guy Debord," *Krisis* 15 (1995). English translation forthcoming
in the journal *SubStance*.

of abstract individuality from premodern constraints. Art conceived of these constraints, however, not just in terms of exploitation and political oppression, as the workers' movement did, but also in terms of the family, morality, and everyday life, as well as structures of perception and thought. What neither art nor the workers' movement perceived was that the process of dissolution was in reality the triumph of the abstract monad of money. Art believed it was witnessing the beginning of a general disintegration of bourgeois society, including the state and the money system; what it was really witnessing was the victory of the most highly developed capitalist forms—among them, precisely, the state and money—over the remains of precapitalism.[52] So it was that modern art unintentionally pointed the way to the complete rout, by a subjectivity structured by value, of all pre-bourgeois forms. The expectation was that the overthrow of prevailing modes of production, precipitated by capitalist development itself, would as a logical consequence bring about the subversion of the traditional superstructures, from sexual morality to the physical aspect of cities. Modern art naturally accused the "bourgeoisie" of resisting change in order to keep its grip on power, yet it was itself grievously mistaken in its view that such subversion should be championed. Mallarmé's "Destruction was my Beatrice" was realized in ways very far removed from anything the poet could have imagined, for it was capitalist society itself that in the end turned everything upside down. We have indeed witnessed the breaking of new paths and the abandonment of old traditions—but, so far from delivering individual lives from archaic and stifling bonds, the aim has been to tear down all obstacles to the total transformation of the world into commodities. Giving free rein to unconscious drives, contempt for logic, the cultivation of surprises, arbitrary and fantastical combinations—the whole Surrealist agenda has been carried through by the juggernaut of state and economy in ways the Surrealists never remotely anticipated. The decomposition of artistic forms has thus become perfectly concordant with the real state of the world and retains no shock effect whatsoever. Meaninglessness, aphasia, incomprehensibility, or irrationality—as, say, in the work of Beckett—can now appear to us only as an integral and indistinguishable part of the world around us, contributing not to a critique but to an apology.

The most conscious elements in the artistic avant-gardes were the first to realize that the continuation of their critical work required a revision of perspective. In 1948, when asked whether the Surrealists of 1925

52. Sometimes art made this belief explicit, as in the cases of the Dadaists, the Surrealists, the Futurists, and the Constructivists; at other times, it was merely implicit.

would not have gone so far as to hail the atomic bomb in their desire to shake up the bourgeois order, André Breton replied as follows: "In *La Lampe dans l'horloge* . . . you'll see that I have no trouble explaining this crucial variation: the lyrical aspiration toward the end of the world and its subsequent retraction, owing to new facts."[53] In 1951 Breton summed up in a few eloquent words the great change that had occurred in less than three decades—a change which, we might add, has continued to occur at an ever increasing pace in the years since: "In France, for example, the mind was threatened back then with coagulation, whereas today it is threatened with dissolution."[54]

The Situationists were heir to this self-criticism of the earlier avant-gardes, whose frequently declared allegiance to "the irrational" had constituted a genuine protest against the tight fetters imposed by so-called rationality on the human possibilities foreshadowed in the realms of the imaginary and the unconscious. It is altogether typical of the course of this century that the critique of life in capitalist society should have been undertaken first by the Surrealists as a critique of excessive *rationalism*, whereas the inheritors of this critique were eventually driven to conclude that even the mean-spirited rationalism of the nineteenth century, so bitterly mocked by the Surrealists, seems like great wisdom as compared with the spectacle's galloping irrationalism. What Debord took the Surrealists to task for was, precisely, their embrace of the irrational, and in this connection he insisted on the need "to rationalize the world more, as the first step to impassioning it" (*Rapp.*, 691–92; *SIA*, 19–20). In 1932 the Surrealists had presented "experimental research on some possible irrational beautifications for cities"; in 1956, *Potlatch* published a humorous "plan for the rational beautification of the city of Paris" (*Pot.*, 203–7; *Dérive*, 56–57). What the Situationists rejected in Surrealism was thus an idealist view of history that sees it as nothing but a struggle between the irrational and the tyranny of the logico-rational (*IS* 2/33). Likewise, the Situationists never cultivated the idea of disorder as an end in itself; in Debord's words, "victory will be for those who have known how to create disorder without loving it" (*IS* 2/21; *Oct.*, 92).

Much the same sort of thing might be said of humanist culture or of the relationship with the past. The Situationists always despised the "beautiful soul" humanism of people who in the last reckoning wanted

53. Breton, *Entretiens*, rev. ed. (Paris: Gallimard, 1969), 271; English translation by Mark Polizzotti as *Conversations: The Autobiography of Surrealism* (New York: Marlowe, 1993), 223.

54. Ibid., 218; Eng., 174.

nothing more than a comfortable niche in the spectacle. They held that it was meaningless to contrast bad mass media with good "high culture" or with artistic fulfillment (*IS* 7/21)—neither of which were in reality any less alienated. Initially the SI argued that a race was on between "free artists and the police" for control of the "new techniques of conditioning," while "the whole humanistic, artistic and juridical conception of the personality as inviolable and unalterable has been abandoned, and we are only too happy to see it go."[55]

On the matter of works of the past, however, Debord changed his mind. In 1955, according to *Potlatch*'s report on the meeting concerned with the aforementioned "plan for the rational beautification of the city of Paris," he declared himself in favor of "the complete demolition of religious buildings of all denominations"; along with his fellow Letterists, he felt that "aesthetic objections should be overruled, that admirers of the great portal of Chartres should be silenced. Beauty, *when it does not hold the promise of happiness*, must be destroyed" (*Pot.*, 204, 205; *Dérive*, 56). Many years later Debord found to the contrary that the most astonishing thing imaginable now would be "to see a Donatello re-emerge" (*OCC*, 225; *In girum*, 30), that "American-style" restoration of the Sistine Chapel or of Versailles was a crime (*Comm.*, 56; Eng., 51), and that a few old buildings and a few old books were perhaps the only things that had not been transformed by modern industry (*Comm.*, 20; Eng., 10). At the outset the Situationists had wanted to be "partisans of forgetting" (*IS* 2/4); they could hardly have foreseen that the spectacle itself would take charge of consigning the whole historical past to oblivion, and destroying everything "old-fashioned" that impeded *its* progress, without helping the revolutionary project in the slightest. In such circumstances, however, the past, as imperfect and even execrable as it might be, becomes a lesser evil and must often be defended. "When 'to be absolutely modern' has become a special law decreed by a tyrant, what the honest slave fears more than anything is that he might be suspected of being behind the times" (*Pan.*, 83; Eng., 76–77).[56] That which in the past had taken itself for a radical challenge to bourgeois society ended up clearing away only things that were obsolete and in any case destined to be swept aside by the victory of the commodity. Debord alludes

55. *IS* 1/8; Eng.: Christopher Gray, ed. and trans., *Leaving the Twentieth Century: The Incomplete Work of the Situationist International* (London: Free Fall, 1974), 12.

56. This does not, however, imply a nostalgia for some lost golden age: "I indicated, in the *Spectacle*, the two or three periods in which it is possible to discern a measure of historical life in the past, and their limits. If you look at things dispassionately, it does not seem as if, out of the entire existence of the old world, we ever had very much to lose"

to this in his last film, *Guy Debord, son art et son temps,* assimilating the Dadaist revolt—that is to say, one of the moments to which the Situationists referred continually—to the most contemptibly modern phenomenon, which he calls "State Dada": David Buren's striped columns at the Palais Royal, compared by Debord to the "bar codes" now widely used to identify merchandise. The fact is that Dada, like other iconoclastic movements, was the all-unknowing precursor of today's urbanists, whose job it is, where they are unable to destroy something outright, at least to strip it of any historical depth and hence of any memory of a past distinct from the spectacle. By introducing utterly unrelated architectural elements into the courtyard of the Louvre or into the Palais Royal, these buildings are reduced to the status of mere backdrops and become in effect as fake as everything else.

For a long time the task of the critique of society was to combat the "old"—from historical city centers to classical philosophers, from the institution of the family to traditional trades and crafts. The first point to be made here is that power appropriates any number of innovations proposed or actualized by its opponents. The practice of *détournement,* as defined by the Situationists, is strictly an epiphenomenon by comparison with the gigantic *détournement* perpetrated upon all the revolutionary tendencies of the century. The Situationists knew this, of course: "Power creates nothing; it co-opts" (*IS* 10/54; *SIA,* 173). The fact remains that the meaning of *détournement* is tied to the *subjectively* subversive intentions of its practitioners, the *objective* content of whose actions so often harmonized with the profound orientation of a society ruled by the commodity. Consider for instance an area where the Situationists were true pioneers: their contempt for the work ethic and conviction that labor was absolutely nothing more than a source of income, still—but only temporarily—an unfortunate necessity. Today this view is almost universally accepted—not that it has in any way affected our "work-based society." On the contrary, the spectacular system has only benefited from the dissolution of all kinds of occupational associations, from the loss of specific skills, and from the general lack of identification with a trade of one's own, all of which encourage the disappearance of all quality from life and justify every sort of aberration. As Debord himself remarks in his *Comments on the Society of the Spectacle,* "it is disorienting to consider what it meant to be a judge, a doctor or a historian not so long

(letter from Debord to Daniel Denevert, 26 February 1972, in *Chronique des secrets publics* [Paris: Centre de Recherches sur la Question Sociale, 1975], 23).

ago, and to recall the obligations and imperatives they often accepted, within the limits of their competence" (*Comm.*, 29; Eng., 20); today, by contrast, we are witnessing the sudden "parodic end of the division of labor" (*Comm.*, 21; Eng., 10). Another point on which the Situationists were ahead of their time, and in tune—as may be seen in hindsight—with the underlying trends of the last few decades, was the fact that they dubbed "alienating" or "spectacular" any activity that did not have as its aim the immediate satisfaction of the individual's needs or desires. However justified it might have been in the sixties to mock political militants who forgot their own misery by identifying with far-off events or with the actions of political leaders, that mockery was in fact a prefigurement of the attitude of those who, today, will hear nothing of wars and disasters that are "no concern of theirs." Clearly such developments were not foreseen, nor could they have been.

In conclusion, it is worth pointing out that some of the most powerful features of Debord's theory belong to the tradition, in its continuity and self-criticism, of Enlightenment philosophy. In other words, they belong to the "dialectic of Enlightenment" in Adorno and Horkheimer's sense: "In the most general sense of progressive thought, the Enlightenment has always aimed at liberating men from fear and establishing their sovereignty."[57] The philosophy of the Enlightenment continually strove to show that the forces dominating society were of human origin, or at least that it is possible for man to bring them under rational control. Religion was long this philosophy's chief target, and Debord considers that the spectacle is "the heir of religion" (*IS* 9/4: *SIA*, 136; *SS* §20): both constitute contemplation by humanity of its own separated powers. It is no coincidence that forms of "fetishism" are present in religion just as they are in the modern system of production. Likewise Debord compared art to religion: material development had now succeeded in removing any justification for all those forms that had hitherto been at once cause and effect of the impossibility of fulfilling individual desires directly; henceforward, however, "the construction of situations will replace the theater only in the sense that the real construction of life has tended more and more to replace religion" (*IS* 1/12; *SIA*, 44). The Situationist program, seeking as it did to abolish whatever had become separate from in-

57. Max Horkheimer and Theodor W. Adorno, *Dialectic of Enlightenment* (New York: Herder and Herder, 1972), 3. The Situationists always had an elective affinity for the philosophy of the Enlightenment; for a time Mustapha Khayati entertained the notion of producing a new *Encyclopédie* (see *IS* 10/50–55; *SIA*, 170–75).

dividuals—the economy, the state, religion, works of art—so that they could proceed unhindered to construct their own everyday life, was without question a continuation of the work of demystification undertaken by Marx and Freud. Kant defined *Aufklärung* as "for man, the way out of his minority status"; according to Debord, the spectacle keeps people in a state of infantilism, producing the conditioned "need to imitate that the consumer experiences" (*SS* §219) and creating a world where "there is no entering into adulthood" (*OCC*, 45; *Films*, 45).

Debord's theory is a critique as much of the unfinished quality of Enlightenment philosophy as of its reversal. Adorno and Horkheimer have described how *Aufklärung* falls back into myth and is transformed into a new form of domination as its rationality becomes autonomous and mutates into a fetishism of quantity. The spectacle, described by Debord as a product of capitalist rationalization, is also a new myth and a new religion generated from an Enlightenment philosophy that has not been thought through. It is *the separation of human potential from the conscious global project* and leads to the state of affairs where, in the terms of *Dialectic of Enlightenment*, "men expect that the world, which is without any issue, will be set on fire by a totality they themselves are and over which they have no control."[58]

The relevance of Debord's thought no longer lies in his desire to generalize a culture of play made possible by technical progress but rather, today, in the fact that he supplies a new foundation for the contention of the young Marx that political economy is "the denial of man accomplished" (*Comm.*, 46; Eng., 39). There is *one* comfort, at any rate, to be gleaned here by the liberatory project: for the first time, this project stands to benefit from man's instinct of self-preservation.[59] In his film *Critique of Separation* (1961), Debord notes that "the problem is not that people live more or less poorly; but that they live in a way that is always beyond their control" (*OCC*, 45; *Films*, 45). Now, so many years later, the consequences for a society organized after this fashion are clear. A new critical theory, so sorely needed at the present time, and the praxis that must accompany it will surely recognize the true value of Debord's contribution.

58. Horkheimer and Adorno, *Dialectic of Enlightenment*, 29.
59. This idea is very well articulated in "Discours préliminaire," *Encyclopédie des Nuisances* 1 (November 1984): 9–10.

Afterword to the English-Language Edition

"If you cannot rid yourself of a bandit," goes an Italian proverb, "make him into a baron." Almost until his death, Guy Debord was the object of a conspiracy of silence; these days his work, and the work of the Situationists in general, seem rather to have fallen prey to a conspiracy of *chatter* that is liable to distort their meaning beyond all recognition. In France, the strong tendency now is to treat Debord as an elegant stylist, the actual content of whose writings is of scant interest. In Great Britain and the United States, by contrast, where in the last decade more has been published on the Situationists than anywhere else, even France, and where the subject was taken up by academic and mainstream commentators sooner than in other countries, the Situationist movement is viewed almost exclusively from the angle of the history of culture.

Practically all current discussions of the Situationists embody an attempt—perhaps not always conscious—to render them innocuous, to normalize them by one means or another. One such means is flatly to present this antipolitical and antiartistic movement as political and artistic, and then concentrate entirely on the SI's aesthetic and "ludic" concerns. Hence the almost complete silence surrounding everything the SI did after breaking with its remaining artist members in 1962. What might be called the official account thus attends with relentless philological rigor to every least pronouncement on such early Letterist and Situationist themes as the *dérive* or "unitary urbanism," only to shy away and take cover behind vague generalities when it comes to characterizing the Situationists' critique of society or explaining its pertinence (to which full lip service is nevertheless paid). The truth is that the unquestionably admirable *forms* of the SI's assault on the established world during the organization's "artistic phase" cannot be fully appreciated if one does not see that this was indeed but a first stage which, had it not been very quickly surpassed by an activity of much wider scope, would have been confined to a purely ornamental role within the prevailing spectacle.

Another consequence of focusing exclusively on the first third of the SI's history is that Debord's role is downplayed, even if he survives as an obsessing and shadowy presence. We should do well to remember the degree to which the SI was truly Debord's creation. It is true that, especially in the early days, others contributed a great deal. Yet even those contributions would never have had the same significance were it not for the unmistakable *style*, the incomparable *language*, and the particular *tone* for which the SI was renowned—and all of these it owed to Debord alone. With the exception of Asger Jorn, all the other Situationists would probably be forgotten today were it not for the association of their names with the SI, and hence with Debord. As for the "Nashists" and other artists expelled from the SI, their later activities are often placed under the rubric of "Situationism"; for some commentators, indeed, some special virtue seems to attach to having been one of these "victims of Debord."

There are people, too, who seem to feel that the ideal heir to the subversive work of the Situationists is something called "transgressive deconstructionism"; at times the tendency variously known as poststructuralism, deconstructionism, postmodernism, or media theory gets an urge to be *critical* and in that mood strives to incorporate Debord. One might do worse, in response, than reiterate (in a slightly updated form) a sentiment first expressed in the Situationist journal in 1967: "We want ideas to become *dangerous* once again. We cannot allow people to support us on the basis of a wishy-washy, fake eclecticism, along with the Derridas, the Lyotards, the Rortys and the Baudrillards." In any case, the present work defends quite another view, namely that Debord's theory is *in essence a continuation of the work of Marx and Hegel* and that its importance inheres for the most part precisely in this fact. Those who have no interest in the Hegelian dialectic and in Marx's interpretation of it, or in the authors chiefly responsible for keeping this line of inquiry alive, run the risk of—or, rather, will succeed in—understanding very little of *The Society of the Spectacle*.[1]

Debord's work itself effectively demonstrates—though none of the academic or subcultural accounts acknowledge this—that Hegelian-Marxist concepts are still the most useful for understanding the modern

1. Whereas this book pays ample attention to Lukács's influence on Debord and to the parallel between Debord and Adorno, I suspect I have delved too little into Debord's debt to Karl Korsch.

world, particularly the self-destructive character of a society driven by the commodity.[2] Only now, in fact—globalization having finally realized the notorious "totality"—is Hegelian-Marxist theory really coming into its own; and it is no doubt for this very reason that our accredited intellectuals have for quite some time, and with rare unanimity, been declaring that nothing could be as out of date and irrelevant as the concepts of Hegel. Hegel is the greatest absentee of the day, surpassing even Marx in this regard, for even Marxism is acceptable to a degree, so long as it is guaranteed Hegel-free—so long as it is analytical, structuralist, or ethical in character (to name the leading variants). Hegelian Marxism is generally dismissed, both within and outside academia, as the deadest of dead dogs, as the supreme instance of the kind of "totalizing theory" and "grand narrative" that modern society has declared itself, loudly and clearly, unwilling to countenance. In resorting to such exorcisms, official knowledge follows a sure instinct, for without the categories of the Hegelian dialectic, no matter how much they need to be reversed, reworked, turned upside down, or transcended, all understanding of capitalist society must remain in the best of circumstances fragmentary and devoid of any possible application: it will be what the SI called "research without directions for use." Even such truths as may be found by means of nondialectical methods will be unusable, or turn into falsehoods, unless they are integrated into an understanding of the *totality*. This concept seemingly constitutes the *horror maximus* of "politically correct" thinkers, but hardly more tolerable to them are the dialectical concepts of the difference between essence and phenomenon and of an objective truth distinct from the empirical one, or indeed any sense that every phenomenon is a *result*, and hence explicable only in terms of its historical genesis. This is not the place to debate whether the Hegelian interpretation, according to which every singular phenomenon is but one *moment* in the process of becoming of a totality, has universal ontological validity and holds good for every historical period. What is indisputable is that such a (negative) totality does indeed exist in the case of capitalist society, because the all-pervading logic of commodities concedes no autonomy to any other reality; and hence that only a form of thinking based on the totality can adequately account for the situation in which we find ourselves. For postmodern thought this conclusion is both forbidden

2. For an interpretation of Marx close to that which informs this book, see the excellent work of Moishe Postone, *Time, Labor, and Social Domination* (Cambridge: Cambridge University Press, 1993).

and strictly meaningless; how exactly Debord's postmodern admirers contrive to blind themselves to the fact that his is a "totalizing theory" is a secret known only to themselves.

The Hegelian dialectic permeates the entire first part of *Capital,* Volume I, where Marx explores the basic determinants constituted by value, commodities, and money, with their profoundly contradictory and ultimately self-destructive character. This analysis of the "cell-form" today represents Marx's most vital legacy, and Debord's recovery of it is undoubtedly one of his main achievements. The best example of a Hegelianizing concept in Marx—a concept for this very reason almost completely ignored in the Marxist tradition—is that of abstract labor, discussed in some detail in this book. The notion that anything could be simultaneously concrete and abstract is of course an affront to the positivist consciousness. Yet the dynamic of abstract labor as an end in itself, driven by a need for continual growth way beyond all consideration of utility, is the only reasonable explanation for the convulsions of the present fin de siècle. This kind of historical thought cannot therefore remain merely contemplative. The shift to praxis is intrinsic to the Hegelian-Marxist dialectic as to no other kind of thinking; nowhere else is thought driven in this way toward its own actualization. It is unsurprising that Hegelian-Marxist theories have come to the fore at times of violent social revolt—around 1920, say, or in 1968. The Surrealists and the Situationists may not have studied the *Science of Logic* in the greatest detail, but they knew perfectly well why Hegel had to be the point of reference.

In contrast, the postmodernist galaxy, whatever its subjective intentions, carries apology for *what exists* to the extreme. Its *index verborum prohibitorum* coincides exactly with the categories of dialectical thought: totality, truth, reason, history, objectivity. All questions concerning the fetishistic forms that govern society are explicitly tabooed. But deconstructionism is canny, and it successfully mimics a radical critique of all received ideas. By means of a now familiar device, it channels the real social need for a thoroughgoing and corrosive critique, applied even to the seemingly most self-evident and neutral ideas, into innocuous forms that always end up willy-nilly obeying "the syntax of the spectacle": a perfect instance of *détournement*—but a *détournement* carried out in this case by power.

A widespread misconception sees Debord as a "precursor" of Baudrillard and Baudrillard's notion of the "simulacrum" as a more radical version of the notion of the spectacle. Feuerbach's assertion that our age

"prefers the copy to the original," used by Debord as an epigraph for
The Society of the Spectacle, thus turns out to hold good even for radical criticism. In response to the threat posed by the emergence of Situationist theory, some apologists for the reigning order of things chose,
immediately after 1968, to speak the language of radical criticism and
indeed to do so in a way that seemed if anything a little bit more extreme and daring; the actual intent and content, however, were opposed
to any radical critique. If it is true that we are immersed in a sea of uncontrollable images barring our way to reality, this may make it seem
all the bolder to assert that reality has completely disappeared and that
the Situationists were still too timid, or too optimistic, because the process of abstraction has now devoured the *whole* of reality and the spectacle has become even more "spectacular," even more totalitarian, than
had at first been supposed, and has even extended its criminal proclivi-
ties to the "murder of reality" itself.[3]

Although Baudrillard hardly ever cites the Situationists, he frequently
speaks of "the spectacle" or of "the society of the spectacle." He adopts
Debord's account of a progressive detachment of the spectacle from reality but remains on the strictly phenomenological plane, never looking
for a reason beyond the spectator's supposedly irresistible and irrational
urge to embrace the spectacle. When Baudrillard asserts that "the abstraction of the 'spectacle' was never irrevocable, even for the Situationists . . . whereas unconditional realization *is* irrevocable," when he
maintains that the spectacle "still left room for a critical consciousness
and demystification" but that we are now "beyond all disalienation," it
becomes quite obvious that the sole purpose of such references is to proclaim the vanity of any resistance to the spectacle.[4]

Pompously presented as an uncomfortable truth, even as a terrifying
discovery, the alleged disappearance of reality is in fact eminently reassuring in a period of crisis. If the tautological character of the spectacle, as denounced by Debord, expresses the automatism of the commodity economy, proceeding in its freedom from any kind of control along
its mad way, then there is indeed much to be afraid of; but if on the
contrary it is a matter of signs that refer only to other signs, which in

3. The differences between Debord and Baudrillard are underscored even by Sadie
Plant, *The Most Radical Gesture: The Situationist International in a Postmodern Age*
(London: Routledge, 1992), and by Steven Best and Douglas Kellner, *The Postmodern
Turn* (New York: Guilford Press, 1997), esp. chapter 3, "From the Society of the Spectacle to the Realm of Simulation: Debord, Baudrillard, and Postmodernity."
4. Jean Baudrillard, *Le Crime parfait* (Paris: Galilée, 1995), 47–48; English translation by Chris Turner: *The Perfect Crime* (London: Verso, 1996), 27.

turn refer to yet others, if there is no original of the unfaithful copy, then there is absolutely no danger of getting entangled with reality. One might claim to pass a radically negative moral judgment on such a state of affairs, but any such judgment would perforce itself be strictly decorative.

But the postmodern is better considered not on a theoretical level but as the reflection of a particular historical moment. The "derealization" so often evoked by postmodern thinkers had a distinctly "real" basis in the purely speculative boom of the nineteen-eighties, financed by debt and refueled by a great mass of capital no longer susceptible of productive investment. The euphoric climate of the times was a big bubble of false pretenses. In a word, the boom and the euphoria were both *simulated*. At the same time, derealization was very much yearned for, and even more so once the euphoria evaporated along with the prospect of indefinitely prolonging the artificial life of a financial system devoid of any basis in production. When the extreme transience of the foundation of one's own life, whether in the individual or the collective sense, becomes apparent, when reality in all its fearsomeness can no longer be kept at bay but is still not wholly perceptible, when your neighbor's house is burning down but your own is barely scorched, then the moment is ripe for theories proclaiming that all is relative and nothing is certain, that nothing is irreparably lost because in every case there is a copy, a prosthesis, a substitute ready to hand, that everything is interchangeable, combinable, dismantleable.

The portion of truth contained in postmodern theory resides in its description of processes of virtualization, in the fact that it took those processes seriously. Viewed simply as a description of the reality of the last decades, postmodernism has indeed often been superior to Marxist-inspired sociology. Postmodernism rightly condemns the positive references of "traditional Marxists" to inherently capitalist categories such as labor, value, and production. But in the end, though it raises real questions, its answers come from nowhere and go nowhere.

A few other misapprehensions need dispelling in regard to the canonical image of Debord that is now rapidly being built up. First of all, Debord was not a run-of-the-mill intellectual, and he chose his "bad boy" role deliberately. His power to scandalize lay, and still lies, not only in what he said but also in the way he lived and the example he set. His effective demonstration that one can get heard without making any of the compromises others consider par for the course is naturally intolerable for most intellectuals today. The admirable thing about Debord, though, is not so much that he never compromised—which might be said, after all, of any sectarian, or for that matter of a backwoods hermit—but rather that he succeeded in living well while still affecting the destinies of the world.

Recently a bizarre cult of Debord has arisen, threatening to transform him into a pop idol, a sort of Che Guevara for the more refined taste. As a Parisian bookseller put it, "there is a lot of money waiting to be made out of Debord tee-shirts and ashtrays." Passive worship of real-life icons as a way of compensating for the wretchedness of one's own life is a quintessentially "spectacular" type of projection. As applied to Debord, it has long plagued the marginal "pro-Situationist" milieu, and it now seems well set to infect a much vaster hip public.

Lastly, it must be stressed that despite the claims of so many of his detractors—and not a few of his admirers—Debord was no nihilist: nothing could be falser than the picture sometimes painted of a dour character mulling hateful and destructive deeds night and day, showering anyone unlucky enough to come in range with insults, denunciations, expulsions, and anathemata, and finally crowning this dismal existence with an act of suicide. The truth is that Debord *loved* many things, among them of course life in the Paris he knew in the nineteen-fifties; in later years, he always contrived to find people and places to savor, particularly in such *quartiers populaires* as still existed. Never having been taken in by the spectacle's false promises of life, he seems to have found some real happiness. For the ostentatious despair that flirts with self-destruction and is so much admired in art galleries and halls of learning Debord had nothing but scorn: as early as 1955 he evoked the "overrated corpse" of Artaud—a barb that can still outrage petty Parisian snobberies forty years later.[5] In his own words, "I have no thought of complaining about anything, and certainly not about the way I have managed to live."

Anselm Jappe
Rome, July 1998

---

5. See Michel Surya, "Le Cadavre surfait de . . . ," *Lignes* 31 (May 1997): 207.

Bibliography 1: Works of Guy Debord

1952–57

"Prolégomènes à tout cinéma futur," followed by a first scenario for the film *Hurlements en faveur de Sade*. *Ion* 1 (April 1952). Reprinted in Berréby, 109–23.

Short articles in *Internationale Lettriste*, nos. 1–4 (1952–54). Reprinted in Berréby, 143–58.

Articles in *Potlatch*, nos. 1–29 (1954–57). Reprinted (with errors) in Berréby, 159–252. Complete run of *Potlatch* reprinted in book form and introduced by Debord: *Potlatch 1954–57* (Paris: Gérard Lebovici, 1985). Slightly expanded edition: *Guy Debord présente Potlatch (1954–1957)* (Paris: Gallimard, Collection Folio, 1996). Another edition (nos. 1–29 only) is *Potlatch* (Paris: Allia, 1996).

Articles in *Les Lèvres Nues* (Brussels, 1954–58), including: "Introduction à une critique de la géographie urbaine," in no. 6 (September 1955); another version of the scenario for *Hurlements en faveur de Sade*, with a preface entitled "Grande fête de nuit," in no. 7 (December 1955); "Mode d'emploi du détournement," with Gil J. Wolman, in no. 8 (May 1956); and "Théorie de la dérive," in no. 9 (November 1956). All these articles reprinted in Berréby, 288–319. "Théorie de la dérive," shorn of its two appendices, "Deux comptes rendus de dérive," was reprinted in *Internationale Situationniste* 2 (December 1958): 19–23; an English translation is in *SIA*, 50–54; the appendices, translated by Thomas Y. Levin as "Two Accounts of the Dérive," are in *Passage*, 135–39; and both article and appendices appear in translation in *Dérive*, 22–32. There have been two facsimile reprints of the complete run of *Les Lèvres Nues* (Paris: Plasma, 1978; and Paris: Allia, 1995).

"Le Labyrinthe éducatif," short internal document of the Letterist International (1956).

Guide psychogéographique de Paris: Discours sur les passions de l'amour. Copenhagen: Le Bauhaus Imaginiste, 1957. Folding map. Frequently reproduced, as for example in Bandini, 126; and in Berréby, 402.

The Naked City: Illustration de l'hypothèse des plaques tournantes en psychogéographique. Map. In Asger Jorn, *Pour la forme* (Paris: Internationale Situationniste, 1958). Frequently reproduced, as for example in Berréby, 535–37; in Bandini, 128–29; and in Libero Andreotti and Xavier Costa. eds., *Situationists, Art, Politics, Urbanism* (Barcelona: Museu d'Art Contemporani/ACTAR, 1996), 56.

(Note: These last two items are "psychogeographical maps" constructed by cutting up a well-known axonometric plan of Paris, rearranging the pieces, and adding directional arrows to suggest psychogeographical itineraries.)

With Asger Jorn. *Fin de Copenhague*. Copenhagen: Le Bauhaus Imaginiste, 1957. Reprinted (in color) in Berréby, 553–91; and in book form (Paris: Allia, 1986).

Rapport sur la construction des situations et sur les conditions de l'organisation et de l'action de la tendance situationniste internationale. Paris: n.p., 1957. Reprinted in Bandini, 278–96; in Berréby (with errors), 607–19; and as an appendix in *Internationale Situationniste 1958–1969* (Paris: Arthème Fayard, 1997), 689–701. Partial English translation in *SIA*, 17–25.

"Remarques sur le concept d'art expérimental," internal SI document (October 1957), partially reprinted in Bandini, 297–99.

1958–72

Articles in *Internationale Situationniste*, nos. 1–12 (1958–69). Eight articles are signed by Debord, but many others are attributable to him. There have been three photographic reprints of the full run of the SI journal: *Internationale Situationniste 1958–69* (Amsterdam: Van Gennep, 1970; Paris: Champ Libre, 1975; Paris: Arthème Fayard, 1997); the last of these editions contains additional material. Complete translations have appeared in German (1976–77) and Italian (1994). The largest selection of translations from *IS* into English is in Ken Knabb, ed. and trans., *Situationist International Anthology* (Berkeley: Bureau of Public Secrets, 1981; reprint edition with updated bibliography, 1995). An earlier large (but unevenly translated) selection is in Christopher Gray, ed. and trans., *Leaving the Twentieth Century* (London: Free Fall, 1974). Other material in English is very widely scattered and often ephemeral, but substantial selections can be found in *Passage, Oct.*, and *Dérive*.

"Dix ans d'art expérimental: Jorn et son rôle dans l'invention théorique." Published in Dutch in *Museum Journaal* 4 (Otterlo, Oct. 1958). Retranslated into French in Luc Mercier, ed. and trans., *Archives situationnistes*, vol. 1 (Paris: Contre-Moules/Parallèles, 1997).

Editorial in *Potlatch*, no. 30/new series no. 1 (15 July 1959). Reprinted in Berréby, 253–54; and in *Guy Debord présente Potlatch (1954–1957)* (Paris: Gallimard, Collection Folio, 1996), 282–84.

With Asger Jorn, *Mémoires*. Copenhagen: Internationale Situationniste, 1959. "Work entirely composed of prefabricated elements." New edition, with introductory note by Debord (Paris: Jean-Jacques Pauvert aux Belles Lettres, 1993).

With P. Canjuers [Daniel Blanchard]. *Préliminaires pour une définition de l'unité du programme révolutionnaire*. Paris, 1960. Pamphlet. Reprinted in Bandini, 342–47. Translated into English as "Preliminaries toward Defining a Unitary Revolutionary Program," in *SIA*, 305–10.

"Les Situationnistes et les nouvelles formes d'action dans la politique et dans l'art." In *Destruktion af RSG-6: En kollectiv manifestation af Situationistisk*

Internationale (Odense, Denmark: Galerie EXI, 1963), 15–18. This catalog
also contains Danish and English versions of Debord's text. Reprinted in
Debord, *Textes rares 1957–1970* (see below), 18–22. Partial English translation in *SIA*, 317–18. Complete English translation, by Thomas Y. Levin, in
Passage, 148–53.

Contre le cinéma. Aarhus, Denmark: Institut Scandinave de Vandalisme Com-
paré, 1964. Preface by Asger Jorn. Contains the scripts, with technical directions, of Debord's first three films (see Filmography below).

"Le Déclin et la chute de l'économie spectaculaire-marchande." Published first
in English as an SI pamphlet (and soon very widely reproduced in the United
Kingdom and the United States): *The Decline and the Fall of the "Spectacular" Commodity-Economy* (Paris: Internationale Situationniste, December
1965). Debord's (unattributed) French text appeared for the first time in *IS*
10 (March 1966): 3–11. Reprinted in book form (Paris: Jean-Jacques Pauvert aux Belles Lettres, 1993). English version reprinted in *SIA*, 153–60; and,
as revised by Ken Knabb, published as the pamphlet *Watts 1965: The Decline and Fall of the Spectacle-Commodity Economy* (Berkeley: Bureau of
Public Secrets, 1992).

Le Point d'explosion de l'idéologie en Chine. Pamphlet. Paris: Internationale
Situationniste, 1966. Reprinted in *IS* 11 (October 1967): 3–12. (Text written by Debord but signed collectively by the SI.)

La Société du spectacle. Paris: Buchet/Chastel, 1967. New edition (Paris: Champ
Libre, 1971). Third edition, with preface by Debord (Paris: Gallimard, 1992;
Paris: Gallimard, Collection Folio, 1996). Foreign editions published notably in Italy (1968, 1979), Denmark (1972), Portugal (1972), West Germany
(1973), Argentina (1974), Holland (1976), Spain, (1977), Greece, Japan
(1993), and Egypt (1993). English translation (unattributed) by Fredy Perl-
man and others: *Society of the Spectacle* (Detroit: Black and Red, 1970; revised edition, 1977). New translation by Donald Nicholson-Smith: *The Society of the Spectacle* (New York: Zone Books, 1994).

With Gianfranco Sanguinetti. *La Véritable Scission dans l'Internationale.* Paris:
Champ Libre, 1972. New edition (Paris: Arthème Fayard, 1998). English
translation: *The Veritable Split in the International* (London: Piranha, 1974);
revised edition (London: Chronos, 1985); again revised, by Lucy Forsyth and
others (London: Chronos, 1990).

Post-1972

"De l'Architecture sauvage." Preface (dated September 1972) to *Jorn/Le Jardin
d'Albisola* (Turin: Edizione d'Arte Fratelli Pozzo, 1974). A photographic
guide, with further text (in Italian) by Ezio Gribaudo and Alberico Sala.
Reprinted in Debord, *Textes rares 1957–1972* (see below), 47–48. English
translation by Thomas Y. Levin: "On Wild Architecture," *Passage*, 174–75.

Translation of "Censor" [Gianfranco Sanguinetti], *Rapporto veridico sulle ultime opportunità di salvare il capitalismo in Italia* (Milan: Ugo Mursia,
1975), as *Véridique Rapport sur les dernières chances de sauver le capitalisme en Italie.* Paris: Champ Libre, 1976.

Oeuvres cinématographiques complètes 1952–1978. Scripts of Debord's first six films (see Filmography below). Illustrated. Paris: Champ Libre, 1978; Paris: Gallimard, 1994. These scripts, with the exception of *In girum imus nocte et consumimur igni* (see below), have been published in English translations by Richard Parry and others as *Society of the Spectacle and Other Films* (London: Rebel Press, 1992).

Preface to the fourth Italian edition of *The Society of the Spectacle*, translated by Paolo Salvadori as *La società dello spettacolo* (Florence: Nuova Vallecchi, 1979). Published in book form as *Préface à la quatrième édition italienne de "La Société du Spectacle"* (Paris: Champ Libre, 1979). Reprinted with *Commentaires sur la société du spectacle* (Paris: Gallimard, 1992; Gallimard, Collection Folio, 1996). Translated into English as *Preface to the Fourth Italian Edition of "The Society of the Spectacle"* by Frances Parker and Michael Forsyth (London: Chronos, 1979); revised edition, trans. Michel Prigent and Lucy Forsyth (London: Chronos, 1983).

Stances sur la mort de son père. Translation of Jorge Manrique, *Coplas de Don Jorge Manrique por la muerte de su padre* (1477 or 1478), with an afterword by Debord. Paris: Champ Libre, 1980. New edition (Cognac: Le Temps Qu'Il Fait, 1996).

"Aux Libertaires." Preface to *Appels de la prison de Ségovie* (Paris: Champ Libre, 1980). An appeal in support of libertarians imprisoned in Segovia.

Considérations sur l'assassinat de Gérard Lebovici. Paris: Gérard Lebovici, 1985; Paris: Gallimard, 1993. An English translation by Thomas Y. Levin and M. Stone-Richards is forthcoming (Los Angeles: Tam Tam Press).

Preface to *Potlatch 1954–1957* (Paris: Gérard Lebovici, 1985). New and slightly expanded edition: *Guy Debord présente Potlatch (1954–1957)* (Paris: Gallimard, Collection Folio, 1996).

With Alice Becker-Ho. *Le "Jeu de la guerre," relevé des positions successives de toutes les forces au cours d'une partie.* Paris: Gérard Lebovici, 1987. Partial English translation by Len Bracken: "The Game of War," in Bracken, *Guy Debord—Revolutionary* (Venice, Calif.: Feral House, 1997).

Commentaires sur la société du spectacle. Paris: Gérard Lebovici, 1988; Paris: Gallimard, 1992; Paris: Gallimard, Collection Folio, 1996. Translated into English by Malcolm Imrie as *Comments on the Society of the Spectacle* (London: Verso, 1990).

Panégyrique, vol. 1. Paris: Gérard Lebovici, 1989; Paris: Gallimard, 1993. Translated into English by James Brook as *Panegyric*, vol. 1 (London: Verso, 1991).

"Les Thèses de Hambourg en septembre 1961 (Note pour servir à l'histoire de l'Internationale Situationniste)." Dated November 1989. In *Internationale Situationniste 1958–1969* (Paris: Arthème Fayard, 1996), 703–4.

In girum imus nocte et consumimur igni. Edition critique. Paris: Gérard Lebovici, 1990. New edition announced for 1999 (Paris: Arthème Fayard). Film script, with sources of quoted material indicated (no illustrations). Translated into English by Lucy Forsyth as *In girum imus nocte et consumimur igni: A Film* (London: Pelagian Press, 1991, illustrated).

Preface to third edition of *La Société du spectacle*. Paris: Gallimard, 1992. English translation by Donald Nicholson-Smith in *The Society of the Spectacle* (New York: Zone Books, 1994).

Preface to new edition of *Considérations sur l'assassinat de Gérard Lebovici* (Paris: Gallimard, 1993).

"Cette mauvaise réputation . . . ." Paris: Gallimard, 1993.

"Attestations." Introductory note to new edition of *Mémoires* (Paris: Jean-Jacques Pauvert aux Belles Lettres, 1993).

Des Contrats. Cognac: Le Temps Qu'Il Fait, 1995. Three film contracts signed by Debord between 1973 and 1984, a preface, and a letter written a few days before his death.

Panégyrique, vol. 2. Paris: Arthème Fayard, 1997. Unpaginated. Mostly photographs, along with a few quotations and an author's note. As an appendix, "Sur les difficultés de la traduction de *Panégyrique.*"

Several internal SI documents signed by Debord may be found in Pascal Dumontier, *Les Situationnistes et mai 68* (Paris: Gérard Lebovici, 1990); two are also appended to *Internationale Situationniste 1958–1969* (Paris: Arthème Fayard, 1996).

Some editorial and introductory matter in books published by Champ Libre may be attributed to Debord.

Nine miscellaneous texts by Debord were published in duplicated typescript: *Textes rares 1957–1970* (Saint-Nazaire, n.p., 1981).

A number of letters from and to Debord will be found at the International Institute of Social History in Amsterdam; these have been published in part in two sets of duplicated documents: *Débat d'orientation de l'ex-Internationale Situationniste 1969–1970* (Paris: Centre de Recherche sur la Question Sociale, 1974); and Jeanne Charles and Daniel Denevert, eds., *Chronique des secrets publics* (Paris: Centre de Recherche sur la Question Sociale, 1975). Some of this material is reprinted in Dumontier.

Other letters from and to Debord appear in Éditions Champ Libre, *Correspondance*, vols. 1 and 2 (Paris: Champ Libre, 1978, 1981).

An exhaustive bibliography seemingly recording every line ever written or co-signed by Debord will be found in Shigenobu Gonzalvez's book of 1998 (see Bibliography 2).

Filmography

Hurlements en faveur de Sade. Films Lettristes, Paris, 1952.

Sur le passage de quelques personnes à travers une assez courte unité de temps. Dansk-Fransk Experimentalfilmskompagni, Paris, 1959.

Critique de la séparation. Dansk-Fransk Experimentalfilmskompagni, Paris, 1961.

La Société du spectacle. Simar Films, Paris, 1973.

Réfutation de tous les jugements, tant élogieux qu'hostiles, qui ont été jusqu'ici portés sur le film "La Société du spectacle." Simar Films, Paris, 1975.

In girum imus nocte et consumimur igni. Simar Films, Paris, 1978.

Guy Debord, son art et son temps. With Brigitte Cornand. Canal Plus Television, Paris, 1995.

Bibliography 2: Selected Works
on Debord and the Situationists

The most complete bibliography, covering works published before 1985, is in
Sanders (1989; see below). Ford's very extensive bibliography on the SI (1995)
is confined to the period 1972–92 and concentrates on English-language publications. Ohrt (1990) has a brief annotated list running up to 1989. The lengthy
bibliography in Dumontier (1990), especially strong on pamphlets, handbills
and the like, also ends at 1989. Important older lists are in Bandini (1977) and
Raspaud and Voyer (1972).

There is a copious literature in several languages, dating for the most part
from the seventies, that is largely made up of insignificant glosses on Situationist ideas written from a very favorable ("pro-Situationist") standpoint. Especially in more recent years, passing mentions of the Situationists often occur in
works on history and art history; likewise entries in works of reference have become more common, as for example in *Encyclopédie des philosophes*, second
edition (Paris: P.U.F., 1993), or in *Dizionario dei filosofi* (Milan: Bompiani,
1991). Articles and commentaries in the French press, especially since 1988,
have become far too numerous to record. A few are cited in Debord's *"Cette
mauvaise réputation . . . "* (1993). What follows is an annotated chronological
list of publications dealing in some detail with Guy Debord and the Situationist
movement.

Ronald Hunt, ed. *Poetry Must Be Made by All! Transform the World!* Catalog
of an exhibition mounted at the Moderna Museet, Stockholm (15 November–21 December 1969), and later in Düsseldorf. The Situationists are presented as the end of a series of movements that begins with the Russian Constructivists and the Surrealists. Excellent iconography.

Richard Gombin. *Les Origines du gauchisme*. Paris: Le Seuil, 1971. English translation by Michael K. Perl: *The Origins of Modern Leftism* (Harmondsworth,
Middlesex: Penguin, 1975). Traces the history, from the end of the Second
World War to 1968, of those groups of the French far Left that rejected economic determinism. Writing with sociological dispassion and supplying plenty
of detail, Gombin gives a good deal of space to *Socialisme ou Barbarie*, but
his main emphasis is on the central part played by the SI in the run-up to
May 1968. Considered by Debord one of the "least bad" commentaries of
the time on the Situationists (*VS*, 36–37; Eng., 33–34).

Mario Perniola. "I situazionisti." *Agar-Agar* 4 (1972): 5–92. One of the rare attempts at theoretical engagement with the SI on its own ground. Perniola feels
that the Situationists failed to escape artistic subjectivity, indeed that they

raised the "signified" aspect of that subjectivity to a paroxysmal level, and that they did not go far enough in their critique of the economy, which they conflated with activity in general (*operare*). Also worthy of note is Perniola's article "Arte e rivoluzione," *Tempo Presente* (December 1966): 69–74, and his presentation of a Situationist text to the Italian public, in a way congenial to the SI, in the review *Fantazaria* (1966). The first part of Perniola's *L'alienazione artistica* (Milan: Mursia, 1971) elaborates on certain Situationist *trouvailles* in an original way.

Jean-Jacques Raspaud and Jean-Pierre Voyer. *L' Internationale Situationniste: Chronologie, bibliographie, protagonistes (avec un index des noms insultés)*. Paris: Champ Libre, 1972. Contains a great deal of useful information, including a fold-out chronology, a list of members of the SI, a bibliography, and a name index of people mentioned in *Internationale Situationniste*—along, where applicable, with the epithets applied to each of those named. (The chroniclers reckon that the number of individuals insulted is only just over half of the total.)

David Jacobs and Christopher Winks. *At Dusk: The Situationist Movement in Historical Perspective*. Berkeley: Perspectives, 1975. A pamphlet by two American ex-pro-Situationists which, amidst much revisiting of well-worn themes, offers a critique, from what might be described as an orthodox Marxist standpoint, of some of the weaker points of Situationist theory.

Mirella Bandini. *L'Estetico, il politico: Da Cobra all'Internazionale Situazionista 1948–1957*. Rome: Officina Edizioni, 1977. An excellent account of the movements that merged to form the SI, and of the early years of the organization. The viewpoint is aesthetic rather than theoretical. Includes a very useful collection of documents, many of them rare when Bandini's book appeared, and illustrations. Though much of the documentary material overlaps, it is worth consulting Bandini's earlier exhibition catalog, also well illustrated: *Pinot Gallizio e il Laboratorio Sperimentale d'Alba del Movimento Internazionale per una Bauhaus Immaginista (1955–57) e del Internazionale Situazionista (1957–60)* (Turin: Galleria Civica d'Arte Moderna, 1974).

Patrick Tacussel. *L'Attraction sociale. Le dynamisme de l'imaginaire dans une société monocéphale*. Paris: Librairie des Méridiens, 1984. Writing from the perspective of the sociology of Maffesoli, in a highly affected style, the author is interested in new explorations of utopian and imaginary themes by marginal groups. He devotes a chapter to Debord, entitled "Profile of a Modern Legend," explaining from the outset that he is more concerned with "atmosphere" and "images" than with Debord's theoretical contribution, which he treats as an afterthought. Tacussel typifies a fairly widespread tendency to present the Letterists and Situationists as charming dreamers.

Gérard Berréby, ed. *Documents relatifs à la fondation de l'Internationale Situationniste*. Paris: Allia, 1985. An imposing and well-produced volume containing an exhaustive but error-ridden mass of reprinted material from the Letterists, CoBrA, the Letterist International, Asger Jorn, and others. Strictly no editorial commentary.

Mark Shipway. "Situationism." In Maximilien Rubel and John Crump, eds., *Non-Market Socialism in the Nineteenth and Twentieth Centuries* (Basingstoke: Macmillan Press, 1987). Shipway argues that Debord developed a universal theory which in reality applied solely to a specific stratum of French society in the nineteen-sixties.

Jean Barrot. *What Is Situationism? Critique of the Situationist International.* London: Unpopular Books, 1987. Essay by a French ultraleftist first published (in English) in *Red Eye* 1 (Berkeley, California, 1979). Barrot upbraids Debord for speaking not of capital but merely of commodities, which are said to be a phenomenon exclusive to the stage of circulation and consumption. The writer has clearly read neither Debord nor Marx.

Stewart Home. *The Assault on Culture: Utopian Currents from Lettrisme to Class War.* London: Aporia Press/Unpopular Books, 1988. For Home, the chief interest of the Situationists is their role as precursors of punk. He favors the "Nashist" group expelled from the SI in 1962 and considers Debord a mystic, an idealist, a dogmatist, and a liar.

Jean-François Martos. *Histoire de l'Internationale Situationniste.* Paris: Gérard Lebovici, 1989. Unsurprisingly, given the publishing house, this is a very "orthodox" account, composed almost entirely of quotations from Situationist texts with a linking commentary. Useful, perhaps, as an introduction to the subject, it does little to deepen our understanding.

Greil Marcus. *Lipstick Traces: A Secret History of the Twentieth Century.* Cambridge, Mass.: Harvard University Press, 1989. Something of a bestseller in the United States, Marcus's book traces the history of underground cultural movements and of cultural transgressiveness from Dada and the early Surrealists, through the Letterists and Situationists, to punk rock, with digressions on the Anabaptists of Munster, on singers of the Paris Commune, and so forth. The style is distinctly journalistic, the narrative and iconography opulent. Marcus writes with a brio quite absent from other works on this subject, and he provides a lively account of the Letterist atmosphere, but some of the connections he makes between very different phenomena—between the SI and the Sex Pistols, for example—are fanciful, and betray a lack of historical understanding,

R. J. Sanders. *Bewegung tegen de schijn: De situationisten, een avant-garde.* Amsterdam: Huis aan de Drie Grachten, 1989. This book, more than the others mentioned here, attempts to place the SI in its historical context and specifically within the history of ideas. Some of the results are of interest, but Sanders takes on so many subjects that he is unable to treat any of them in depth. The style makes for hard going, but the book is valuable for its rich bibliography and the precision of its information and references.

Elizabeth Sussman, ed. *On the Passage of a Few People through a Rather Brief Moment in Time: The Situationist International 1957–1972.* Cambridge, Mass.: MIT Press/Boston: Institute of Contemporary Art, 1989. Catalog to the large exhibition on the Situationists mounted (in slightly different forms) at the Centre Georges Pompidou, Paris (21 February–9 April 1989), at the Institute of Contemporary Arts, London (23 June–13 August 1989), and at the Institute of Contemporary Art, Boston (20 October 1989–7 January 1990). Debord had nothing good to say about this event, which he saw as an attempt to eradicate the last two-thirds of the SI's history (see *"Cette*

mauvaise réputation . . . " [Paris: Gallimard, 1993], 41–42). Apart from list-
ing and illustrating materials displayed, *Passage* contains a dozen or so
texts and articles, notably Thomas Y. Levin's analysis of Debord's films; an
interpretation of *Mémoires* by Greil Marcus; Peter Wollen's "Bitter Victory:
The Art and Politics of the Situationist International," which sees the SI as a
fusion of the historical artistic avant-gardes and the "Western Marxist" tradition; a description by Mirella Bandini of Jorn and Gallizio's "Experimental Laboratory" in Alba; a discussion of Jorn and the SI by Troels Andersen;
and a few Situationist writings in translation. Another, highly illustrated
miscellany published in connection with this exhibition is Iwona Blazwick
and others, eds., *An Endless Adventure . . . An Endless Passion . . . An Endless Banquet: A Situationist Scrapbook* (London: ICA/Verso, 1989).

Pascal Dumontier. *Les Situationnistes et mai 68: Théorie et pratique de la révolution (1966–1972).* Paris: Gérard Lebovici, 1990. Like those of Sanders and
Ohrt, Dumontier's book began as an academic thesis. An account of the years
between the Strasbourg scandal and the SI's self-dissolution, it draws on documents that are difficult to find, including those pertaining to the group's internal debate during the final crisis. The perspective is historiographical.

Roberto Ohrt. *Phantom Avantgarde: Eine Geschichte der Situationistischen
Internationale und der modernen Kunst.* Hamburg: Nautilus, 1990. Chiefly
concerned with the relationship of the SI to modern art up to about 1960.
Ohrt adopts the point of view of the German painters known as the SPUR
group, expelled from the SI in 1962, and he never misses an opportunity to
castigate Debord. Despite his ambition to write the first serious critical account of the SI, all Ohrt's conclusions are highly questionable. His book can
nevertheless be recommended for its magnificent iconography and docu-
mentation.

Various authors. *I Situazionisti.* Rome: Manifestolibri, 1991. This little book
reprints some brief pieces first published in *Il Manifesto* for 6 July 1989,
along with other contributions. French translation: *Retour au futur: Des
situationnistes* (Marseilles: Via Valeriano, 1990).

"Abrégé." *Encyclopédie des Nuisances* 15 (April 1992): 62–73. Reveals the
importance of the artistic origins of the SI and the limitations that they
imposed. For Debord's response to this article, see *"Cette mauvaise réputation . . . "* (Paris: Gallimard, 1993), 79–84.

Sadie Plant. *The Most Radical Gesture: The Situationist International in a Postmodern Age.* London: Routledge, 1992. As the title suggests, Plant seeks to
bring the Situationists into conjunction with the so-called postmodernists.

Gérard Guégan. *Debord est mort* [etc.]. Paris: Société des Saisons, 1995. Ran-
corous diatribe from a superannuated Leftist. (On Guégan, see Debord,
"Cette mauvaise réputation . . . " [Paris: Gallimard, 1993], 71–79.)

Simon Ford. *The Realization and Suppression of the Situationist International:
An Annotated Bibliography 1972–1992.* Edinburgh and San Francisco: AK
Press, 1995. Demonstrates how surprisingly vast the literature now is, espe-
cially in English.

Cécile Guilbert. *Pour Guy Debord.* Paris: Gallimard, 1996. This essay garnered much approval in the French press by reducing Debord to a charming dandy and an elegant literary stylist.

Gianfranco Marelli. *L'amara vittoria del situazionismo*. Pisa: Biblioteca Franco Serantino, 1996. Umpteenth history of the Situationist movement, this time from an orthodox anarchist standpoint.

Stewart Home, ed. *What Is Situationism? A Reader*. Edinburgh and San Francisco: AK Press, 1996. A ragbag collection of twelve texts concerned in one way or another with the SI. The confusion is unsurprising, given the editor (see above).

Libero Andreotti and Xavier Costa, eds. *Situacionistes: Art, política, urbanisme/Situationists: Art, Politics, Urbanism*. Barcelona: Museu d'Art Contemporani/ACTAR, 1996. Catalog, in Catalan and English, of a show on Situationist activity in the fields of urbanism and art. Fine color iconography. Several essays (including contributions by Andreotti, Thomas Y. Levin, and Mirella Bandini) testify to the progress made in the art of defanging even the most "dangerous" of the SI's theses. A volume complementing the catalog is a collection of Letterist and Situationist texts translated into English: Libero Andreotti and Xavier Costa, eds., *Theory of the Dérive and Other Situationist Writings on the City*, trans. Paul Hammond, Gerardo Denís, and others (Barcelona: Museu d'Art Contemporani/ACTAR, 1996).

Thomas F. McDonough, ed. *October* 79 (winter 1997). Special issue on "Guy Debord and the *Internationale Situationniste*." Suffers from the usual overemphasis on exclusively aesthetic aspects. Includes an interesting polemical contribution, by T. J. Clark and Donald Nicholson-Smith, evoking the failure of "the Left" to confront the history of the SI.

Lignes 31 (May 1997). Contains ten articles on Debord. One wonders why so many French authors, when they elect to write about Debord, insist on doing it in a style so mannered that as a rule it masks whatever thoughts—perhaps even very pertinent ones—they may have wished to convey.

Len Bracken. *Guy Debord—Revolutionary*. Venice, Calif.: Feral House, 1997. This supposed biography is hugely derivative and has nothing new to convey except for wild insinuations and a few truly hilarious errors.

Shigenobu Gonzalvez. *Guy Debord ou la beauté du négatif*. Paris: Mille et Une Nuits, 1998. More useful for its bibliography than for its observations.

In May 1996 the radio station France Culture broadcast a four-part program, "Nuits magnétiques: L'Internationale Situationniste," composed mainly of interviews with people who had known Debord. Cassette version marketed by Chronos Publications, London.

Index

Compositor:	Prestige Typography
Text and display:	Sabon
Display:	Franklin
Printer and binder:	IBT